Instructor's Manual
and Test Bank

for

Western Civilizations
Thirteenth Edition

D1622745

Instructor's Manual
and Test Bank

for

Robert E. Lerner
Standish Meacham
Edward McNall Burns

Western Civilizations
Thirteenth Edition

Meredith Veldman
Louisiana State University

W. W. NORTON & COMPANY, INC.
New York • London

ISBN 0-393-97193-7 (pbk.)

W. W. Norton & Company, Inc., 500 Fifth Avenue, New York, NY 10110
http://www.wwnorton.com
W. W. Norton & Company Ltd., 10 Coptic Street, London WC1A 1PU

1 2 3 4 5 6 7 8 9 0

CONTENTS

Preface

This Instructor's Manual and Test Bank aims to provide university and college teachers with a guide for assessing their students' mastery of the thirteenth edition of *Western Civilizations* by Robert E. Lerner, Standish Meacham, and Edward McNall Burns. It assumes, as does the textbook which it accompanies, that students enter a course in history with little to no background in the subject. This lack of background results in some serious difficulties for the university-level teacher. Any course that reduces the complexities and contradictions of history to a list of names, dates, and terms will rob the subject of its inherent excitement, and will affirm the all-too-prevalent misconception of history as irrelevant. Yet the student who thinks that Hitler was responsible for the First World War or who cannot identify John Calvin lacks the necessary tools for a critical understanding of the history of civilization. Therefore, this manual attempts to strike the proper balance between emphasis on the so-called objective elements of the historical record—the "facts"—and stress on concepts and context. Thus, the questions focus not only on testing the students' ability to think critically about historical relationships, but also on the underpinnings of such ability: acquisition of the *essential* names, dates, and terms of the story.

Each chapter follows the same format. First, an outline provides an overview of the corresponding chapter in *Western Civilizations*. Sets of multiple-choice, true-or-false, and identification questions test the students' mastery of the material. These short-answer questions are also available in a computerized test bank designed for use on IBM-compatible and Macintosh microcomputers. A set of essay and discussion questions aims at involving the student in historical debate as well as honing his or her critical faculties. As a result, these questions have no "right" answers, but instead demand that the student take a stand and formulate an argument. The final section in each chapter supplies a list of possible classroom and feature films. The American Historical Association's *Teaching History through Film* would be helpful to the teacher who chooses to utilize the vast resources available in this area.

BIBLIOGRAPHY

Baer, D. Richard (ed.) *The Film Buff's Checklist of Motion Pictures (1912–1979).* Hollywood: Hollywood Film Archive, 1979.

Educational Film and Video Locator of the Consortium of College and University Media Centers and R.R. Bowker Company. Vols. I and II. New York: R.R. Bowker, 1990.

Gifford, Denis. *The British Film Catalogue. 1895–1970. A Reference Guide*. New York: McGraw-Hill, 1973.

Halliwell, Leslie. *Halliwell's Film Guide*, 3rd ed. New York: Scribner's, 1982.

History Films. Champaign, Ill.: University of Illinois, 1979.

Magill, Frank (ed.) *Magill's Cinema Annual, 1982–1986*. Englewood Cliffs, N.J.: Salem Press, 1982–1986.

Parlato, S.J. *Superfilms: An International Guide to Award-Winning Educational Films*. Metuchen, N.J.: Scarecrow Press, 1976.

Pickard, Roy. *The Award Movies*. London: Frederick Muller, 1980.

_____. *Dictionary of the 1000 Best Films*. New York: Association Press, 1971.

Rosenstone, Robert. *Visions of the Past: The Challenge of Film to Our Idea of History*. Cambridge, Mass.: Harvard University Press, 1995.

Seltz-Petrash, Ann (ed.) *AAAS Science Film Catalog*. Washington, D.C.: American Association for the Advancement of Science and R.R. Bowker, 1975.

Schipman, David. *The Good Film and Video Guide*. London: Consumer's Association, 1984.

USEFUL ADDRESSES

Facets Multimedia Inc.
1517 West Fullerton Avenue
Chicago, Illinois 60614
(312) 281-9075

Filmic Archives
The Cinema Center
Botsford, Connecticut 06404
(800) 366-1920

Films for the Humanities and Sciences
P.O. Box 2053
Princeton, New Jersey 08543-2053
(800) 257-5126

Insight Media
2162 Broadway
New York, New York 10024
(212) 721-6316

Instructor's Manual
and Test Bank

for

Western Civilizations
Thirteenth Edition

PART ONE.   THE DAWN OF HISTORY

CHAPTER 1.   FROM THE ICE AGE TO THE EARLIEST CITIES

Outline

I. The nature of history
II. Early human art and early human survival
    A. Cave paintings and their interpretation
    B. Specialization and differentiation of labor
III. The origins of food production
    A. End of the Ice Age
    B. Shift from food-gathering to food production
    C. Spread of sedentary agriculture
IV. The age of villages
    A. Development of restricted women's roles
    B. Handicraft production
    C. Development of long-distance trade
    D. Warfare and its benefits
V. The birth of cities in western Asia
    A. Cities versus villages
    B. The emergence of Mesopotamian cities
    C. The birth of civilization

MULTIPLE CHOICE

Choose the best response.

1. How has the discipline of history changed within the last few decades?
    (a) It has become more politically oriented.
    (b) Historians have realized that the actions of elites are very insignificant.
    (c) It has become an exact science that uses quantitative skills and methods.
    *(d) Historians have tried to record past human actions in a much wider range of spheres.

2. The study of history might most meaningfully be pursued to
    (a) celebrate ways of life that are now lost forever.
    (b) understand more thoroughly modern institutions and events.
    (c) demonstrate humanity's unbroken chain of progress.
    *(d) learn how past peoples solved their problems and lived their lives in the context of their particular environments.

2

3. The earliest humanlike species originated in
    (a) Southeast Asia.
  *(b) Africa.
    (c) western Europe.
    (d) South America.

4. The cave murals of southern France and northern Spain
    (a) depict human beings engaged in ritualistic activity.
    (b) provide the earliest evidence of a written language.
  *(c) picture species of game in various modes of activity.
    (d) show the earliest myths about the creation of the world.

5. The most likely explanations for the cave murals is that the cave painters were
  *(a) working sympathetic magic.
    (b) women who desired a more prominent role in primitive society.
    (c) trying to overthrow their priestly rulers.
    (d) constructing temples for the gods.

6. The early human hunting societies, such as those that produced the cave paintings, did NOT include the following specialists:
    (a) Handicraft workers
  *(b) Merchants
    (c) Hunters
    (d) Painters

7. The end of the Ice Age brought
    (a) a transition from food-gathering to hunting as a means of survival.
    (b) violent social conflict between priests and cave painters.
    (c) a shift in human civilization from Asia to Europe.
  *(d) the disappearance of large game species from western Asia.

8. The transition from food-gathering to food production
  *(a) gradually evolved over about 3,000 to 4,000 years.
    (b) resulted in greater leisure time for human societies.
    (c) led to nomadism.
    (d) was made possible by the development of slavery.

9. A crucial intermediary step in the systematic production of plant food was
    (a) foraging.
  *(b) stockpiling.
    (c) creating a merchant class.
    (d) developing a slave trade.

10. _____ constituted the most advanced form of human organization in western Asia from about 6500 to about 3500–3000 B.C.E.
    (a) Small nomadic groups
    (b) Cities
    *(c) Villages
    (d) Warrior clans

11. For most of human history, women (and women alone) have been responsible for cloth production because
    (a) spinning and sewing were respectable occupations for females.
    (b) as a highly skilled occupation, weaving required a long apprenticeship.
    (c) religious beliefs restricted male participation.
    *(d) the rhythms of cloth production are compatible with the demands of child care.

12. Pottery emerged as an important village handicraft because
    (a) it had ritualistic uses and significance.
    (b) nomadic peoples had already developed and refined the necessary techniques.
    (c) its products were handy objects of barter.
    *(d) it met the crucial storage needs of villagers.

13. After the discovery of smelting, _____ was used for manufacturing containers, tools, and weapons.
    (a) gold
    (b) steel
    (c) woven cloth
    *(d) copper

14. Village life fostered trade because
    *(a) the practice of storing food and goods created surpluses, which could then be bartered to obtain more goods.
    (b) of competition between villages.
    (c) settled peoples had more time for leisure activities and the enjoyment of material goods.
    (d) religious rituals demanded the acquisition of rare metals and silks.

15. Settled life and ongoing warfare marched hand in hand because
    (a) land became scarce.
    *(b) villagers had material possessions to tempt attackers.
    (c) nomadic peoples had neither the time nor the tools to construct weapons.
    (d) captured peoples were needed as slaves to work in the fields.

16. Warfare stimulated the progress of technology and trade for all the following reasons EXCEPT:
    (a) To protect themselves and attack others more effectively, villagers achieved technological advances.
    (b) To acquire weapons and metals, villagers strove to produce greater surpluses for trading.
    *(c) Captured peoples gave new techniques and technologies to their captors.
    (d) Village "arms races" stimulated the advance in metallurgy.

17. The presence of which social group does NOT differentiate cities from villages?
    (a) administrators
    *(b) handicraft workers
    (c) priests
    (d) professional warriors

18. The earliest cities arose in
    (a) southeastern Europe.
    (b) central Anatolia.
    (c) modern-day France.
    *(d) Mesopotamia.

19. Which of the following is NOT true of the development of artificial irrigation systems in Mesopotamia?
    (a) They were needed to make the region inhabitable for the population overflow from neighboring regions.
    (b) Their success depended on coercion, and thus on the division of society into rulers and ruled.
    *(c) They decreased the priests' influence on society by showing that humanity could manipulate the environment without supernatural aid.
    (d) They required an unprecedented degree of organization and administration that led to the development of government.

20. The emergence of a full-time priesthood was most likely linked to
    (a) the invention of religion in Mesopotamia.
    (b) the need to find respectable occupations for men too frail to hunt or wage warfare.
    *(c) the need to establish social cohesion in larger, less equal societies.
    (d) a new desire to manipulate natural forces.

IDENTIFICATIONS

Homo sapiens   obsidian
sympathetic magic   Mesopotamia
Ice Age   sedentary agriculture
village   civilization

TRUE OR FALSE

F   1.   Because history is a science, historians can ask what happened in the past, but not why it happened.
F   2.   The cave paintings of France and Spain show that nomadic peoples regularly engaged in warfare.
F   3.   The lack of sophisticated artistic technique in the cave paintings reveals that no differentiation of labor existed in the societies that produced these paintings.
T   4.   In the period around 10,000 B.C.E., after the disappearance of the large game herds, the coastal areas of western Asia produced such great quantities of wild grain and other foods that they could support permanent settlements.
T   5.   The first farm animals were sheep and goats.
F   6.   Nomadic peoples produced many more children than did settled peoples.
T   7.   Copper became important in the production of tools and weaponry, and therefore in the newly developing trading economy of western Asia.
F   8.   Until the emergence of cities (around 3200 B.C.E.), trade was restricted to limited exchanges involving villages clustered within a ten-mile radius.
F   9.   Human beings chose to settle in the Mesopotamian region because of its fertile soil and abundant rainfall.
T   10. The origins of "civilization" are closely connected with the origins of cities.

DISCUSSION AND/OR ESSAY QUESTIONS

1.   What is "history"? What is the point of learning about the customs and beliefs of long-dead peoples?
2.   Why is the shift from food-gathering to food production often called the "first Agricultural Revolution"? What was "revolutionary" about a development so gradual that the peoples involved did not even notice that they were participating in anything important?
3.   Explain the connections among the emergence of villages, the development of trade, and the rise of a culture of warfare.

4. What is the difference between a village and a city? Why are cities regarded as fundamental for the emergence of "civilization"?
5. Consider the evolution of a Mesopotamian *civilization*. What was the role of warfare in this evolution? Were individuals better off in this civilized society, or did this evolution result in a decline in the quality of life for most people?

SUGGESTED CLASSROOM FILMS

The Agricultural Revolution: Man as a Food Producer. 19 min. Color. 1982. McGraw-Hill. Explores the transition from hunting to farming.

The Birth of Civilization: 6000 B.C.–2000 B.C. 26 min. Color. 1985. Insight Media. Explores the links among technological developments, social structures, and political arrangements.

Colliding Continents and the Age of Bronze. 55 min. Color. 1991. Insight Media. This BBC production explores the interaction between the use of bronze and the history of early humanity.

Hunters and Gatherers. 60 min. Color. 1989. Insight Media. A look at the arrival and dispersal of the first human beings in Australia.

Out of the Ice. 55 min. Color. 1991. Insight Media. A BBC production that chronicles the story of humanity from the end of the last Ice Age to the first civilizations.

CHAPTER 2. THE MESOPOTAMIAN CIVILIZATION

Outline

I. Ancient Sumer: the world of the first cities
   - A. Sumerian political history: city-states, Sargon, and the Sumerian revival
   - B. The subjugation of nature
   - C. Sumerian contributions to civilization
     1. The invention of the wheel
     2. The invention of the lunar calendar
     3. The invention of writing
   - D. The Sumerian religion
     1. Evolution of the gods
     2. The temples
   - E. The Sumerian social structure
II. Old Babylonian developments
   - A. Sumerian economic decline and the Old Babylonian dominance
   - B. The rise of the Amorites
   - C. Old Babylonian law: the Code of Hammurabi
   - D. Old Babylonian literature: the Epic of Gilgamesh
   - E. The development of personal religion
   - F. Old Babylonian mathematics
III. The Kassite and Hittite interlude
   - A. Decline of the Old Babylonian empire
   - B. The Mesopotamian dark age
   - C. The Hittite empire
     1. Misconceptions
     2. Sources of strength
IV. The might of the Assyrians
   - A. The development of the Assyrian empire
   - B. The reign of Sennacherib
   - C. Assyrian culture
     1. Intellectual dependency on Sumerian and Old Babylonian knowledge
     2. Frightfulness: brutality in art and policy
V. The New Babylonian revival
   - A. The Chaldeans
   - B. Nebuchadnezzar's Babylon
   - C. New Babylonian astronomy and astrology
VI. The Mesopotamian legacy
   - A. Influences on the Hebrews
   - B. Technological and intellectual legacy

MULTIPLE CHOICE

Choose the best response.

1. Sumer was located in
    (a) Anatolia (modern-day Turkey).
    *(b) southern Mesopotamia.
    (c) northern Palestine.
    (d) Egypt.

2. Around 3200 B.C.E., the earliest forms of writing were invented in
    (a) Babylon.
    *(b) Sumer.
    (c) Akkad.
    (d) Assyria.

3. During the first nine centuries of the Sumerian era
    *(a) several independent city-states, rather than a single unified government, existed in Sumer.
    (b) Sumer was peopled by nomadic tribes and had no cities.
    (c) the dynasty of Nebuchadnezzar made Sumer into a mighty military power.
    (d) the city of Babylon emerged as one of the seven wonders of the world.

4. The victories of Sargon
    (a) freed Sumer from foreign domination.
    (b) placed the Amorites in control of Sumer.
    (c) established a period of peace that allowed the development of a legal and judicial code.
    *(d) placed Sumer under Akkadian domination for almost two centuries.

5. Climate and geography shaped Sumer's accomplishments because
    *(a) a harsh climate and a lack of natural resources made the Sumerians perceive nature as an enemy to be subdued.
    (b) an abundance of natural resources provided the incentive for development.
    (c) year-round flooding made centralized control a necessity.
    (d) accessibility to harbors made the region a trading center.

6. Which of the following statements CORRECTLY describes the development of wheeled transport?
    (a) It led to the use of the wheel in pottery-making.
    (b) It was first discovered by the Egyptians.
    (c) It radicalized military techniques but had little effect on economic or political developments.
    *(d) It proved crucial in Sumerian irrigation and building projects.

7. Sumerian contributions to civilization did NOT include
   - (a) the wheel.
   - (b) writing.
   - *(c) duodecimal time reckonings (time based on units of twelve).
   - (d) the lunar calendar.

8. As Sumerian religion evolved, it moved away from viewing the gods as part of nature to imagining
   - (a) God as a unitary, omnipotent Being.
   - (b) the gods as superheroes.
   - (c) a world without supernatural intervention.
   - *(d) the gods as guardians of various regions.

9. Sumerian temples were usually built in the form of a terraced tower surmounted by a shrine, called a _____.
   - (a) cuneiform
   - (b) sargon
   - *(c) ziggurat
   - (d) tabernacle

10. Sumerian economic and political decline was caused by
   - (a) overly greedy and incompetent rulers.
   - (b) civil wars resulting from an unjust legal system.
   - (c) failure to develop irrigation techniques.
   - *(d) the deterioration of the soil because of salinization.

11. The Code of Hammurabi did NOT
   - (a) divide society into two legal and clearly unequal classes.
   - (b) enforce the principle of exact retaliation.
   - (c) serve as the point of departure for the evolution of Western concepts of justice.
   - *(d) preserve social order by insisting that the aristocratic class was above the law.

12. The Epic of Gilgamesh reveals
   - (a) the dominance of the priestly class in Mesopotamian society.
   - (b) that the Hittites developed startling new artistic forms.
   - (c) that the Mesopotamians followed a rigid moral code based on the principle of "an eye for an eye."
   - *(d) a secular philosophy of life that affirmed human experience and action on earth.

13. Before the Old Babylonians, religious commitment had not included
    (a) the concept of the gods as superhuman.
    *(b) prayer to personal gods who watched over the daily affairs of ordinary people.
    (c) the notion of the priests as a separate class.
    (d) worship of individual deities as the patron gods of cities.

14. Our division of the day into two sets of twelve hours, the hour into sixty minutes, and the minute into sixty seconds is derived from the mathematical achievements of the
    (a) Sumerians.
    *(b) Old Babylonians.
    (c) Hittites.
    (d) Chaldeans.

15. Hittite strength depended on
    (a) racial superiority.
    *(b) availability of resources.
    (c) monopoly of the technology of the wheel.
    (d) monopoly of the manufacture of iron.

16. To display his might and seal his military victories, Sennacherib constructed
    (a) the ziggurat.
    *(b) Nineveh.
    (c) the Code of Hammurabi.
    (d) the Hanging Gardens.

17. The Assyrian reputation for "frightfulness"
    (a) is somewhat unjust since they were no more or less cruel than other primitive nations.
    (b) is based on an early-twentieth-century misreading of an Assyrian document.
    (c) rested on their unprecedented use of chariots in warfare.
    *(d) made the Assyrians a hated race and drove subject peoples to revolt.

18. Which of the following places the Mesopotamian civilizations in CORRECT chronological order?
    *(a) the Sumerians, the Assyrians, the New Babylonians
    (b) the Hittites, the Sumerians, the New Babylonians
    (c) the New Babylonians, the Assyrians, the Sumerians
    (d) the Assyrians, the Hittites, the Sumerians

19. Which of the following was NOT true of New Babylonian astrology?
    (a) It bore witness to the New Babylonian belief that the universe could be measured and interpreted for humanity's benefit.
    (b) It served as a point of departure for Greco-Roman astronomy.
    *(c) It served as a personal religion for people who relied on their individual horoscopes for comfort and for guidance.
    (d) It enabled the New Babylonians to compile a careful record of astronomical observations.

20. The Mesopotamian legacy to the modern world includes all of the following EXCEPT
    (a) influence on Old Testament theology.
    *(b) artistic and architectural styles.
    (c) technological breakthroughs such as the wheel.
    (d) mathematics and jurisprudence.

IDENTIFICATIONS

Tigris	Hammurabi
Sargon	Epic of Gilgamesh
Ur	Kassites
Akkad	Sennacherib
Sumerian Revival	Nineveh
cuneiform	Medes
ziggurat	Chaldeans
salinization	Nebuchadnezzar
Amorites	Hanging Gardens

TRUE OR FALSE

T   1. Southern Mesopotamia was entirely lacking in natural resources such as stone, minerals, and trees.

T   2. The lunar calendar resulted from the need for precise agricultural planning in Mesopotamia's perilous climate.

F   3. Cuneiform refers to writing through the use of pictures.

T   4. Sumerian temple complexes served as centers of not only religious practice but also economic production and trade.

F   5. The Code of Hammurabi was a step in the direction of the concept of equality before the law because it accorded even slaves the right to "an eye for an eye."

T   6. Old Babylonian arithmetic and algebraic concepts were so advanced that the Old Babylonians must be considered the most accomplished mathematicians of antiquity.

T 7. The Old Babylonian Empire declined because of a combination of a series of rulers lacking governing skills and the inability to adjust to new fighting techniques.

T 8. Some early-twentieth-century scholars assumed that the Hittites' power rested in part on their racial superiority.

T 9. The fame of Sennacherib's Nineveh rested on its size, its system of aqueducts, and its immense library, which contained all of Sumerian and Old Babylonian learning and literature.

F 10. The New Babylonians developed sophisticated military technologies but achieved no significant intellectual advancements.

DISCUSSION AND/OR ESSAY QUESTIONS

1. Discuss this statement: "The 'first chapter of history,' which the Mesopotamians wrote by their exploits and their documents, was surely one of the most important chapters in the entire book of human events." (p. 17)

2. Defend or refute this statement: "Although historians often concentrate on the exploits of individuals like Sargon the Great, Hammurabi, Sennacherib, and Nebuchadnezzar, the achievements of the anonymous persons who invented the wheel and developed the lunar calendar and cuneiform were much more significant in shaping human history."

3. Agree or disagree, in whole or in part: "The Code of Hammurabi reveals the Old Babylonians to be a primitive and savage people, with no concept of justice or notion of equality."

4. In what ways did the New Babylonian development of astrology contribute to a scientific worldview?

5. How did climate and geography shape the history of the Mesopotamian civilizations? To what degree were human beings free to determine the course of their destiny, and to what degree did the impersonal forces of climate and geography control events?

SUGGESTED CLASSROOM FILMS

Ancient Cultures of Mesopotamia: I. The Sumerian Kingdom of Ur. II. Babylon: The Gate of the Gods. III. Assurnasirpal: The Assyrian King. 25 min. each. Color. 1989. Insight Media.

Mesopotamia. 30 min. Color. 1989. Insight Media. A look at the political, religious, and social structures of the empires of Mesopotamia.

Sumer, Babylon, Assyria: The Wolves. 26 min. Color. 1991. Films for the Humanities. Uses collections of Near Eastern antiquities to explore the militarism of ancient civilizations.

CHAPTER 3. EGYPTIAN CIVILIZATION

Outline

Introduction: Comparison of Egyptian and Mesopotamian civilizations
  I. Political history under the pharaohs
      A. The pre-archaic period: the development of hieroglyphic
      B. Egyptian unification
      C. The Old Kingdom
          1. The absolute power of the pharaohs
          2. Nonmilitarism
          3. Downfall of the Old Kingdom and the first intermediate period
      D. The Middle Kingdom
          1. Egypt's golden age
          2. The second intermediate period: the invasion of the Hyksos
      E. The New Kingdom
          1. The rise of aggressive imperialism
          2. The decline of Egypt and the end of Egyptian independence
 II. Egyptian religion
      A. Early religious evolution
          1. The solar faith
          2. The Osiris cult
          3. The hereafter and the development of ethical religion
      B. The debasement of religion under the empire
          1. The rise of magic
          2. The reforms of Akhenaton
          3. The restoration of the old religion
III. Egyptian intellectual achievements
      A. Egyptian writing
          1. The alphabet
          2. The use of papyrus
      B. Egyptian science
          1. Astronomy and the calendar
          2. Medicine and the belief in natural causes
          3. Mathematics and measurement
 IV. The splendor of Egyptian art
      A. The pyramids
      B. The temples
      C. Sculpture
      D. Akhenaton's artistic revolution

V. Social and economic life
   A. The class system
   B. The role of women
   C. Agriculture, trade, and industry
   D. Economic collectivism
VI. The Egyptian achievement

MULTIPLE CHOICE
Choose the best response.

1. The stability and serenity of Egyptian civilization is explained by all of the following EXCEPT
    (a) the regular flooding of the Nile.
    *(b) the most powerful standing army of the ancient world.
    (c) a predictable and bountiful growing season.
    (d) geographical isolation.

2. The most important development during the archaic period was the
    *(a) unification of Upper and Lower Egypt.
    (b) invention of the hieroglyphic system.
    (c) shift from nomadic to settled farming.
    (d) creation of a standing army.

3. During the period of the Old Kingdom, the pharaohs
    (a) lost much power to the warring nobles.
    (b) relied on military power as the basis of their absolute rule.
    (c) succeeded in redirecting Egyptian religion from magic to ethics.
    *(d) had nearly unlimited powers because of the lack of separation between religious and political life.

4. The reign of the Twelfth Dynasty (the Middle Kingdom) is considered to be Egypt's classical or golden age because
    (a) it was the only period in Egyptian history in which military values did not predominate.
    (b) it was the period in which the pyramids were built.
    (c) of the great victory over the Hyksos.
    *(d) it was a time of economic prosperity and social responsibility.

5. During both the first and second intermediate periods,
    *(a) Egypt endured both foreign invasion and political chaos.
    (b) Egyptian rulers focused on public works that benefited ordinary people.
    (c) Egypt was subject to Greek rule.
    (d) democratic revolts abolished the rule of the pharaoh.

6. A spirit of aggressive imperialism characterized which period in Egyptian history?
   (a) the Old Kingdom
   (b) the first intermediate period
   (c) the Middle Kingdom
   *(d) the New Kingdom

7. After the unification of Egypt, the various gods who personified the powers of nature were fused into a deity called
   *(a) Osiris.
   (b) Aton.
   (c) Amon.
   (d) Tut.

8. During the period of the Old Kingdom, the solar faith
   (a) gave common people a personal god to which to pray.
   *(b) was the official state religion through which the state and the people collectively gained immortality.
   (c) was an attempt to reform the magical religion.
   (d) gave way to the cult of Osiris.

9. The Osiris legend offered Egyptians comfort and inspiration for all the following reasons EXCEPT
   (a) they could see that the gods also suffered terrible trials.
   *(b) the overthrow of Seth promised a future of democratic equality and social justice.
   (c) Osiris's resurrection promised personal immortality.
   (d) Horus's victory foreshadowed the ultimate triumph of good over evil.

10. The religious revolution of Akhenaton failed because
    *(a) it was rejected by the pharaohs who followed Akhenaton and restored the old religion.
    (b) although welcomed by ordinary people, it was rejected by elites who refused to give up any of their power.
    (c) its polytheism offended the priests.
    (d) it lacked an ethical emphasis.

11. Unlike most ancient systems of medicine, the Egyptian system
    (a) relied on priests for medical information and treatment.
    (b) held that illness was controlled by astrological and magical forces.
    (c) viewed disease as a sign of divine displeasure.
    *(d) held that diseases had natural causes and thus could be diagnosed and treated.

12. The first pyramid was that of the pharaoh
    (a) Ramses.
    (b) Ahmose.
    (c) Akhenaton.
    *(d) Zoser.

13. The pyramids were built largely by
    (a) slave labor.
    (b) professional and much-honored construction teams.
    *(c) agricultural laborers during the unproductive summer months.
    (d) hired armies from foreign countries.

14. Which of the following is NOT true of the pyramids?
    (a) They were believed to be the "stairways" by which the pharaohs ascended to eternal life.
    *(b) They were seen as the avenues by which individuals could find personal salvation.
    (c) Their builders found pride in teamwork.
    (d) The Egyptians believed that their completion meant that earthly prosperity would increase.

15. Which of the following was NOT a characteristic of mainstream Egyptian art?
    (a) Anatomical distortion
    *(b) Naturalism
    (c) Rigid figures
    (d) Lack of emotional expression

16. Akhenaton's artistic revolution was characterized by
    (a) the use of anatomical distortion.
    (b) an emphasis on larger-than-life figures.
    (c) depiction of gods rather than human beings.
    *(d) a naturalistic style.

17. During the period of the Empire or New Kingdom, a sixth class was added to the social structure, that of the
    *(a) professional soldiers.
    (b) priests.
    (c) scribes and merchants.
    (d) slaves.

18. The stability of Egyptian history did NOT rest on
    (a) favorable natural resources.
    *(b) lack of a great gulf between rich and poor.
    (c) geographical location.
    (d) religious cohesion.

19. Unlike in most ancient societies, women in Egypt were
    (a) considered slaves.
    (b) treated as men's equals.
    *(c) allowed to own property.
    (d) permitted many husbands.

20. Economic collectivism in Egypt meant
    (a) the Egyptians organized the first socialist state.
    (b) the pharaoh owned all the land and businesses.
    *(c) the interests of the individual and of society were conceived as identical.
    (d) all goods were held in common.

IDENTIFICATIONS

Old Kingdom	Osiris
hieroglyphic	Akhenaton
Zoser	Nefertiti
Twelfth Dynasty	papyrus
Hyksos	the pi ratio
Ahmose	Pyramid of Khufu (Cheops)
Ramses III	Great Sphinx
Amon	

TRUE OR FALSE

F   1. The annual pattern by which the Nile overflowed and receded made the Egyptians believe nature to be capricious and hostile.

T   2. Even before the beginning of the archaic period the Egyptians had begun to engage in settled farming.

T   3. The Old Kingdom fell because of a combination of the exhaustion of governmental revenues and climatic disasters.

F   4.   The invasion of the Hyksos destroyed the Middle Kingdom and ushered in several centuries of anarchy and disunity.

T   5.   The cult of Osiris gave ordinary Egyptians a personal god through whom one could achieve immortality.

T   6.   Among the doctrines established by Akhenaton in his religious reformation was the belief that the new god Aton was a heavenly father who took loving care of his children.

F   7.   The Egyptians were the first people to devise an exclusively alphabetical system of writing.

T   8.   The Egyptians were the first people to discover the pi ratio.

T   9.   Religious psychology and group dynamics rather than coercion appear to explain why laborers undertook the arduous task of constructing the pyramids.

F   10.   During the later years of the Empire, the collectivist ethos of the Egyptians broke down and the government withdrew from all business and construction enterprises.

DISCUSSION AND/OR ESSAY QUESTIONS

1. Agree or disagree, in whole or in part: "Although the Egyptian civilization is more appealing to modern eyes, the civilization of the Mesopotamians played a much more significant role in shaping human history."

2. Consider the relationship among natural resources, climate, and the history of Egypt. Do you agree that environment, rather than human endeavor, decided the course of events?

3. Trace the evolution of Egyptian religion from the archaic period through the time of the New Kingdom. What function did religion serve in Egyptian society? What was the relationship between religious practices and political events?

4. How do you explain the achievement of the pyramids? What role did these structures play in Egyptian religious and social life?

5. Discuss: "The history of Egypt is best read as a morality play, one which warns us of the dangers of militarism and imperialism."

SUGGESTED CLASSROOM FILMS

Ancient Egypt: The Sun and the River. 58 min. Color. 1971. University Films Library Holder. Explores the art and architecture of Egyptian culture.

The Ancient Egyptian. 27 min. Color. 1967. Insight Media. Uses art and artifacts to explore religious beliefs and cultural values. Winner of the Blue Ribbon, American Film and Video Festival.

Egypt: The Gift of the Nile. 29 min. Color. 1977. Centron Educational Films. Explores Egyptian history and the role of the Nile.

The Glory That Remains. No. 10—A Matter of Life and Death. 31 min. Color. 1969. BBC/Time-Life Films. Focuses on the daily life of ancient Egypt. *No. 11—The 1000 Year Walk.* 31 min. Color. 1969. BBC/Time-Life Films. The history of Egypt from 1800 to 800 B.C.E.

Hymn to Aton. 15 min. Color. 1977. Phoenix. Examines the reign of Akhenaton and his attempts to introduce monotheism to Egypt.

Life Under the Pharaohs. 21 min. Color. 1989. Insight Media. Uses ancient paintings to depict everyday life.

Mysteries of the Great Pyramid. 50 min. Color. 1977. Wolper Productions. Looks at still-unanswered questions regarding the construction and purpose of the Great Pyramid.

Tut: The Boy King. 2 parts, each 26 min. Color. 1977. Films, Inc. Uses the treasure of his tomb to examine his reign.

CHAPTER 4. THE HEBREW AND EARLY GREEK CIVILIZATIONS

Outline

   I. Importance of Hebrews and early Greeks

  II. The record of political hopes and frustrations

      A. The struggle for Canaan

      B. The reign of King Saul

      C. The reign of King David

      D. Solomon, Jerusalem, and the Temple

          1. The need for a capital and a temple

          2. Northern antagonism and secession

      E. The Kingdoms of Israel and Judah

          1. The destruction of Israel

          2. The Babylonian Captivity

      F. Palestine from Persian overlordship to the diaspora

 III. Hebrew religious development

      A. The stage of national monolatry

          1. The figure of Yahweh

          2. Contributions to Western thought

          3. Moral precepts, rituals, and tabus

      B. The prophetic revolution

          1. The prophets

          2. Basic doctrines

      C. The postexilic stage

          1. This-worldly eschatology

          2. Otherworldly eschatology

          3. Expectations of the Messiah

  IV. Hebrew law and literature

      A. Hebrew law: the Deuteronomic Code

      B. Hebrew literature

          1. The Song of Songs

          2. The Book of Job

          3. The Book of Ecclesiastes

          4. The Book of Malachi

   V. The magnitude of the Hebrew influence

  VI. The Minoan and Mycenaean civilizations

      A. Rediscovery of the first Greeks

      B. The rise and fall of the Minoan and Mycenaean civilizations

C. Characteristics of Minoan civilization
1. The bureaucratic monarchy
2. Social and sexual equality
3. Matriarchal religion
4. Scientific and artistic achievements
D. Comparison of Minoan and Mycenaean civilizations
E. The significance of the Minoan and Mycenaean civilizations

MULTIPLE CHOICE
Choose the best response.

1. During their migration from Mesopotamia to Egypt, the Hebrew tribe began to call themselves
    (a) Canaanites.
    *(b) Israelites.
    (c) Palestinians.
    (d) Jews.

2. Which of the following is NOT true of Hebrew history before the period of national monarchy?
    (a) The Hebrews were a nomadic pastoral tribe who originated in Mesopotamia.
    *(b) The Hebrews were conquered in war by the Egyptians and forced to leave Syria for slavery in Egypt.
    (c) The Hebrews became worshippers of Yahweh.
    (d) The Hebrews failed in their attempt to claim Canaan for their own.

3. The Hebrews adopted a monarchical instead of tribal system of organization as a response to
    (a) the threat of enslavement by the Egyptians.
    (b) their desire to shift from a nomadic to a settled existence.
    *(c) the need to defend themselves against the Philistines.
    (d) their acceptance of a religion characterized by monolatry.

4. During the reign of King Saul the
    (a) building of the temple was completed.
    (b) Hebrews destroyed the might of the Philistines.
    *(c) king was faced with the challenge of a popular contender for the throne.
    (d) northern tribes seceded to form their own nation.

5. All of the following occurred in David's reign EXCEPT the
   *(a) Babylonian Captivity.
   (b) subjugation of the Canaanites.
   (c) shift from pastoralism to farming and urban occupations.
   (d) use of forced labor and the collection of taxes.

6. Solomon's Temple was
   (a) actually constructed during the reign of Saul.
   (b) the name given the portable tent that housed the Ark of the Covenant.
   (c) first discovered by Arthur Evans in 1899.
   *(d) one of the reasons the northern tribes seceded from the Hebrew state.

7. The northern Hebrew kingdom was called _____; the southern
   remnant was called _____.
   (a) Palestine; Israel
   (b) Minoa; Crete
   (c) Judah; Egypt
   *(d) Israel; Judah

8. The Northern Kingdom was destroyed by the
   (a) Palestinians.
   (b) Minoans.
   *(c) Assyrians.
   (d) Romans.

9. The four stages in the growth of the Hebrew religion were
   *(a) polytheism, monolatry, the prophetic revolution, the post-exilic stage.
   (b) atheism, monolatry, polytheism, the prophetic revolution.
   (c) polytheism, monolatry, the prophetic revolution, atheism.
   (d) the post-exilic stage, matriarchy, monolatry, the prophetic revolution.

10. One of the most important Hebrew contributions to Western thought that
    emerged during the stage of monolatry was
    *(a) transcendent theology.
    (b) pacifism.
    (c) feminism.
    (d) a concept of God as exclusively righteous.

11. The writer of the Book of Daniel taught that
    (a) the chief deity was not a god but a goddess.
    (b) marriage is a symbol of the love between God and humanity.
    *(c) the messiah would preside over a Last Judgment.
    (d) everything is cyclical and nothing adds up to lasting achievement.

12. The major repository of Hebrew law is called the
    (a) Odyssey.
    *(b) Deuteronomic Code.
    (c) Book of Ecclesiastes.
    (d) Code of Hammurabi.

13. Which of the following books of the Old Testament probably originated as a collection of secular wedding poems?
    (a) The Psalms.
    (b) The Book of Isaiah.
    (c) Ecclesiastes.
    *(d) The Song of Songs.

14. Which of the following is NOT true of the Book of Job?
    (a) The story concerns a virtuous man who is overtaken by a series of disasters.
    *(b) Job is proven blameless by his refusal to despair or to blame God.
    (c) Job's friends argue that all suffering must be understood as a punishment for sin.
    (d) God is shown to be far above the understanding of humanity.

15. The Hebrew legacy to Western civilization includes all of the following EXCEPT
    (a) monotheism.
    *(b) some of the world's greatest painting and sculpture.
    (c) a system of morality.
    (d) a sense that nature can be mastered for humanity's purposes.

16. Because of the research of Heinrich Schliemann
    *(a) Homer's *Iliad* has been shown to be based on historical fact.
    (b) scholars now believe the Book of Isaiah to be the work of three authors.
    (c) the Psalms have been shown to have been written over several centuries.
    (d) Linear B has been deciphered.

17. When the Minoan civilization was at its peak
    (a) the island of Crete served as the hub of a vast empire.
    (b) Crete was ruled by Israel.
    (c) a prophetic revolution called the people back to traditional religious beliefs.
    *(d) several prosperous cities co-existed peacefully on Crete.

18. Which of the following did NOT characterize Minoan civilization?
    (a) Minoan painting served to teach religious doctrines to apparently illiterate workers.
    (b) Communal games and sports formed an important part of their culture.
    *(c) Women took part in public activities.
    (d) Trade and handicrafts played an important role in the Minoan economy.

19. Compared to Minoan civilization, that of Mycenae was
    (a) much more decentralized.
    (b) rural rather than urban.
    *(c) geared more toward warfare.
    (d) much less dependent on slave labor.

20. The Mycenaean and Minoan civilizations are historically significant for all the following reasons EXCEPT:
    (a) They were the earliest European civilizations.
    (b) They exhibited a worldly and progressive outlook.
    (c) Their art shared certain characteristics with that of later European peoples.
    *(d) Their religious systems passed almost unaltered into the later Greek civilization.

IDENTIFICATIONS

Jacob	Amos
Philistines	messiah
Samuel	Song of Songs
Ark of the Covenant	Malachi
tabernacle	Heinrich Schliemann
Babylonian Captivity	Agamemnon
Judas Maccabeus	Arthur Evans
diaspora	Knossos
monolatry	Linear B
transcendent theology	Dorians

TRUE OR FALSE

F   1. Under Joshua the Hebrews established themselves as the dominant people of Canaan.

T   2. Solomon's building projects overstrained the nation's resources and contributed to the secession of the northern tribes.

F   3.   After the Babylonian Captivity the Judean tribes were annihilated and so disappeared from history.

T   4.   The prophets effected a religious revolution when they declared that Yahweh desired justice and righteousness more than ritual and sacrifices.

T   5.   The Jews came to believe in the coming of the messiah during the period that they were under direct or indirect rule by the Persians and the Greeks.

T   6.   No Hebrew sculpture or painting exists because the Hebrew religious code prohibited the making of likenesses.

F   7.   Like the Code of Hammurabi, the Deuteronomic Code allowed no rights to slaves.

T   8.   The writer of Ecclesiastes taught that human life has little meaning or purpose.

F   9.   Archeological and linguistic research since the late nineteenth century has shown Homer's *Iliad* to be wholly fictional.

F   10.   Unlike the Minoan state, the Mycenaean government was a bureaucratic monarchy.

DISCUSSION AND/OR ESSAY QUESTIONS

1. "The Hebrews exerted the greatest influence of any ancient western Asian peoples on the thought and life of the modern world" (p. 59). Discuss those areas in which you believe the Hebrews had the greatest impact.

2. What was the role of the Temple in the rise, decline, and continued survival of the Jewish people?

3. "But what does the Lord require of thee but to do justice, to love mercy, and to walk humbly with thy God?" (Micah 6:8). Discuss this verse in the context of the prophetic revolution.

4. Consider the Song of Songs, the Book of Job, and Ecclesiastes. What picture of the Hebrew people would you draw from these sources? What are the problems with using these works for such an assignment?

5. Discuss: "The history of the Minoan and Mycenaean civilizations shows that the idea of historical 'progress' is an illusion—the Minoan civilization was far more 'progressive.' "

SUGGESTED FEATURE FILMS

Ulysses. 103 min. Color. 1954. Lux Film. Kirk Douglas stars in this generally faithful version of the *Odyssey*.

SUGGESTED CLASSROOM FILMS

The Age of Minos. 38 min. B/W. 1969. BBC/Time-Life Films. Explores the legends of Zeus, Minos, and Theseus and the Minotaur.

The Bible as Literature. Part One: Saga and Story in the Old Testament; Part Two: History, Poetry, and Drama in the Old Testament. 26 min. each. Color. 1974. Encyclopaedia Britannica Educational Corporation. Examines the Bible from a literary perspective.

Enigma of the Dead Sea Scrolls. 50 min. Color. 1993. Insight Media. Features leading scholars in this look at the history, significance, and controversy of the Scrolls.

The Glory That Remains. No. 1—The Sudden Empire. 30 min. Color. 1969. BBC/Time-Life Films. Persia under the Archaemid dynasty. *No. 2—Invaders and Converts.* 28 min. Persia during the Mongol Invasions.

The Greeks (I): The Greek Beginning. 52 min. Color. Films for the Humanities. From the Mycenaean Age to the death of Alexander the Great. With Sir Kenneth Dover of Corpus Christi College, Oxford.

The Myth of Masada. 28 min. Color. Films for the Humanities. Was Masada an episode in Roman siege warfare or a proto-nationalist myth?

The Search for Ulysses. 53 min. Color. 1965. Carousel. Follows Ulysses' journey in the *Odyssey.*

Secrets of the Dead Sea Scrolls. 60 min. Color. 1991. Films for the Humanities. A WGBH production that examines historical significance of and controversy surrounding the Scrolls.

PART TWO. THE CLASSICAL CIVILIZATIONS OF GREECE AND ROME
CHAPTER 5. GREEK CIVILIZATION

Outline

I. The Greek Dark Ages
  A. Political patterns
  B. Social and economic life
  C. Religious life
    1. The gods
    2. Life after death
II. The emergence of the city-states
  A. Origins
  B. Economic development
  C. Colonization
  D. Government: participatory, military, male
III. The armed camp of Sparta
  A. Government and politics
  B. Military values and culture
IV. The Athenian political partnership
  A. Development of democracy
    1. Solon's reforms
    2. Pisistratus's benevolent tyranny
    3. Clisthenes and democracy
  B. Workings of democracy
    1. Structure
    2. Differences from modern democracies
V. The Persian War and the Peloponnesian War
  A. The Persian War
  B. The Peloponnesian War
    1. Origins
    2. Outcome
VI. Women and men in the daily life of ancient Athens
  A. The female experience
    1. Exclusion from political life
    2. A life of childbirth and seclusion
  B. The shadow of slavery
  C. Simple living
VII. Greek philosophy
  A. The Pre-Socratics
  B. The Pythagoreans
  C. The Sophists: Protagoras
  D. Socrates

MULTIPLE CHOICE
Choose the best response.

1. Our knowledge of the Greek Dark Ages is based on
    (a) the Bible.
    (b) deciphered Linear B tablets.
    *(c) the *Iliad* and the *Odyssey*.
    (d) archaeological findings.

2. During the Greek Dark Ages, political and economic power was held by
    (a) women.
    (b) priests.
    (c) Minoan rulers.
    *(d) kings and warriors.

3. Which of the following statements was NOT true of Greek religion during the Dark Ages?
    (a) It was polytheistic.
    (b) It lacked dogmas, commandments, and professional priests.
    *(c) It promised eternal life to believers.
    (d) It revealed confidence in human greatness.

4. The rise of the polis rested on the
    *(a) revival of trade and the invention of the alphabet.
     (b) formation of a professional priesthood.
     (c) shift from democratic to monarchical government.
     (d) collapse of the Egyptian empire.

5. What important change in military techniques brought about wider
    participation in Greek political affairs?
    *(a) a shift from chariot warfare to battles dominated by phalanxes
     (b) a shift from the dominance of infantry to the dominance of cavalry
     (c) the use of the catapult
     (d) the use of swords and armor instead of spears and shields

6. Unlike in modern forms of democracy, in the Greek city-states
     (a) only propertied women had the vote.
     (b) the executive was elected by the legislature.
    *(c) no difference existed between the state and its citizens.
     (d) only military leaders could vote and hold office.

7. A political system based on checks and balances was first introduced by
     (a) Athens.
    *(b) Sparta.
     (c) Crete.
     (d) Corinth.

8. The vast majority of Sparta's population were unfree farm laborers called
     (a) polis.
     (b) thebes.
    *(c) helots.
     (d) thales.

9. The Spartans were able to avoid overseas political and military
    entanglements because
     (a) their military might made them the most feared power in Asia Minor.
     (b) of their alliance with Persia.
    *(c) they did not need imported goods and so engaged in little international
          trade.
     (d) the citizens voted annually against war.

10. The reforms of Solon
    (a) introduced a system of dual monarchy to Athens.
    (b) placed political power in the hands of a military dictatorship.
    (c) gave slaves the vote.
*(d) regarded wealth rather than birth as the main qualification for political participation.

11. The father of Athenian democracy was
    (a) Plato.
    (b) Pisistratus.
    (c) Socrates.
*(d) Clisthenes.

12. In _____, executive authority was given to a small number of magistrates, chosen annually by lot.
*(a) Athens
    (b) Sparta
    (c) Crete
    (d) Corinth

13. Which of the following statements describes the Persian War INCORRECTLY?
    (a) Sparta and Athens were allies.
    (b) The war can be seen as a victory for Greek ideals of freedom.
    (c) The war created the conditions for the emergence of the Athenian empire and ultimately war between Sparta and Athens.
*(d) The military resourcefulness of the Greeks prevented the Persians from winning a single battle.

14. As a result of the Peloponnesian War
*(a) the city-states entered a period characterized by civil strife and unending warfare.
    (b) the supremacy of the Athenian empire was established.
    (c) the city-states were forced to submit to Persia.
    (d) Athens formed naval and defensive alliances that ultimately led to war with Sparta.

15. The emergence of democracy worsened the lives of Athenian women for all the following reasons EXCEPT
    (a) the emphasis on the infantry led to exaltation of male friendships and sexual relationships.
    (b) women were expected to produce children to serve the state.
    (c) the development of public spaces for "male" activities.
*(d) women were not expected to do any useful work.

16. Athenians idealized homosexual rather than heterosexual love because
    (a) they feared overpopulation.
    *(b) they believed men were superior to women.
    (c) men did not live with their wives until they were thirty years old.
    (d) they feared that love for a woman would make a man "soft."

17. Which of the following was NOT a characteristic feature of Athenian life?
    (a) simple ways of living
    *(b) leisured way of life for women
    (c) dependence on slavery
    (d) respect for intellectual endeavor

18. The Pre-Socratics
    *(a) believed that all things could be reduced to some primary substance.
    (b) argued that supernatural forces could be discerned in natural events.
    (c) believed that the only purpose in life is pleasure.
    (d) condemned the Athenian subjugation of women.

19. The _____ were professional teachers who focused on practical wisdom and were frequently relativists.
    (a) Thebans
    (b) Corinthians
    *(c) Sophists
    (d) Platonists

20. _____ was put to death on a charge of "corrupting the youth" of Athens.
    (a) Protagorus
    *(b) Socrates
    (c) Plato
    (d) Aristotle

21. _____ taught that a higher, spiritual realm exists that cannot be comprehended with our physical senses.
    (a) Protagorus
    (b) Socrates
    *(c) Plato
    (d) Aristotle

22. _____ argued for an elitist state ruled by intellectually superior "guardians."
    (a) Protagorus
    (b) Socrates
    *(c) Plato
    (d) Aristotle

23. _____ believed that everything in nature has a purpose, and that this purpose can be known through systematic observation and rational inquiry.
    (a) Protagorus
    (b) Socrates
    (c) Plato
    *(d) Aristotle

24. Greek medicine was based on the assumption that
    (a) the material world is only a reflection of the real world of ideas.
    *(b) every disease has a natural cause.
    (c) only free men feel pain.
    (d) human health, like the rest of the universe, is in the hands of a capricious god.

25. The father of history was
    (a) Pisistratus.
    (b) Plato.
    (c) Euripides.
    *(d) Herodotus.

26. Sappho was
    (a) believed by the Greeks to have written the *Iliad*.
    (b) the first woman to be immortalized in sculpture.
    (c) the leader of the successful Athenian uprising against Sparta.
    *(d) one of the most gifted of the Greek lyric poets.

27. Which of the following was NOT characteristic of Greek tragic drama?
    *(a) Interest in plot led to a proliferation of subplots and so to very complicated scripts.
    (b) Tragedy was meant to inspire pity and fear in the audience.
    (c) The plot often depicted a terrible change in the central character's fortunes.
    (d) All the roles were played by men.

28. The Greek playwright who displayed a notable sense of sympathy for women was
    (a) Socrates.
    (b) Pythagoras.
    *(c) Euripides.
    (d) Thucydides.

29. The sudden appearance in Greek art of well-proportioned, naturalistic statues depicting naked human figures is linked to what political event?
   * (a) the Greek triumph in the Persian War
   (b) the establishment of the Theban empire
   (c) Sparta's victory over Crete
   (d) the emancipation of women

30. The Greeks passed on to Western civilization
   (a) the idea that all dissenting opinions should be tolerated.
   (b) the concept of the equality of the sexes.
   (c) the concept of the state as an abstract entity.
   * (d) a high regard for secular inquiry and human capability.

IDENTIFICATIONS

Iliad	Pythagoras
Peloponnesian War	Protagoras
polis	Socrates
phalanx	doctrine of ideas
helot	Aristotle
Solon	Hippocrates
Clisthenes	Sappho
Helen of Troy	Sophocles
Pre-Socratics	Aristophanes

TRUE OR FALSE

T 1. During the Dark Ages Greek women had more freedom than during the classical period.

T 2. Despite their belief in the capriciousness of the gods, the Greeks perceived no need for a professional priesthood.

F 3. In the Greek city-states, only the scribal class was literate.

T 4. Although the Spartans kept themselves in a state of perpetual military preparedness, they managed better than most other Greeks to avoid war.

T 5. Clisthenes is known as the father of Athenian democracy because in the system he introduced every free man has some role in influencing Athenian affairs.

F   6.   In Athens, the father selected his daughter's spouse, but she retained the right to veto his choice.

T   7.   Except in the state-owned silver mines, Athenian slavery was small in scale.

T   8.   Socrates, Plato, and Aristotle all belonged to the philosophic movement that opposed Sophist relativism and argued that truth is real and absolute standards do exist.

T   9.   Socrates insisted on the importance of sound definition as the basis for a system of truth.

F   10.   Unlike the temple architecture of ancient Egypt, that of Greece stressed the vertical rather than the horizontal and sought to create an impression of energy and uncontrollable emotion.

DISCUSSION AND/OR ESSAY QUESTIONS

1. Greek civilization can be regarded as the basis of much of the best in modern Western society. Defend the counterargument: that Greek society possessed great weaknesses, many of which continue to trouble human society.
2. Discuss: "Athenian democracy was born in war and was destroyed by war."
3. Write an essay entitled "Victory in the Persian War: A Turning Point for Athens." In what ways can the Persian War be seen as pivotal in the evolution of Athenian politics, foreign relations, intellectual endeavors, and artistic achievements?
4. Compare and contrast the ideas of Socrates, Plato, and Aristotle. Why does your textbook author regard the three as members of a single philosophical movement?
5. What role did slavery play in the economic, political, and cultural development of Sparta and Athens?

SUGGESTED FEATURE FILMS

Aeschylus: The Oresteia (*Agamemnon*, 90 min.; *The Libation Bearers*, 70 min.; *The Furies*, 70 min.). Color. 1985. Films for the Humanities. The National Theatre of Great Britain production, directed by Peter Hall.

Antigone. 88 min. B/W. 1962. Fleetwood. Greek dialogue with English subtitles.

Euripides' Medea. 90 min. Color. 1982. Films for the Humanities. A Kennedy Center production with Zoe Caldwell as Medea. English text by Robinson Jeffers.

Oedipus the King. 105 min. Color. 1967. Alfredo Bini. Filmed in Morocco and set in modern times.

Orpheus and Eurydice: The Appia Staging. 91 min. Color. 1985. Films for the Humanities. Richard Beachame's re-creation of the opera as staged by Appia in 1912. With the University of Warwick Chamber Orchestra and Chorus.

Sophocles: The Theban Plays (Oedipus the King, Oedipus at Colonus, Antigone). 120 min. each. Color. 1987. Films for the Humanities. Films for the Humanities joined up with the BBC to coproduce these modern versions of classical Greek drama. Performers include John Gielgud, Claire Bloom, Anthony Quayle, and Juliet Stevenson.

Thucydides: The Peloponnesian Wars and Plato: Alcibiades I. 72 min. Color. 1991. Films for the Humanities. Seventeen British classical actors (including Ben Kingsley and Alex McCowen) from the National Theatre and the Royal Shakespeare Company enact the story. Set as a contemporary news program.

SUGGESTED CLASSROOM FILMS

The Ancient Games. 28 min. Color. 1972. ABC. Modern athletes recreate the ancient Olympics in this documentary written and narrated by Erich Segal.

The Ancient World: Greece, Part II. 29 min. Color. 1955. New York University. Examines the art and literature of Greece in the fifth century B.C.E. with narration drawn entirely from Greek authors.

Classical Comedy. 60 min. Color. 1976. Films for the Humanities. Performance of excerpts from Aristophanes's *Ecclesiazusai* and Plautius's *Miles Gloriosus.*

Conversations with Ancient History. 60 min. 1991. Insight Media. The classics scholar Edith Hamilton hosts a series of "conversations" with ancient figures.

Death of Socrates. 45 min. B/W. 1968. Time-Life Films. Modern-dress dramatization of Plato's account of Socrates's death.

Greek Myths. Part One—Myth as Fiction, History and Ritual. Part Two—Myth as Science, Religion and Drama. 25 min. each. Color. 1971. Encyclopaedia Britannica Educational Corporation. Uses films of sculptures, animation, and re-enactments.

Greek Thought. 2 parts, 30 min. each. 1989. Color. Insight Media. Dr. Eugen Weber's look at Greek art, science, and philosophy.

The Greeks: In Search of Meaning. 26 min. Color. 1971. Learning Corporation of America. Dramatized conversations with Sophocles, and performances from *Antigone* and *Lysistrata.*

The Greeks: II. The Classical Age. III. Heroes and Men. IV. The Minds of Men. 52 min. each. Color. 1982. Films for the Humanities. Sir Kenneth Dover of Corpus Christi College, Oxford, narrates this series.

Plato's Apology: The Life and Teachings of Socrates. 29 min. Color. 1962. Encyclopaedia Britannica Educational Corporation. Includes dramatizations of selections from Plato.

Plato's Drinking Party. 40 min. B/W. 1969. Time-Life Films. Sets Plato's dialogue on love at a college reunion.

The Rise of Greek Tragedy: Oedipus the King. 45 min. Color. 1975. Films for the Humanities. Greek tragedy staged as Greek tragedy. Filmed in the theatre of Amphiaraion with the Athens Classical Theatre Company. English soundtrack includes Claire Bloom and Ian Richardson.

The Temple of Apollo at Bassae. 16 min. Color. 1971. International Film Bureau. Features the temple built by the designer of the Parthenon.

The Trial of Socrates. 29 min. Color. 1971. Insight Media. A dramatization.

CHAPTER 6. THE HELLENISTIC CIVILIZATION

Outline

Introduction: The Hellenistic synthesis
- I. The Persian empire
  - A. The victories of Cyrus
  - B. The reign of Darius I
    - 1. Administrative achievements
    - 2. The Persian Wars
  - C. Persia's religious legacy: Zoroastrianism
    - 1. Universalism
    - 2. A personal religion
    - 3. Similarities to Judaism and Christianity
  - D. Persia's cultural legacy: universalism
- II. Philip of Macedon and Alexander the Great
  - A. The achievements of Philip of Macedon
  - B. Alexander the Great and the foundations of Hellenistic civilization
- III. Political and economic trends
  - A. Political organization of the Hellenistic state
    - 1. Oriental despotism
    - 2. City-state federalism
  - B. The economy of the Hellenistic states
    - 1. The growth of trade
    - 2. The growth of finance
    - 3. The growth of cities
    - 4. An economy of extremes
- IV. Hellenistic culture: philosophy and religion
  - A. Trends in philosophy: Stoicism, Epicureanism, Skepticism
  - B. Hellenistic religion
    - 1. Mystery cults
    - 2. Mithraism
- V. Hellenistic culture: literature and art
  - A. Hellenistic literature
    - 1. Drama and the pastoral
    - 2. History, biography, and utopias
  - B. Hellenistic architecture
  - C. Hellenistic sculpture
- VI. The first great age of science
  - A. Reasons for the advance
  - B. Astronomy, mathematics, and geography
  - C. Medicine, physiology, and physics

VII.   The balance sheet
    A. Hellenistic achievements
    B. Hellenistic cosmopolitanism and modernity

MULTIPLE CHOICE
Choose the best response.

1.   "Hellenistic" civilization receives its name from the fact that
   *(a) it was "Greek-like," composed of both Greek and Asian elements.
   (b) its greatest king was named Hellenes.
   (c) its mythology centered on Helen of Troy.
   (d) it possessed a purely Greek culture.

2.   The Persians acquired an unprecedented empire under the leadership of
   (a) Alexander the Great.
   (b) Philip.
   (c) Seleucus.
   *(d) Cyrus.

3.   Darius the Great's accomplishments included all of the following EXCEPT the
   *(a) defeat of the Athenians and incorporation of Greece into the Persian Empire.
   (b) division of the empire into satrapies.
   (c) construction of irrigation canals, a system of roads, and a new capital city.
   (d) development of the first postal system.

4.   In Zoroastrianism, the one supreme god in the universe is called
   (a) Croesus.
   (b) Philip.
   (c) Mithra.
   *(d) Ahura-Mazda.

5.   Which of the following is CORRECT regarding Persian culture?
   *(a) It embraced a tolerance of other peoples that expressed itself in intellectual and artistic eclecticism.
   (b) The influence of the Zoroastrian doctrine that "might makes right" made it an especially cruel society.
   (c) It differed from the other ancient cultures in its stress on the equality of the sexes.
   (d) It stressed Persian superiority and therefore tried to impose Persian ways on conquered peoples.

6. By the time Philip of Macedon died, he had
   (a) established Greek rule over Asia Minor.
   (b) extended his empire as far as India.
   *(c) installed his despotic rule throughout Greece.
   (d) led Athens to victory over Sparta.

7. The advantages that a professional army gave to Philip of Macedon in his quest to rule Greece did NOT include
   (a) a wide range of specialists.
   (b) strict discipline.
   *(c) unity and enthusiasm inspired by idealism.
   (d) elimination of large numbers of noncombatant servants.

8. Historians now agree that Alexander was motivated by
   *(a) the desire for personal power and glory.
   (b) a sense of mission to bring Greek enlightenment to Asia.
   (c) the desire to defend his father's empire from its enemies.
   (d) the need to expand because of the overpopulation of Greece.

9. Which of the following was NOT a result of Persian or Asiatic influence upon Alexander the Great?
   (a) Alexander's decision to proclaim himself a god
   (b) the encouragement of intermarriage between Greeks and conquered peoples
   (c) a lavish style of dress
   *(d) the extreme respect accorded to philosophers

10. The dominant form of government in the Hellenistic Age in all the lands conquered by Alexander except mainland Greece was
    (a) city-state federalism.
    *(b) despotism.
    (c) democracy.
    (d) oligarchy.

11. The Hellenistic world was generally prosperous for all the following reasons EXCEPT the
    (a) growth of trade.
    (b) promotion of manufacturing by autocratic rulers.
    (c) rise of cities.
    *(d) replacement of agriculture by trade and industry as the major source of wealth.

12. Cities grew enormously during the Hellenistic Age for all the following reasons EXCEPT
    (a) the Greek practice of founding urban centers as bases of imperial rule.
    (b) the growth of trade and manufacturing.
    *(c) the mistaken belief that only urban centers could provide safety from barbarian invasion.
    (d) governmental promotion of industry meant the proliferation of governmental offices.

13. Which of the following argued that all events are rigidly determined and that therefore no individual is in control of his or her destiny?
    (a) The Epicureans
    (b) The Skeptics
    (c) The Mithras
    *(d) The Stoics

14. Which taught that the state is a mere convenience, that absolute justice is a fiction, and that no wise man would take an active part in politics?
    *(a) The Epicureans
    (b) The Skeptics
    (c) The Mithras
    (d) The Stoics

15. Mithraism appealed to the lower classes because it
    *(a) offered an elaborate ritual and the promise of salvation.
    (b) taught the equality of all men and encouraged violent revolution.
    (c) condemned slavery and war.
    (d) rejected the spiritual world and emphasized physical pleasures.

16. Who invented the pastoral?
    *(a) Theocritus
    (b) Mithras
    (c) Aristarchus
    (d) Herophilus

17. The historian who argued that nations pass through predictable cycles of growth and decay was
    (a) Theocritus.
    (b) Thucydides.
    *(c) Polybius.
    (d) Aristarchus.

18. All of the following are characteristics of Hellenistic sculpture EXCEPT
    (a) extreme naturalism.
    (b) the desire to create something unique.
    *(c) understated restraint.
    (d) exaggerated postures.

19. Hellenistic rulers patronized scientists because
    (a) in order to develop healthy economies, they needed new industrial technologies.
    (b) they wished to make use of labor-saving devices.
    (c) they lived in an intellectual climate that stressed this-worldly activity and the possibility of creating utopia.
    *(d) they desired to add to their personal prestige.

20. Herophilus of Chalcedon achieved significant breakthroughs in the field of
    *(a) medicine.
    (b) mathematics.
    (c) astronomy.
    (d) physics.

IDENTIFICATIONS

Philip of Macedon	Seleucus
Hellenistic	Achaean League
Lydia	Diogenes
Croesus	Skeptics
Darius I	Mithras
Royal Road	pastoral
Xerxes I	Corinthian column
Ahriman	Euclid
magi	Archimedes

TRUE OR FALSE

F   1. Alexander laid the foundations for the Hellenistic civilization by his effort to impose not only Greek rule but Greek customs and culture throughout his empire.

F   2. In his career, Alexander sought to realize the ideals taught him by his tutor, Aristotle.

T	3.	After establishing himself as ruler of all the Persians, Cyrus founded the Persian Empire by overthrowing the lordship of the Medes and conquering Lydia and Babylon.
T	4.	By taking the title "King of Kings" Persian rulers implied their acceptance of the continued existence of various peoples with various rulers under the Persian imperial canopy.
T	5.	After the death of Alexander, the successors to the various Asian portions of his empire ruled as semi-divine despots.
T	6.	Despite the vast expansion in the number and size of cities during the Hellenistic Age, agriculture remained the major form of occupation and the primary source of wealth.
F	7.	The Cynics taught that because knowledge is limited to sense impressions, and because sense impressions can be deceptive, no truth can be certain.
T	8.	For most ordinary people, Hellenistic religion took the form of an emotional, personal faith that offered escape from present-day commitments.
F	9.	The *Almagest* of Ptolemy, which taught that the earth revolves around the sun, was handed down to medieval Europe as the classic summary of ancient astronomy.
T	10.	In its role as intermediary between Greece and Rome, Hellenistic culture both preserved and transmuted Greek civilization.

DISCUSSION AND/OR ESSAY QUESTIONS

1. Trace the development of the Persian Empire before the reign of Alexander the Great. What were the key events or turning points in this history?
2. Why was the Hellenistic Age characterized by economic expansion, innovation, and vitality?
3. Why is Alexander's reign called Hellenistic rather than Hellenic or Asian? Support your answer with specific examples.
4. Write an essay titled "The Hellenistic Era: The Quest for Escape." Be sure to consider philosophical, religious, literary, and artistic developments in your paper.
5. Defend or refute, in whole or in part: "In the Hellenistic age we see a decaying civilization, one in which the strengths of Greek society are taken to such extremes that they become weaknesses."

SUGGESTED CLASSROOM FILMS

The Age of Victory (Greece). 38 min. B/W. 1969. BBC/Time-Life Films. Discusses the revolt of Greece against Persian rule. Filmed on site.

Alexander the Great and the Hellenistic Age. 2 parts. 30 min. each. Color. 1989. Insight Media. Empire building and its cultural and social impact.

Alexander the Great: The Battle of Issus. 45 min. Color. Filmic Archives. Uses 3-D computer graphics to explore the terrain and tactics of this pivotal battle.

Heroes or History. 58 min. Color. 1978. Insight Media. From the *Crossroads of Civilization* series. Examines Alexander the Great's political and personal motives in his quest for power.

Macedonia: The Land of a God. 2 parts. 90 min. each. Color. 1995. Insight Media. Explores the cultural history of Macedonia under Philip II and Alexander.

CHAPTER 7.   ROMAN CIVILIZATION

Outline

Introduction: The Roman synthesis
- I. Early Italy and the Roman monarchy
    - A. Geography and Roman history
    - B. Early immigrations: the Etruscans and the Greeks
    - C. The founding of Rome
    - D. The government of Rome under the monarchy
- II. The early Republic
    - A. Expansion and warfare
    - B. Patricians versus plebeians
    - C. Roman religion and morality
- III. The fateful wars with Carthage
    - A. The empire of Carthage
    - B. Causes and course of the Punic Wars
    - C. Results of the wars with Carthage
- IV. The social struggles of the late Republic
    - A. The revolt of the Gracchi
    - B. The rule of Marius and Sulla
    - C. The rise and significance of Julius Caesar
- V. Rome becomes sophisticated
    - A. Epicureanism: Lucretius
    - B. Stoicism: Cicero
    - C. Roman literary achievements
    - D. Social conditions
    - E. The spread of slavery
- VI. The Principate or early Empire (27 B.C.E.–180 C.E.)
    - A. The struggle between Octavian and Antony
    - B. The reforms of Augustus
    - C. Good and bad emperors after Augustus
- VII. Culture and life in the period of the Principate
    - A. Philosophy and literature
    - B. Art and architecture
    - C. Science and technology
    - D. Negative aspects of Roman life: status of women and slaves
    - E. Spread of Mithraism and Christianity
    - F. Economic prosperity and weakness
- VIII. Roman Law
    - A. The influence of the jurists
    - B. The three divisions of law

IX. The crisis of the third century (180–284 C.E.)
    A. Civil war and its consequences
    B. The culture of the age of anxiety: Neoplatonism
X. Causes for Rome's decline
    A. Theories of decline
    B. Internal causes of decline
XI. The Roman heritage
    A. Comparison of Rome with the modern world
    B. Influence of Roman civilization

MULTIPLE CHOICE
Choose the best response.

1. Geography played a role in Roman history in which of the following ways?
    (a) The peninsula's extensive resources provided the necessary base for empire.
    (b) Easy access to water encouraged the Romans in their maritime exploits.
    (c) Scarcity of fertile land drove the Romans to expansionism.
    *(d) The ease with which the peninsula could be invaded encouraged militarism.

2. Which was NOT one of the dominant peoples on the Italian peninsula before the sixth century B.C.E.?
    (a) Romans
    (b) Etruscans
    (c) Greeks
    *(d) Egyptians

3. Annual warfare during the early Republic had all the following consequences EXCEPT it
    (a) enabled Rome to conquer almost all of the Italian peninsula.
    (b) provided land for agricultural colonization.
    (c) reinforced the Roman military ideal.
    *(d) provided incentives for the development of industry and commerce.

4. The plebeian victories
    *(a) won for the plebeians a larger share in government, including admission to the Senate.
    (b) shaped the Roman Republic along the lines of the Greek democracies.
    (c) proved short-lived as the plebeians were soon declared enemies of the state by the Senate.
    (d) deprived the Senate of all its power.

5. UNLIKE the Greeks, the Romans
   (a) believed they would be rewarded with eternal life if they regularly partook of the sacraments.
   (b) thought of God as an impersonal force rather than as a deity with a name and personality.
   *(c) literally revered their ancestors.
   (d) carefully separated religious and political life.

6. The results of the Punic Wars did NOT include
   (a) enormous increases in Roman territory.
   (b) the beginning of Rome's westward expansion.
   *(c) an increase in the number of small, independent farmers.
   (d) legal changes that gave Roman wives greater independence.

7. The Gracchus brothers proposed to alleviate social and economic stress by
   *(a) granting government lands to the landless.
   (b) abolishing slavery.
   (c) forming state-owned agricultural collectives.
   (d) strengthening the legislative power of the Senate.

8. The achievements of Julius Caesar did NOT include
   (a) settlement of unused land to relieve economic inequities.
   (b) policies that aimed to eliminate the distinction between Italians and provincials.
   (c) recognition of the possible significance of northwestern Europe.
   *(d) the rescue of the Republic from dictatorship.

9. Lucretius is usually described as a(n) _____ philosopher.
   (a) Stoic
   *(b) Epicurean
   (c) Christian
   (d) Neoplatonist

10. Which was NOT true of slavery in the Roman Empire?
    (a) Most of the productive labor was performed by slaves.
    (b) Slavery made possible the emergence of a lifestyle of luxury.
    *(c) Slaves were treated well because they cost so much.
    (d) A huge influx of slaves was one of the results of the Punic Wars.

11. The battle of Actium is significant because it
    (a) established Julius Caesar rather than Pompey as the ruler of Rome.
    (b) led to the Roman occupation of Spain.
    *(c) solidified Rome's Western orientation.
    (d) gave Romans a lasting distrust of monarchical government.

12. Augustus's reforms did NOT include
    (a) a new coinage system.
    (b) a program of incentives for colonization of the provinces.
    *(c) restrictions on gladiatorial combat.
    (d) abolition of tax farming.

13. Which of the following was NOT a Stoic?
    (a) Seneca
    (b) Cicero
    (c) Marcus Aurelius
    *(d) Commodus

14. The literature of the golden age
    *(a) sought to instruct and uplift its readers.
    (b) focused on bawdy entertainment.
    (c) savagely indicted the political corruption of the age.
    (d) emphasized the superiority of Greek over Roman culture.

15. Which of the following is INCORRECT concerning the period of the Principate?
    (a) Upper-class women were free to engage in intellectual and artistic pursuits.
    *(b) The Romans achieved great advances in science.
    (c) The "circuses" became more violent and bloody.
    (d) The Romans achieved great triumphs in engineering and public works.

16. The branches or divisions of Roman law did NOT include
    (a) civil law.
    *(b) royal law.
    (c) natural law.
    (d) law of the peoples.

17. The crisis of the third century
    (a) occurred as a result of the succession struggle following Augustus's death.
    (b) refers to the philosophical conflict between Stoics and Epicureans over the nature of things and human beings.
    *(c) was marked by civil war, economic chaos, and pestilence.
    (d) ended Rome's leading role in Western history.

18. The doctrines of Neoplatonism do NOT include
    (a) emanationism.
    (b) asceticism.
    (c) mysticism.
    *(d) humanism.

19. The best explanation for Rome's decline is that
    (a) the immorality and love of violence embedded in Roman culture weakened Roman civilization.
    (b) lead poisoning weakened Rome, both physically and mentally.
    *(c) Rome's internal political, economic, and cultural failings led to collapse.
    (d) the German invasions proved too severe for Roman resistance.

20. Your textbook author argues that Rome's *most important* contribution to the future was its
    (a) architectural and artistic legacy.
    (b) system of jurisprudence.
    (c) role as organizational model for the Catholic Church.
    *(d) transmission of Greek civilization to the European West.

IDENTIFICATIONS

Etruscans	Octavian
consul	Mark Antony
Law of the Twelve Tables	Trajan
Carthage	Seneca
Hannibal	Marcus Aurelius
Cato the Censor	Virgil
Marius	Juvenal
Ides of March	Pliny the Elder
Lucretius	Commodus
equestrians	Plotinus

TRUE OR FALSE

F   1. The Etruscans were the ancestors of the Romans.
T   2. In the time of the early Republic, morality was a matter of patriotism and respect for authority and tradition.
F   3. In the Third Punic War, Hannibal led the Romans to final victory over Carthage.
F   4. As a result of the Gracchan riots, Gaius Gracchus was able to establish a personal dictatorship over the Roman state.

T	5.	Growth of luxury, a widened gap between rich and poor, and an increase in slavery characterized the late Republic.
T	6.	After being branded as an enemy of the state, Julius Caesar established himself as the sole ruler of Rome through a series of stunning military victories.
F	7.	The *Pax Romana* refers to the ending of civil war in Rome and the period of political stability during the reign of Augustus.
T	8.	Upper-class women during the period of the Principate were—by the standards of the ancient world—relatively liberated.
T	9.	During the third-century crisis, Rome's lines of defense were broken through in both the East and the West.
T	10.	Rome's worst economic problems derived from its slave system and manpower shortages.

DISCUSSION AND/OR ESSAY QUESTIONS

1. In what ways was Rome "the builder of a great historical bridge between East and West"?
2. Why did Stoicism appeal to the Romans? How did Roman Stoicism differ from Greek Stoicism? Can you explain the reasons for these differences?
3. Agree or disagree, in whole or in part: "Economic factors explain both the rise and decline of Rome."
4. Was Augustus the savior or the destroyer of the Roman Republic?
5. Discuss the relationship between Roman intellectual and cultural achievements, and its political and economic structures.

SUGGESTED FEATURE FILMS

I, Claudius. 13 parts. 58 min. each. Color. Filmic Archives. Derek Jacobi heads the cast of this now-classic dramatization of Robert Graves's unforgettable books.

Julius Caesar. 121 min. B/W. 1953. MGM. This version of Shakespeare's play was selected by the National Board of Review as one of the Ten Best Films of 1953. With John Gielgud and Marlon Brando.

Terence: That Girl from Andros. 115 min. Color. Filmic Archives. This performance of *Andria* uses the earliest English verse translation (c. 1500).

SUGGESTED CLASSROOM FILMS

The Etruscans. 27 min. Color. 1982. Films for the Humanities. Uses tomb frescoes
to explore Etruscan culture.

Four Views of Caesar. 22 min. B/W. 1964. BFA Educational Media.
Interpretations by Caesar himself, Plutarch, Shakespeare, and Shaw.

Julius Caesar: The Battle of Alesia. 45 min. Color. Filmic Archives. Uses 3-D
computer graphics to explore the terrain and tactics of this pivotal battle.

Julius Caesar: The Forum Scene. 17 min. B/W. 1961. International Film Bureau.
Act III, Scene II from Shakespeare.

The Rise of Rome, Fall of Rome. 4 parts. 30 min. each. Color. 1989. Insight Media.
Traces the rise, decline, and fall of the Empire.

The Romans: Life, Laughter, and Laws. 22 min. Color. 1971. Learning
Corporation of America. Uses excerpts from Roman satire.

CHAPTER 8. CHRISTIANITY AND THE TRANSFORMATION OF THE ROMAN WORLD

Outline

   I. The reorganized empire
      A. Diocletian's policies: reform and orientalization
      B. The rule of Constantine
      C. From Constantine to Theodosius the Great
  II. The emergence and triumph of Christianity
      A. The context and career of Jesus of Nazareth
      B. Jesus' teachings
      C. The Apostle Paul and the development of Christianity
      D. Christianity's appeal
      E. Christianity's triumph
 III. The new contours of Christianity
      A. Doctrinal disputes
         1. Arius versus Athanasius
         2. Results of doctrinal quarrels
      B. Organizational development
         1. The clerical hierarchy
         2. The rise of the papacy
         3. Effects of ecclesiastical organization
      C. The development of monasticism
         1. Fourth-century context
         2. Monastic asceticism
         3. St. Basil and communal monasticism
         4. The Benedictine rule
      D. Negative attitudes toward women and marriage
  IV. The Germanic invasions and the fall of the Roman Empire in the West
      A. Character of the Germans
      B. The Visigoths and the Vandals
      C. Fall of the Western Empire and survival of the Eastern
      D. Consequences of the Germanic invasions
      E. The political map of sixth-century Europe
   V. The shaping of Western Christian thought
      A. St. Jerome and the Vulgate
      B. St. Ambrose: *On the Duties of Ministers*
      C. St. Augustine
         1. The doctrine of predestination
         2. *On the City of God*
         3. Compromise with classical learning
      D. Boethius: influence and Augustinianism

VI. Eastern Rome and the West
   A. The reign of Justinian and plans for Roman revival
   B. Codification of Roman law
   C. The failure of the western campaigns

MULTIPLE CHOICE
Choose the best response.

1. Diocletian's reforms "orientalized" the Roman Empire in all the following ways EXCEPT
    (a) the shift of administrative power eastward.
    *(b) the growth of military influence in state affairs.
    (c) the adoption of the titles and ceremonies of an Oriental ruler.
    (d) an increasing reliance on an imperial bureaucracy.

2. Constantine
    (a) confirmed Rome as the imperial capital.
    (b) earned the title "Great" by defeating the Germanic tribes.
    (c) abandoned the practice of hereditary succession.
    *(d) accepted and favored Christianity but did not outlaw paganism.

3. Which of the following was NOT true of the Roman Empire during the age of antiquity?
    (a) Its center of gravity shifted from West to East.
    (b) It became characterized by growing regionalism.
    (c) It witnessed a widening gap between rich and poor.
    *(d) It was characterized by peace and political stability.

4. During the time of Jesus of Nazareth
    (a) Christianity emerged as a powerful new religion.
    *(b) political and religious fervor found expression in the legalism of the Pharisees, the pacifism of the Essenes, and the revolutionism of the Zealots.
    (c) the Jews achieved independence from Rome.
    (d) the toleration imposed by Constantine created a favorable climate for new religious teachings.

5. Jesus' teachings included all of the following EXCEPT
    *(a) the exclusion of women from salvation.
    (b) the fatherhood of God and the brotherhood of all humanity.
    (c) self-denial.
    (d) the necessity of forgiving one's enemies.

6. The Apostle Paul
    (a) viewed Christianity as a Jewish religion.
    (b) developed the clerical hierarchy of the Church.
    *(c) defined Christianity as a religion of personal salvation through Jesus.
    (d) taught that women have no souls.

7. One of the reasons that Christianity triumphed over other religions in western Europe was that
    (a) it was the only religious alternative to emphasize the dominance of spiritual forces in this world.
    (b) none of its rivals promised otherworldly salvation.
    (c) it allowed its converts to continue worshipping their old gods.
    *(d) it offered the poor respect and a better life.

8. Doctrinal disputes
    (a) severely weakened Christianity's appeal.
    *(b) increased local differences and regional hostilities.
    (c) resulted in the development of a nondogmatic, tolerant religion.
    (d) threatened to destroy Christianity in its early years but lessened after the new religion won state support.

9. Monasticism emerged
    (a) as part of the developing clerical hierarchy.
    *(b) in the East as extreme asceticism.
    (c) as one of the earliest and strongest of Christianity's rivals.
    (d) to answer the need to reconcile classical and Christian teachings.

10. The Benedictines did NOT
    (a) convert England and most of Germany to Christianity.
    (b) contribute to the economic advancement of the West.
    (c) preserve much of classical culture.
    *(d) view manual labor as a distraction from the contemplative life.

11. The changes that took place in Christian institutions and attitudes during the fourth century did NOT include the
    *(a) acceptance of women into the priesthood.
    (b) emergence of bitter disagreements over doctrine.
    (c) growth of hierarchical organization among the clergy.
    (d) development of monasticism.

12. The Germans easily conquered the Roman Empire in the West because of
    (a) superior manpower.
    (b) superior weaponry and military tactics.
    *(c) demoralization within the imperial territories.
    (d) Germanic hatred of Roman culture.

13. As a result of the German conquests
    * (a) the de-urbanization of the West accelerated.
      (b) Constantinople decayed due to lack of trade.
      (c) Christians faced renewed persecution.
      (d) Diocletian instituted drastic political, economic, and military reforms.

14. The Western Christian thinker whose Latin translation of the Bible is known as the Vulgate version was
      (a) Augustine.
    * (b) Jerome.
      (c) Ambrose.
      (d) Theodoric.

15. Ambrose taught that
      (a) a life of extreme asceticism and isolation characterized the true Christian.
      (b) Christians must avoid the temptations of classical learning.
    * (c) even emperors must submit to Church discipline.
      (d) the Bible should be read as an allegory.

16. St. Augustine's theology included all of the following EXCEPT
      (a) emphasis on human depravity.
      (b) the principle of God's omnipotence.
      (c) the concept of predestination.
    * (d) emphasis on humanity's freedom to choose salvation.

17. St. Augustine's teachings helped maintain the practice of education in the Western world because he taught that
    * (a) a liberal education would help a Christian elite to understand the Bible.
      (b) classical thought was worthy of study in and of itself.
      (c) all men should be liberally educated.
      (d) the "City of God" could be built only if all men were educated.

18. Boethius
    * (a) combined classical expression and ideas with an Augustinian worldview.
      (b) described his interpretation of history in his work *On the City of God*.
      (c) influenced Latin style and thought through his translation of the Bible.
      (d) argued that monks should turn from isolation and self-torture to communal living and devotion to useful labor.

19. Justinian's legal work was later used to support all of the following EXCEPT
      (a) absolutism.
      (b) constitutionalism.
      (c) the modern concept of the state as public and secular.
    * (d) the modern concept of equality before the law.

20. As a result of Justinian's western campaigns
    (a) the focal point of the Empire shifted permanently to Rome.
    *(b) Italy was left in economic chaos and on the verge of political disintegration.
    (c) Constantinople fell to the Persians.
    (d) the Germanic tribes were forced to flee from the Continent and settle in Britain.

IDENTIFICATIONS

Maximian	Alaric
Theodosius I (the Great)	The Vulgate
Galerius	St. Jerome
Arians	*On the Duties of Ministers*
Council of Nicea	predestination
Doctrine of the Petrine Succession	*On the City of God*
St. Basil	*The Consolation of Philosophy*
St. Benedict	Theodora
Cassiodorus	*Corpus Juris Civilis*
Theodoric the Ostrogoth	

TRUE OR FALSE

F   1. The severity of the Roman persecutions of the Christian Church strengthened the unity and resolve of Christians and so aided the spread of Christianity.

T   2. Diocletian abandoned the pretense of being a constitutional ruler and adopted the trappings and tactics of an Oriental autocrat.

F   3. Christianity began to gain a substantial number of converts during the third century because its optimistic message accorded with the political stability and economic prosperity of the era.

T   4. The ecclesiastical structure of the Church served as one source of stability in an increasingly chaotic West.

T   5. The extreme self-torture characteristic of early monasticism substituted for martyrdom in a world where Christians now had state approval.

F   6. The emergence of asceticism in the Church improved attitudes toward women since both males and females underwent extreme self-torture to prove their faith.

T   7. Before the invasions by the barbarians that began in the second half of the fourth century, trade relations, military alliances, and common religious ties ensured that the Germanic tribes both knew and respected Roman culture.

F   8.   Augustine argued that God, in his mercy, elected to give each indi-
         vidual the capacity to perform good deeds and so choose salvation or
         damnation.

T   9.   In *The Consolation of Philosophy,* Boethius concluded that human life
         should be spent in pursuit of God.

T   10. A view of the state as a public and secular entity emerged with the
         codification of Roman law.

DISCUSSION AND/OR ESSAY QUESTIONS

1.   The period of late antiquity "saw a steady shift in the weight of civilization
     and imperial government from West to East," (p. 190). Explain.

2.   Defend or refute this statement: "The high taxation and oppressive
     legislation which Diocletian and Constantine instituted to preserve the
     Roman Empire instead ensured the Empire's fall in the West."

3.   The itinerant preacher Jesus of Nazareth preached a pacifistic religion that
     one would have expected to have died with him. Instead, by the end of the
     fourth century, Christianity had conquered Europe. Compare and contrast the
     religion of Jesus with the Christianity of the fourth century. How do you
     account for Christianity's appeal and internal development?

4.   Using the theme "Christianity and Classical Teaching" as your focus,
     compare and contrast the ideas and works of Jerome, Ambrose, Augustine,
     and Boethius.

5.   You have been asked to deliver a lecture on the topic "The Fall of Rome."
     Outline your main points.

SUGGESTED FEATURE FILMS

Ben Hur. 217 min. Color. 1959. MGM. William Wyler's production of Lew
     Wallace's novel. Featuring Charlton Heston, along with 300 sets, 365 speaking
     parts, and 78 horses! Winner of eleven Academy Awards.

The Gospel According to St. Matthew. 142 min. B/W. 1964. Acro/Lux. Directed by
     Italian novelist and poet Pier Paolo Pasolini and acted by nonprofessionals, with
     dialogue from the Gospel of Matthew.

Jesus of Nazareth. 300 min. Color. 1977. Independent Television Corp. A beautiful
     film with Olivia Hussey as the Virgin Mary.

Quo Vadis. 171 min. Color. 1951. MGM. This production of Henry Sienkiewicz's
     novel highlights the physical brutality of the Roman world.

SUGGESTED CLASSROOM FILMS

Augustine. 53 min. Color. 1974. BBC/Time-Life Films. Malcolm Muggeridge narrates Augustine's life and achievements.

The Beginnings of Christianity . 25 min. Color. 1991. Insight Media. Examines the lives of Jesus and Paul, and looks at the emergence of Christianity out of first-century Judaism.

The Christians: A Peculiar People (27 B.C.–300 C.E.). 39 min. Color. 1979. McGraw-Hill. This survey from the ministry of Jesus to the establishment of Christianity as a legal religion also includes a look at mystery religions.

The City of God. 39 min. Color. 1988. Films for the Humanities. Explores the role of the Christian Church in creating European medieval civilization.

Early Christianity and the Rise of the Church. 2 parts. 30 min. each. Color. 1989. Insight Media. Covers early history and beliefs.

Saint Augustine: Late Have I Loved Thee. 35 min. Color. 1992. Insight Media. James O'Donnell of the University of Pennsylvania narrates passages from the *Confessions* and *The City of God.*

PART THREE.   THE WORLD IN THE MIDDLE AGES
CHAPTER 9.   ROME'S THREE HEIRS: THE BYZANTINE, ISLAMIC,
            AND EARLY-MEDIEVAL WESTERN WORLDS

Outline

I. The Byzantine Empire and its culture
   A. The Byzantine struggle against invasions
      1. Invasions from the east and the reign of Heraclius
      2. The Arab threat and Leo's relief of Constantinople
      3. Byzantine revival and the Battle of Manzikert
      4. The rise of western Europe and the decline of the Byzantine Empire
   B. Elements of stability in the Byzantine Empire
      1. Rulers
      2. Bureaucratic machinery
      3. Economic base
   C. Byzantine religion
      1. Importance and effect of religious disputes
      2. Involvement of the emperors
      3. The Iconoclastic Controversy
   D. Secular Byzantine culture
      1. Cultivation of the classics
      2. Lay and women's education
      3. Architecture: The Church of Santa Sophia
      4. Art
   E. The conversion of Russia
   F. Byzantine contributions to Western civilization
II. The flowering of Islam
   A. Arabia before Islam
   B. Muhammad's career and the consolidation of his religion
   C. Islamic doctrines and the Judeo-Christian influence
   D. The unification of Arabia under the caliphs
      1. Abu-Bakr and Umar
      2. Division between Shiites and Sunnites
      3. The Umayyads and the Abbasids
   E. Islamic culture and society
      1. Women
      2. Religious life
      3. Philosophy
      4. Science
      5. Art
      6. Economy

III. Western Christian civilization in the early Middle Ages
    A. The Merovingian period
        1. Gregory the Great and the Benedictines
        2. The alliance of the Frankish monarchy and the papacy
        3. Consolidation under Charlemagne
        4. The decline of the Carolingian Empire
    B. The beginnings of national entities
        1. England
        2. France
        3. Germany
    C. Early medieval culture
        1. Economy
        2. Intellectual life and literature: *Beowulf*
        3. Art
    D. The emergence of a western European civilization

MULTIPLE CHOICE
Choose the best response.

1. Which of the following is NOT true of the Emperor Leo's relief of Constantinople in 717?
    (a) It marked the beginnings of a three-centuries-long Byzantine revival.
    (b) It owed much to both Leo's talents and "Greek fire."
    (c) It may well have saved western Europe from the Muslim domination.
  *(d) It marked the end of the Muslim threat to the Byzantine Empire.

2. Factors that contributed to the stability of the Byzantine empire included
    (a) the weakness of the empire's Arab enemies.
    (b) alliance with western Europe.
  *(c) a sophisticated and effective governmental bureaucracy.
    (d) separation of church and state.

3. Which of the following was NOT true of the Byzantine economy?
    (a) Long-distance trade continued to flourish.
    (b) Industries such as silk-making prospered.
    (c) Agriculture was at the heart of economic life.
  *(d) Cities declined as populations dispersed.

4. The destruction of large amounts of Byzantine religious art and a re-emphasis on traditionalism in Byzantine religion were results of the
  *(a) Iconoclastic Controversy.
    (b) Battle of Manzikert.
    (c) sack of Constantinople.
    (d) Battle of Tours.

5. All of the following were characteristics of Byzantine civilization EXCEPT
   (a) an emphasis on contemplation as the road to religious truth.
   (b) a commitment to female education.
   *(c) the rejection of secular literature and learning.
   (d) very abstract and formal styles of art.

6. One example of the vitality and creativity of Byzantine culture is the
   *(a) Church of Santa Sophia.
   (b) Dome of the Rock.
   (c) Book of Kells.
   (d) *Rubaiyat.*

7. Islam was born in
   (a) Africa.
   *(b) Arabia.
   (c) India.
   (d) eastern Europe.

8. In what way did Muhammad's message contrast with traditional Arab beliefs?
   (a) the rejection of the religious significance of Mecca
   *(b) the insistence on monotheism
   (c) the contempt displayed for tradesmen
   (d) the elevated status of women

9. Islamic doctrine does NOT teach that
   (a) there is no divinity but God (or Allah).
   (b) Muhammad was a prophet but not a god.
   (c) men and women can choose whether or not they will follow God.
   *(d) an ordained priesthood is necessary to guide believers to God.

10. After Muhammed's death, Abu-Bakr became the supreme religious and political leader of the Muslims called the
    *(a) Caliph.
    (b) Quraish.
    (c) Kabah.
    (d) Shia.

11. Explanations for the rapidity of Muslim expansion in the seventh and eighth centuries include
    (a) superior weaponry and military tactics.
    (b) the political and religious unity of the Muslim world.
    *(c) the military exhaustion, religious divisions, and political disunity of the Persians and Byzantines.
    (d) the greater sophistication of the Islamic trade and industrial systems as compared to both the Byzantine and western European cultures.

12. After 750, Islam shifted toward a more Eastern or Persian orientation as a result of the takeover of a new family called the
    (a) Umayyads.
    (b) Shiites.
    (c) Sunnites.
    *(d) Abbasids.

13. Important characteristics of Islamic culture include
    (a) a rigid class system.
    *(b) a view of religious experience tolerant enough to include both the tradition-bound *ulama* and the frenzy of the dervishes.
    (c) commitment to lay and female education.
    (d) cultivation of scientific knowledge at the expense of literature and art.

14. The *faylasufs*
    (a) were influential Islamic scholars who stressed study of and obedience to the Koran.
    (b) were mystics devoted to the contemplative life.
    *(c) made notable progress in both astrology and medicine.
    (d) were heretics who abandoned Islam for ancient Greek philosophy.

15. The economy of Islamic culture
    (a) remained largely agricultural.
    (b) rested on the self-supporting landed estate.
    *(c) expanded on the urban culture of the Persians and made use of Arabia's location at the center of world trade.
    (d) stagnated as a result of the struggles between the free peasants and the large landowners.

16. Gregory the Great deserves the adjective "Great" because
    (a) by founding the Merovingian dynasty he paved the way for a strong French monarchy.
    (b) by fostering the Carolingian Renaissance he preserved literacy and some degree of intellectual life in western Europe.
    (c) his interpretation of Aristotle established the outlines of European philosophy and theology.
    *(d) he allied the Roman papacy with Benedictine monasticism, thus reinvigorating the western Church.

17. The increasing stability of Frankish Gaul in the eighth century rested on
    *(a) a series of powerful and able rulers who recognized the benefits of allying with the western papacy.
    (b) the dynamic intellectual influence of Islam.
    (c) a new sense of unity sparked by the Crusades.
    (d) the removal of the pope as competitor to Frankish kings as a result of the triumph of the Eastern Church.

18. The Carolingian Renaissance
    (a) was part of Charlemagne's efforts to destroy the Church's monopoly on education.
    (b) was centered in the cities of the Italian peninsula where commercial wealth could fund artistic endeavors.
    *(c) was practical and intellectually limited in its aims, yet achieved the preservation of Latin literature.
    (d) produced such literary and artistic wonders as the *Book of Kells* and *Beowulf.*

19. Reasons why Charlemagne ranks as one of the most important medieval rulers do NOT include
    (a) dramatically extending the amount of territory controlled by the Franks.
    *(b) turning back the Muslim forces at the Battle of Tours and thus halting the Muslim advance in Spain.
    (c) establishing an effective system of government based on local officials called "counts."
    (d) assuming the title of emperor as a declaration of Western independence from the Byzantines.

20. England became unified in the late ninth century through the work of
    (a) Charlemagne.
    (b) Averroës.
    *(c) Alfred the Great.
    (d) Charles Martel.

IDENTIFICATIONS

Heraclius	*Rubaiyat*
Ottomans	Clovis
Church of Santa Sophia	Merovingians
Hijrah (Hegira) of 622	"Mayor of the Palace"
Medina	Battle of Tours
Shiites	Boniface
Umayyads	Venerable Bede
Moses Maimonides	Alfred the Great
sufis	Otto the Great
Avicenna	*Beowulf*

TRUE OR FALSE

T   1. The Byzantine Empire played a crucial role in the preservation of ancient Greek philosophy and literature.

T   2.   The defeat of the Byzantine army at the battle of Manzikert in 1071 signaled the beginning of the contraction and decline of the Byzantine Empire.

F   3.   The Crusades strengthened the alliance between western Europe and the Byzantine Empire.

F   4.   Eastern Christianity is marked by an activist spirit and a greater impulse toward reform than is characteristic of the Christianity of the West.

T   5.   Islam stresses the connection between religious beliefs and social and political organizations.

T   6.   The Koran outlines the practical steps that an Islamic believer must follow in order to serve the one God.

T   7.   Islamic science made important contributions to medicine, optics, chemistry, and mathematics.

T   8.   The Eastern orientation of the Abbasid caliphate allowed the revival of the Byzantine Empire and the development of western Europe.

T   9.   Charles Martel's alliance with the Benedictines helped expand Frankish territory and strengthen his dynasty's hold over the French empire.

T   10.   The crowning of Pepin the Short as Frankish ruler marked the end of the Merovingian dynasty and the point at which the papacy fully aligned with the Frankish state.

DISCUSSION AND/OR ESSAY QUESTIONS

1.   Defend or refute this statement: "The Iconoclastic Controversy serves to illustrate the fact that political developments in the Byzantine Empire cannot be understood without recognition of the important role of religion."

2.   Agree or disagree, in whole or in part: "The emergence of Islamic civilization as a world power rests on its remarkable degree of tolerance and eclecticism." Consider religious, political, intellectual, and artistic developments in your answer.

3.   How do you account for the fact that in comparison to the Byzantine and Islamic civilizations, the Western Christian world "was a laggard"? How did both the Byzantines and the Muslims contribute to western European development?

4.   What is the historical significance of Charlemagne?

5.   An Arab, a Byzantine, and a Frank have met in the year 950 in the Church of Santa Sophia. They begin to discuss the relationship between art and religion. Describe their conversation.

SUGGESTED FEATURE FILMS

Alfred the Great. 122 min. Color. 1969. MGM. Aims for a realistic portrayal of Alfred's reign. With David Hemmings and Michael York.

SUGGESTED CLASSROOM FILMS

Al Andalus. 34 min. Color. 1975. University Films Library. Covers the intermingling of Spanish and Moorish cultures through the reign of Ferdinand and Isabella. Includes on-site photography.

Anglo-Saxon England. 22 min. Color. 1971. International Film Bureau. Uses aerial photographs, artifacts, and excavations to explore England between the end of Roman rule to 1066.

The Birth of Europe. 39 min. Color. 1979. McGraw-Hill. The early Middle Ages, with the spread of Christianity as the focus.

The Book of Kells. 21 min. Color. 1974. Ulster TV/Picture Films Corporation. With photographs of the manuscript at Trinity College.

The Byzantine Empire. 2 parts. 30 min. each. Color. 1989. Part 1 focuses on the forces that shaped the Byzantine Empire and enabled it to endure for over one thousand years. Part 2 looks at the role of religion in weakening the empire.

Byzantium: From Splendor to Ruin. 43 min. Color. Films for the Humanities. From the founding of Constantinople to 1453.

The Christian Empire. 45 min. Color. 1978. Contemporary Films. Traces the Christian Empire from Rome to Constantinople to Russia.

Civilisation: A Personal View by Kenneth Clark. No. 1. The Frozen World. 52 min. Color. 1970. BBC/Time-Life Films. Traces Europe from 400 to 1000; views this period as the "Dark Ages."

The Dark Ages and the Age of Charlemagne. 2 parts. 30 min. each. Color. 1989. Insight Media. Part 1 contrasts western Europe after the fall of the Roman Empire to Byzantium. Part 2 looks at Charlemagne's rise.

The End of the Ancient World. 26 min. Color. 1989. Insight Media. Covers the period from 100 to 600 C.E.

Living Islam. 6 parts. 50 min. each. Color. 1993. Insight Media. This BBC series explores the history, practice, and politicization of Islam from its origins to the present.

Orient/Occident. 30 min. Color. 1982. Films for the Humanities. Examines Islam's impact on Western culture, and the West's impact on Islam. Part IV of the series *The World of Islam.*

The Ottoman Empire. 28 min. Color. 1991. Insight Media. Covers the early history through the sixteenth century.

The Shadow of God on Earth. 58 min. Color. 1978. Insight Media. Explores both Muhammad's initial conquests and the nature of Islam today.

Spain: The Moorish Influence. 28 min. Color. 1990. Insight Media. Explores the role of the Moors in shaping Spanish culture. Received a "Highly Recommended" rating in the *Video Rating Guide.*

The Triumph of the West. 13 parts. 50 min. each. Color. 1987. Insight Media. BBC series featuring the British historian John Roberts in a discussion of the interactions between Western and non-Western cultures.

CHAPTER 10. THE HIGH MIDDLE AGES (1050–1300): ECONOMIC, SOCIAL, AND POLITICAL INSTITUTIONS

Outline

I. The first agricultural revolution
  A. Prerequisites for the agricultural revolution
  B. Technological breakthroughs
  C. Extension and intensification of land cultivation
  D. Consequences of the agricultural revolution
II. Lord and serf: social conditions and quality of life in the manorial regime
  A. Definitions of manorialism and feudalism
  B. The typical manor
  C. Decline of serfdom
  D. Improvements in noble life: the code of chivalry
III. The revival of trade and the urban revolution
  A. Sophistication of patterns of trade and commercial techniques
  B. The urban revolution
  C. The guild system
  D. Significance of the urban revolution
IV. Feudalism and the rise of the national monarchies
  A. Decentralization and decline in Germany
    1. Strengths under Otto the Great
    2. Henry IV versus Gregory VII
    3. The Italian obsessions of Frederick Barbarossa and Frederick II
  B. Divisions in Italy
  C. Feudalism
    1. Definition and development
    2. Contribution to political stabilization
    3. The example of the Norman Conquest
  D. Growth of the national monarchy in England
    1. The reign of Henry II
    2. The development of bureaucracy and the idea of limited monarchy
    3. The reign of Edward I
  E. Political centralization in France
    1. Obstacles and aids
    2. The reign of Philip Augustus
    3. The reign of Philip IV
    4. Comparison with English developments
  F. Spain in the High Medieval Ages
  G. Significance of the national monarchies

MULTIPLE CHOICE
Choose the best response.

1. Prerequisites for the agricultural revolution did NOT include
    (a) warmer and drier weather.
    (b) ending of invasions.
    (c) peace and political stability.
    *(d) shift of the weight of European civilization from the North Atlantic to the Mediterranean region.

2. As a result of the agricultural revolution
    (a) wealth concentrated in the countryside, thus impoverishing the already weak towns.
    (b) increasing wealth enabled the nobility to tighten their hold on the serfs.
    (c) a system of agricultural production developed that historians term "manorialism."
    *(d) agricultural production became more diverse and specialized.

3. Unlike slaves, serfs
    (a) could leave their lands at will.
    (b) received wages for their work.
    *(c) were given land that normally could not be taken away.
    (d) were equal to the lords in the eyes of the law.

4. The agricultural system that divided the land into narrow strips belonging to the lord, serfs, and sometimes the Church is called
    *(a) the open-field system.
    (b) feudalism.
    (c) the fallow system.
    (d) the demesne.

5. The typical manor
    (a) would most likely be found in Italy.
    *(b) fostered a spirit of community and solidarity among the serfs.
    (c) fostered the spirit of initiative and entrepreneurship that spurred on the agricultural revolution.
    (d) ensured an adequate standard of living for serfs.

6. As a result of the agricultural revolution, the nobility
    (a) abandoned their traditional role as rural landowners and congregated in the newly emerging cities.
    (b) were more frequently involved in military conflicts because of greater competition for the accumulating wealth.
    *(c) adopted a more cultivated and gentle style of living.
    (d) shifted their main source of income from rents to land sales.

7. During the High Middle Ages, noble women
   (a) became prominent characters in literature.
   (b) became the objects of chivalric adoration.
   (c) on rare occasions achieved influential political positions.
   *(d) all of the above.

8. The revival of trade
   (a) established transportation and communication patterns that bypassed the Mediterranean.
   (b) is best understood as the result of technological innovations.
   *(c) led to the development of capitalist commercial techniques.
   (d) was the primary cause of the urban revolution.

9. In twelfth-century Europe, urban life was concentrated most of all in
   (a) Germany.
   (b) France.
   *(c) Italy.
   (d) England.

10. The guilds
    (a) are best understood as early trade unions.
    (b) sought to ensure the prosperity of their members by enforcing the principles of free trade.
    *(c) aimed at the establishment and preservation of a stable and ordered economic system.
    (d) were supported by the Church in their opposition to usury.

11. The strength and stability of the early-medieval German emperors depended on
    *(a) cooperation between the emperors and the papacy.
    (b) the flexibility provided by the feudal system.
    (c) establishment of a base of operations in southern Italy.
    (d) a sophisticated and complex bureaucratic machinery.

12. Frederick Barbarossa advanced the political disintegration of Germany by
    (a) setting up a feudal system of governing.
    (b) allying with the pope against the German princes.
    *(c) endeavoring to make northern Italy his power base.
    (d) leading Germany into a fruitless war against England.

13. Under the system that your textbook writer labels *feudalism*
    (a) the lords' and the serfs' lands were intermixed, and cultivated by the serfs.
    *(b) local loyalties could be transformed into larger political loyalties.
    (c) knights accepted the obligation to fight in defense of honorable causes.
    (d) all of the above.

14. The Norman Conquest placed _____ on the throne of England.
    (a) Frederick II
    (b) Gregory the Great
    *(c) William the Conqueror
    (d) Richard

15. The reforms of the English king Henry II did NOT include
    (a) expansion of the system of traveling circuit judges.
    (b) an early form of the grand jury.
    *(c) the establishment of a representative government via Parliament.
    (d) the use of sheriffs to establish royal control.

16. During the reign of Edward I
    *(a) the development of the national monarchy reached its culmination.
    (b) England fell under Norman control.
    (c) the quarrel between Church and State led to the martyrdom of Thomas Becket.
    (d) legal and judicial innovations made justice more uniform and equitable throughout England.

17. As in England, the emergence of political stability in France depended on
    *(a) the ability of strong monarchs to utilize and then move beyond the feudal system.
    (b) lack of strong regional differences.
    (c) a loyal aristocracy.
    (d) development of a parliamentary system.

18. The French king who acquired large amounts of territory for the monarchy and developed an effective system for administering these new territories was
    (a) Frederick Barbarossa.
    (b) William the Conqueror.
    (c) Edward I.
    *(d) Philip Augustus.

19. In Spain in the early-medieval period
    *(a) Aragon and Castile emerged as the dominant states.
    (b) Islam continued its Reconquista of the peninsula.
    (c) lack of strong regional differences aided political centralization.
    (d) feudalism stabilized the political situation and led to the development of a strong national monarchy by 1300.

IDENTIFICATIONS

climatic optimum	fief
three-field system	Battle of Hastings
demesne	Thomas Becket
chivalry	Constitutions of Clarendon
Eleanor of Aquitaine	John
journeymen	Edward I
usury	Louis VI (the Fat)
Otto the Great	*baillis*
Pope Gregory VII	Louis IX (St. Louis)
Frederick Barbarossa	Philip IV (the Fair)

TRUE OR FALSE

T 1. The use of the heavy plow eased the shift of European civilization from the Mediterranean to the North.

F 2. The manorial system served to revive the money economy in Europe.

T 3. Serfdom came to an end in western Europe during the thirteenth century in part because landlords realized they could earn greater profits from rent than they had from manorial duties.

F 4. The primary cause of the medieval urban revolution was the revival of long-distance trade.

T 5. The humiliation of Henry IV at Canossa aided the German princes in their struggle to gain independence from the emperor.

F 6. Frederick II helped bring political stability to Germany by concentrating his efforts on solidifying his power base there rather than in Italy.

T 7. The Magna Carta was a feudal document that set forth the king's responsibilities as overlord to his vassals.

T 8. Parliament began as a feudal court called mainly for the purpose of raising royal revenues.

T 9. The basic pattern of French government, set during the reign of Philip Augustus, was that of local diversity balanced against bureaucratic centralization.

T 10. Agricultural prosperity and an increase in trade around the region of the Île de France contributed to the growth of the French monarchy.

DISCUSSION AND/OR ESSAY QUESTIONS

1. "I judge those who write at this time to be in a certain measure happy. For, after the turbulence of the past, an unprecedented brightness of peace has dawned again" (p. 275). Explain what could have motivated Otto of Freising to write this statement in 1158.
2. Agree or disagree, in whole or in part: "The history of Europe in the High Middle Ages demonstrates that technology, rather than people or ideas, determines the route a society follows."
3. Compare and contrast economic life in Europe during the early Middle Ages with that of the high-medieval period. How do you explain the differences?
4. Why have recent historians rejected the traditional view of feudalism as a divisive force in the history of western Europe? How do political developments in high-medieval Europe support the newer interpretation?
5. "Around 1050 Germany was unquestionably the most centralized and best-ruled territory in Europe, but by 1300 it had turned into a snake pit of warring petty states" (p. 295). What happened?

SUGGESTED FEATURE FILMS

Becket. 149 min. Color. 1964. Paramount. Film version of Jean Anouilh's play, with Richard Burton, Peter O'Toole, and Sir John Gielgud.

The Lion in Winter. 134 min. Color. 1968. Avco Embassy. Katharine Hepburn as Eleanor of Aquitaine and Peter O'Toole as Henry II.

The War Lord. 121 min. Color. 1965. Universal. Fictional story of a Norman warrior and his feudal obligations. With Charlton Heston.

SUGGESTED CLASSROOM FILMS

Civilisation: A Personal View by Kenneth Clark. No. 2—the Great Thaw; No. 3—Romance and Reality. 52 min. each. Color. 1970. BBC/Time-Life Films. Covers the twelfth and thirteenth centuries.

Feast and Famine. 55 min. Color. 1991. Insight Media. This BBC production explores the agricultural underpinnings of medieval Europe.

The Norman Conquest of England. 20 min. Color. 1971. Radim Films. Discusses the causes and consequences of the Norman conquest.

The Rise of Nations in Europe. 13 min. Color. 1978. Coronet. The origins of modern European nations are traced to the rise of the monarchies.

CHAPTER 11. THE HIGH MIDDLE AGES (1050–1300): RELIGIOUS AND INTELLECTUAL DEVELOPMENTS

Outline

I. The consolidation of the papal monarchy
   A. Corruption of religious life in the tenth century
   B. Religious revival
   C. The papacy of Gregory VII
   D. The development of the papal monarchy
   E. The papacy of Innocent III
   F. The papacy and political crusades
   G. Boniface VIII and the fall of the papal monarchy
   H. Positive results of the papal monarchy
II. The Crusades
   A. The First Crusade
      1. Causes and motives
      2. Results
   B. Subsequent Crusades
   C. Interrelationship between the papal monarchy and the Crusades
   D. Effects of the Crusades
III. The outburst of religious vitality
   A. The revitalizing impact of Gregorian reform
   B. The Cistercian movement
   C. Emergence of new devotional forms: the cult of the Virgin Mary
   D. The rise of heresy
      1. The Albigensians and Waldensians
      2. Innocent III's response
      3. The Dominicans and Franciscans
IV. The medieval intellectual revival
   A. The spread of primary education
   B. The emergence of universities
   C. Acquisition of Greek and Arabic knowledge
   D. Scholasticism
      1. Definition
      2. Peter Abelard
      3. Peter Lombard
      4. The influence of Aristotle
      5. Thomas Aquinas
   E. Misconceptions of medieval intellectual life
V. The blossoming of literature, art, and music
   A. Latin literature: the Goliards

    B. Vernacular literature
        1. The heroic epic
        2. The troubadours
        3. The romances
        4. The *fabliaux*
        5. The *Romance of the Rose*
        6. Dante and the *Divine Comedy*
    C. Architecture
        1. The Romanesque
        2. The Gothic
    D. Drama and music

MULTIPLE CHOICE
Choose the best response.

1.   The Benedictine house that began the movement for monastic reform was the monastery of
    *(a) Cluny.
    (b) the Cistercians.
    (c) the Carthusians.
    (d) Carthage.

2.   Which of the following best describes Gregory VII's new conception of the role of the Church in human society?
    *(a) The Church is responsible for creating "right order in the world."
    (b) The ideal Christian is the monk who withdraws from involvement in secular affairs.
    (c) The Church must be subject to the State.
    (d) The ideal Christian is an impoverished beggar.

3.   The conflict between Pope Gregory VII and the Emperor Henry IV is usually called the
    (a) First Crusade.
    *(b) investiture struggle.
    (c) Divine Comedy.
    (d) Battle of Tours.

4.   The pope whose reign was the zenith of the papal monarchy but who also sowed some of the seeds of future ruin was
    (a) Gregory VII.
    (b) Urban II.
    *(c) Innocent III.
    (d) Boniface VIII.

5. The papal monarchy toppled during the reign of
    (a) Gregory VII.
    (b) Urban II.
    (c) Innocent III.
    *(d) Boniface VIII.

6. Beneficial effects of the papal monarchy did NOT include
    (a) greater unity in Europe through improved international communications.
    (b) increased respect for the rule of law.
    (c) revitalization of popular religion.
    *(d) stabilization and unification of the Holy Roman Empire.

7. The Crusades
    (a) never achieved their objective of capturing Jerusalem for Christianity.
    (b) unified the Eastern and Western Churches.
    *(c) provided another arena for the struggle for power between the papal and secular monarchies.
    (d) resulted in mass conversions of Muslims to Christianity.

8. The First Crusade
    (a) marked the papacy's move away from Gregorian reform and idealism.
    *(b) began as a response to the Byzantine Empire's need for aid against the Turks.
    (c) was called by Urban II to eliminate the Jews from Christendom.
    (d) resulted in the sack of Constantinople.

9. Which event demonstrated that the papacy had fully sacrificed the crusading ideal to political interests?
    (a) the call of the crusade against European heretics
    (b) the inflation of indulgences
    *(c) the launch of the crusade against Frederick II and his heirs
    (d) the sack of Constantinople

10. The Gregorian reform movement reinvigorated lay religion by
    *(a) granting the laity an important role in disciplining corrupt members of the clergy.
    (b) rejecting the doctrine that only ordained priests could administer the sacraments.
    (c) outlawing the Franciscan order.
    (d) increasing the role of secular leaders in the Church and thus capitalizing on rising nationalist loyalties.

11. The emergence of the cult of the Virgin Mary during the High Middle Ages was significant because it
     (a) led to the admission of women into the priesthood.
     (b) made Christian conversion more appealing to Muslims.
     (c) revealed the low level of theological understanding among churchgoers.
     *(d) was part of the general rise of optimism during the twelfth century.

12. Unlike the Waldensians, the Franciscans
     (a) endeavored to imitate Christ and the Apostles in their daily practice.
     (b) devoted themselves to a life of poverty.
     (c) believed preaching of the Gospel to be their central mission.
     *(d) were granted papal approval.

13. In order to combat heresy Innocent III did NOT
     (a) call a crusade to exterminate the Albigensians.
     (b) encourage the use of often brutal inquisitorial procedures.
     (c) support the new orders of friars.
     *(d) demand the University of Paris be closed.

14. Important features of the medieval intellectual revival included all of the following EXCEPT
     (a) development of lay education outside the Church's control.
     (b) the rise of universities.
     (c) translation and absorption of the works of Aristotle.
     *(d) the use of laboratory experimentation in the sciences.

15. Which of the following was NOT one of the changes that occurred in education during the High Middle Ages?
     *(a) the insistence on the education of women
     (b) the development of cathedral schools
     (c) the broadening of the curriculum
     (d) the growth of lay education

16. Scholasticism is best understood as the
     (a) belief that the laity rather than the Church should control education.
     *(b) belief in the compatibility of classical philosophy and Christianity and the attempt to synthesize the two.
     (c) assertion that sensory evidence serves as a more certain basis of knowledge than abstract reason.
     (d) four-year course of study in the liberal arts typical of the medieval university curriculum.

17. Abelard
    (a) called for the First Crusade in the Holy Land.
  * (b) was one of the first thinkers to try to harmonize religion with rationalism.
    (c) challenged the papacy by forming a new order of friars.
    (d) wrote the bawdy *Romance of the Rose.*

18. Which of the following is NOT true of high-medieval literature?
    (a) Heroic epics highlighted the emergence of vernacular literature.
    (b) Southern French courtier poets focused on romantic love as a central literary theme.
  * (c) Dante's *Divine Comedy* is a series of anticlerical and earthy short stories.
    (d) The satires of the Goliards displayed an optimistic spirit and celebration of life opposed to the ascetic Christian ideal.

19. The Gothic style of architecture
    (a) stressed systematic, uniform construction in an effort to display God's glory.
    (b) with its vertical lines and simple interiors expressed the other-worldly outlook of the High Middle Ages.
  * (c) provides evidence of both growing naturalism in art and medieval respect for the human mind.
    (d) used a plain facade and elaborate interior to emphasize the inward character of Christianity.

20. The great high-medieval contribution to musical development was
    (a) the fabliau.
  * (b) polyphony.
    (c) the Gregorian chant.
    (d) choral music.

IDENTIFICATIONS

simony	Albigensian Crusade
college of cardinals	friar
Henry IV	Roger Bacon
canon law	Heloise
Fourth Lateran Council	Thomas Aquinas
Philip IV	*Song of Roland*
Urban II	fabliaux
plenary indulgence	*Romance of the Rose*
Cistercian movement	*Divine Comedy*
transubstantiation	Romanesque

TRUE OR FALSE

T 1. Centralization of Church administration and reform of Church practice went hand in hand in the High Middle Ages.

T 2. The Cluniacs, the Cistercians, and the Carthusians all serve as evidence of the important role of monasticism in high-medieval religious reform and revival.

F 3. By placing his candidate Frederick II on the throne of the Holy Roman Empire, Innocent III gained the papacy a valuable political ally and ensured papal control over the Italian peninsula.

F 4. "Recapturing the Holy Land for Christianity" was a motive that meant little in the call for the First Crusade.

T 5. The Crusades both stimulated European trade and banking, and nourished the development of bureaucratic and administrative techniques necessary for the government of the emerging nation-state.

T 6. During the High Middle Ages emphasis on the worship of Jesus increased.

F 7. The Dominicans' focus on eliminating heresy and converting Jews and Muslims led them to reject the theoretical and intellectual concerns of the new universities.

T 8. Nourished by political stability and agricultural prosperity, the University of Paris became the model for northern European universities.

T 9. Thomas Aquinas had great confidence in the value of human reason and human experience.

T 10. Although varied in form and content, the many literary innovations of the High Middle Ages share an increasing worldliness and focus on humanity.

DISCUSSION AND/OR ESSAY QUESTIONS

1. You are a visiting professor and have been asked to give a lecture entitled "Innocent III at the Turning Point." What are the "turning points" you will describe?

2. Before the middle of the twelfth century, most popes had been monks. Afterward, most were trained canon lawyers. How does this shift reflect much larger developments in the institutional religious life and political structure of western Europe?

3. Defend or refute this statement: "Although the Crusades spanned a century and are an extremely colorful episode in European history, they had little lasting impact on Western society."

4. Why does your textbook writer regard the cult of the Virgin Mary and the emergence of the Dominican and Franciscan orders as evidence of an "outburst of religious vitality" in the high-medieval period?

5. Consider the following cultural artifacts: Aquinas's *Summa Theologica*, Dante's *Divine Comedy*, and the Gothic cathedral at Rheims (photograph, p. 354). What interpretations of the High Middle Ages would you construct on the basis of these artifacts?

SUGGESTED FEATURE FILMS

Alexander Nevsky. 112 min. B/W. 1938. Mosfilm. Eisenstein's depiction of the battle in 1242 between Russian peasants and the Teutonic Knights.

Brother Sun, Sister Moon. 122 min. Color. 1972. Paramount. St. Francis as flower child.

Die Nibelungen. 115 min. B/W. 1924. Decla-Bioscop. Silent. Dramatization of the thirteenth-century verse epic.

El Cid. 160 min. Color. 1961. Samuel Bronston. With the ubiquitous Charlton Heston.

Excalibur. 140 min. Color. 1981. Orion. John Boorman's retelling of *Morte d'Arthur.*

The Knights of the Teutonic Order. 180 min. Color. 1960. Studio Unit. Film of the fourteenth-century conflict between the Polish state and the Teutonic Knights; includes scenes of ordinary peasant life.

The Name of the Rose. 128 min. Color. 1986. Columbia/Tri-Star. Jean-Jacques Annaud directed and Sean Connery starred in this version of Umberto Eco's explanation of the conflict between reason and faith.

SUGGESTED CLASSROOM FILMS

Common Life in the Middle Ages. 2 parts. 30 min. each. 1989. Insight Media. A look at the consequences of the conflicts between church and secular rulers for ordinary people. Also looks at the cities and cathedrals of the medieval period.

The Crusades. 23 min. Color. 1989. Insight Media. Explores the three major crusades.

The Crusades: Saints and Sinners. 26 min. Color. 1970. Insight Media. A reenactment of the First Crusade.

The Disputation: A Theological Debate between Christians and Jews. 65 min. Color. Films for the Humanities. Re-creation of the Barcelona Disputation of 1263.

Early English Drama: The Second Shepherd's Play. 52 min. Color. 1975. Films for the Humanities. Traces the development of medieval theater through three reenactments: a tenth-century mystery play, the *Story of Abraham and Isaac,* and a fourteenth-century shepherd's play.

Everyman. 53 min. Color. 1991. Insight Media. A medieval morality play staged in period costume.

Faith and Fear. 39 min. Color. 1979. Insight Media. A look at religious responses to an uncertain world.

The Fall of Constantinople. 34 min. Color. 1970. Time-Life Films. Filmed on location.

The Flower of the Tales: The Burgundian Miniatures in the Royal Library of Belgium. 17 min. Color. 1975. International Film Bureau. Uses manuscript illustrations to describe medieval life.

Medieval Women. 24 min. Color. 1989. Insight Media. Historian Joyce Salisbury leads this exploration of the lives of medieval women.

The Middle Ages and the Feudal Order. Part Two. 30 min. Color. 1989. Explores the artistic and intellectual aspects of the feudal system.

Triumph in Stone. 42 min. Color. 1979. Alec McCowen narrates this study of Romanesque and Gothic architecture.

CHAPTER 12. THE LATER MIDDLE AGES (1300–1500)

Outline

I. Economic depression and the emergence of a new equilibrium
   A. The crisis
      1. Agricultural shortages and adverse weather conditions
      2. Overpopulation
      3. The Black Death
   B. The revolution: the economic consequences of the Black Death
II. Social and emotional dislocation
   A. Lower-class revolts
      1. The Jacquerie of 1358
      2. The English Peasants' Revolt of 1381
      3. The Ciompi Uprising of 1378
   B. The crisis of the aristocracy
   C. The need for escape and the obsession with sorrow
III. Trials for the Church and hunger for the divine
   A. The institutional crisis of the Church
      1. The Babylonian Captivity and the advantages of Avignon
      2. The Great Schism
      3. The emergence of the Italian territorial papacy
   B. Popular religious developments
      1. Anticlericalism and extra-clerical routes to piety
      2. Pilgrimages and the cult of flagellation
      3. Orthodox and heterodox mysticism: Master Eckhart and Thomas à Kempis
      4. Heresy: Wyclif and Hus
IV. Political crisis and recovery
   A. Italy: the fifteenth-century balance of power
   B. Germany: the triumph of the princes
   C. France and England: the Hundred Years' War
      1. Causes and course
      2. The strengthening of the French monarchy
      3. The Wars of the Roses
      4. English political developments
   D. Spain: internal consolidation and external expansion
V. The formation of the empire of Russia
   A. Early Westernization under the Kievan state

   B. The halt of Westernization
       1. The Mongol conquests
       2. The triumph of Moscow
       3. Religious hostilities
   C. Ivan the Great and Byzantine imperialism
VI. Turkish expansion and the Ottoman Empire
   A. Origins and Islam
   B. From military service to political power
   C. The Seljuk dynasty
   D. The Ottoman Empire
       1. Conquest and expansion
       2. Styles of government
       3. Social structure
       4. Cultural continuity
VII. Thought, literature, and art
   A. The crisis of doubt: William of Ockham
   B. Naturalism and vernacular composition: Boccaccio and Chaucer
   C. Naturalism and piety in art: Giotto and the Flemish painters
VIII. Advances in technology
   A. New weaponry and the nation-state
   B. Optical and navigational advances and overseas expansion
   C. Mechanical clocks and rationalization
   D. Printing and literacy

MULTIPLE CHOICE
Choose the best response.

1. The economic crisis at the beginning of the fourteenth century was NOT the consequence of
    (a) overworking the land.
    (b) overpopulation.
    (c) poor weather.
    *(d) overly specialized agricultural production.

2. The Black Death played a role in all of the following EXCEPT
    (a) the growth of advanced business and financial techniques.
    (b) the emergence of popular anticlericalism.
    (c) the growing importance of cities.
    *(d) England's victory in the Hundred Years' War.

3. All of the following were late-medieval lower-class revolts EXCEPT the
    *(a) Great Schism.
    (b) Jacquerie.
    (c) English Peasants' Revolt.
    (d) uprising of the Ciompi.

4. Which of the following did NOT contribute to the late-medieval aristocratic obsession with luxury and status?
   (a) the Black Death
   (b) the economic and social rise of merchants and financiers
   *(c) land shortages
   (d) falling grain prices and rents

5. The Babylonian Captivity
   *(a) diminished public respect for the papacy.
   (b) drove Russia further from the West.
   (c) strengthened the power of the English crown at the expense of the French.
   (d) halted the centralization of Church government.

6. Conciliarism
   (a) championed the absolute power of the pope.
   (b) sought to reform the Church by the formation of new orders of wandering friars.
   (c) insisted that secular rulers had the right to appoint bishops.
   *(d) argued that a general council of top Church officials, not the pope, possessed supreme earthly authority in the Church.

7. Which of the following did NOT contribute to anticlericalism (hostility toward Church officials and leaders)?
   (a) the Church's greater financial demands
   (b) lay literacy
   *(c) the decline of religious belief
   (d) mysticism's stress on inner holiness

8. John Wyclif
   (a) wrote the popular *Imitation of Christ*.
   (b) led the Bohemian revolt that separated the Bohemian from the Catholic Church until the seventeenth century.
   *(c) argued that according to the standards of the New Testament, most Church officials were damned.
   (d) believed that material wealth was a sign of God's blessing.

9. The country that emerged from the late-medieval political turmoil earlier than any other part of Europe was
   (a) Germany.
   (b) France.
   (c) England.
   *(d) Italy.

10. The Hundred Years' War strengthened the French crown for all of the following reasons EXCEPT
    (a) expelling the English from French territory.
    (b) granting the king the right to collect national taxes.
    (c) granting the king the right to maintain a standing army.
    *(d) weakening the political power of the pope in France.

11. The fifteenth-century struggle between two competing factions for the kingship of England is known as the
    (a) English Civil War.
    (b) Jacquerie.
    (c) Hundred Years' War.
    *(d) Wars of the Roses.

12. Obstacles to the Westernization of Russia did NOT include
    (a) Moscow's distance from western Europe.
    *(b) Russia's absorption of the Eastern-oriented kingdom of Poland.
    (c) religious differences and hostilities.
    (d) Ivan the Great's imitation of the Byzantine style of government.

13. Russian hostility to Roman Catholicism was in part the result of
    (a) fear of military invasion from Italy.
    (b) a long-standing alliance with Palestinian Muslims against European Crusaders.
    (c) suspicion of the hierarchical structure of authority in the Roman Catholic Church.
    *(d) resentment of Catholic Poland's expansion.

14. The man who did the most to turn the Grand Duchy of Moscow into the empire of Russia was
    (a) Henry VII.
    (b) Ferdinand.
    *(c) Ivan III.
    (d) Urban VI.

15. In 1453, Constantinople fell to
    (a) western European Crusaders.
    (b) forces of the Seljuk dynasty.
    (c) the Byzantine army.
    *(d) the Ottoman troops.

16. Which of the following is NOT correct concerning William of Ockham?
   (a) He denied that man's reason could prove God's existence.
   (b) He emphasized God's absolute freedom.
   (c) He contributed to the development of Western science.
 *(d) He believed that the material world is an illusion.

17. Late-medieval art and literature
 *(a) celebrated what is distinctly human.
   (b) broke sharply with that of the High Middle Ages.
   (c) displayed the devastating effects of the Black Death in its lack of creativity.
   (d) serves as evidence of late-medieval piety in its exclusive focus on religious themes.

18. The spread of literary composition in European vernaculars did NOT
   (a) arise in part from a greater sense of national self-identification.
   (b) result in large part from the spread of lay education.
   (c) benefit from the invention of printing.
 *(d) result from the Church's emphasis on the need to communicate with ordinary people.

19. _____ was/were the first to conceive of the painted space in fully three-dimensional terms.
   (a) Boccaccio
   (b) The troubadours
 *(c) Giotto
   (d) John Hus

20. The invention of printing
   (a) reinforced the Church's intellectual dominance by aiding the spread of religious education.
   (b) had little impact because of the low literacy rates.
 *(c) ensured that book culture became basic to the European way of life.
   (d) hindered the development of standardized national languages because of the proliferation of books printed in dialects.

21. Late-medieval technological achievements included all of the following EXCEPT
   (a) artillery and firearms.
   (b) optical and navigational instruments.
   (c) mechanical clocks.
 *(d) the heavy plow.

IDENTIFICATIONS

Black Death	John Hus
Hanseatic League	Hundred Years' War
Jacquerie	Wars of the Roses
Avignon	Ferdinand and Isabella
Great Schism	the Kievan state
Council of Constance	Ivan the Great
flagellants	nominalism
mysticism	empiricism
The Imitation of Christ	*The Decameron*
Lollardy	Giotto

TRUE OR FALSE

T   1.   The combined effects of famine, war, and the Black Death reduced the total population of western Europe by at least one-half between 1300 and 1450.

T   2.   Exaggerated weeping, the recurrence of the theme of Christ's Passion in literature and art, and an obsession with death can all be seen as evidence of the emotional dislocation brought about by the crisis of the fourteenth century.

T   3.   The English Peasants' Revolt is best understood as a revolt of frustrated rising expectations.

T   4.   Late-medieval aristocrats sought to escape the horrors of their age by retreating into a world of excessive luxury.

F   5.   The *Decameron*, an important manual of lay mysticism still widely read by Christians today, is evidence of lay piety in the later Middle Ages.

F   6.   The elimination of foreign influence from Italian soil by 1500 removed a major obstacle to Italy's development as a strong nation-state.

F   7.   Although important for the study of French national mythology, Joan of Arc's role in the Hundred Years' War has little basis in historical fact.

F   8.   With the capture of Bordeaux in 1453, the Hundred Years' War finally drew to a close, and England found itself in a position of international strength and internal stability.

T   9.   Ferdinand and Isabella strengthened their hold on Spain by quelling aristocratic revolt, expelling the Jews, and fostering overseas exploration.

T   10.   By adopting the title of tsar, Ivan the Great claimed to be the successor of the Byzantine emperors and signaled his autocratic ambitions.

DISCUSSION AND/OR ESSAY QUESTIONS

1. "The Black Death serves as a major turning point in the history of European civilization." Discuss this statement in the context of late-medieval economics, social relations, popular religion, and art.
2. Near the end of the fourteenth century, Geoffrey Chaucer began his *Canterbury Tales* by describing how in springtime "people long to go on pilgrimages, and pious wanderers to visit strange lands and far-off shrines in different countries." Describe the late-medieval piety that drove people to set off on such pilgrimages. How do you account for this "hunger for the divine"?
3. "The trials of the later Middle Ages put the existence of these monarchies to the test, but after 1450 they emerged stronger than ever" (p. 385). Discuss this statement in reference to France and England. What were the trials through which they passed? In what ways did these nation-states emerge stronger than ever?
4. "By about 1500 Russia had taken the first decisive steps on its way to becoming Europe's leading Eastern-style empire" (p. 385). Describe these steps. Why did Russia not evolve into a Western-style monarchy?
5. "Historians expend a great deal of time and effort studying ideas, yet it is technology that shapes the way humanity lives, and ultimately, the way individuals think. The invention of clocks, for example, contributed more to the emergence of scientific rationality than did the philosophy of William of Ockham, and certainly had a deeper impact on the lives of ordinary people." Defend or refute this statement. Be sure to consider both late-medieval intellectual and technological developments.

SUGGESTED FEATURE FILMS

Chimes at Midnight. 119 min. B/W. 1966. Internacional Films Espanola/Alpine. Orson Welles stars in this film of *Henry IV, Part II*.

Henry V. 137 min. Color. 1944. Rank Distributors. Laurence Olivier's screen version of Shakespeare's work, which begins as a filmed play in a reconstruction of the Globe Theatre and gradually moves outward until the viewer finds himself in the midst of fifteenth-century war.

Henry V. 138 min. Color. 1989. Festival. Kenneth Branagh's brilliant rendition of Shakespeare.

Ivan the Terrible. Part One. 100 min. Part Two. 88 min. B/W. 1944–1946. Mosfilm. Eisenstein's celebrated depiction of the sixteenth-century tsar.

The Passion of Joan of Arc. 85 min. B/W. 1928. M. J. Gourland. The silent film classic based on actual transcripts of Joan's trial.

Richard III. 161 min. Color. 1956. London Films. Considered by many to be the best of Olivier's film versions of Shakespeare's plays.

The Seventh Seal. 95 min. B/W. 1957. Svensk Filmindustri. Ingmar Bergman's masterful allegory of man's quest for meaning, in which the Crusading Knight returns to plague-stricken Europe to battle Death in a game of chess.

The Virgin Spring. 87 min. B/W. 1959. Svensk Filmindustri. Bergman's version of a fourteenth-century folktale.

A Walk with Love and Death. 90 min. Color. 1970. Twentieth Century Fox. Directed by John Huston, this film is about two people in a fourteenth-century peasants' revolt.

SUGGESTED CLASSROOM FILMS

Al Andalus. See Chapter 9.

Chaucer's England. 30 min. Color. 1969. Encyclopaedia Britannica Educational Corporation. Relates the background of the *Canterbury Tales* and dramatizes the "Pardoner's Tale" in its entirety.

Expansion of Europe: 1250–1500. 26 min. Color. 1985. Insight Media. Explores the internal devastation caused by the Black Death and the external expansion into East Asia and the New World.

Faith and Fear. See Chapter 11.

From Every Shire's Ende: The World of Chaucer's Pilgrims. 38 min. Color. 1969. International Film Bureau. Recreates the trip to Canterbury with wood carvings, illuminated manuscripts, and films of historic sites.

Giotto and the Pre-Renaissance. 47 min. Color. 1969. Universal Educational and Visual Arts. Highlights Giotto's innovations.

The Late Middle Ages and the National Monarchies. 2 parts. 30 min. each. Color. 1989. Insight Media. Focuses on the economic and political changes of the fifteenth century.

Medieval England: The Peasants' Revolt. 31 min. Color. 1969. Learning Corporation of America. Reenactment of the 1381 revolt.

Medieval Theatre: The Play of Abraham and Isaac. 26 min. Color. 1974. The Movie Show Company. Dramatization of a mystery play performance at an English estate in 1482. Features actor Will Geer as Abraham.

The Mongols: Storm from the East. Part Two: World Conquerors. 50 min. Color. Films for the Humanities. Looks at the expansion of the Mongol empire into Russia and Europe.

Once Upon a Wall: The Great Age of Fresco. 18 min. Color. 1969. BFA Educational Media. The Metropolitan Museum of Art exhibit of Italian fresco paintings.

Queen Isabel and Her Spain. 32 min. Color. 1978. International Film Bureau. Covers Isabella's reign with special focus on the defeat of the Moors in Granada, the Spanish Inquisition and the expulsion of the Jews, and Columbus's expedition.

PART FOUR.   THE EARLY-MODERN WORLD
CHAPTER 13.   THE CIVILIZATION OF THE RENAISSANCE
(c. 1350–c. 1550)

Outline

Introduction: The term "Renaissance"
  I. The Italian background
      A. Italy as Europe's most advanced urban society
      B. Italy's classical past and quest for an independent cultural identity
      C. Italy's wealth: civic and private patronage
  II. The Renaissance of thought and literature in Italy
      A. Petrarch, the first humanist
      B. Civic humanism
      C. Lorenzo Valla and the study of language
      D. Ficino and Pico della Mirandola: Neoplatonism
      E. Machiavelli and political thought
      F. Castiglione and the ideal of the Renaissance man
  III. The artistic Renaissance in Italy
      A. The coming of age of Italian painting
      B. The Florentines: philosophical and psychological themes
          1. Masaccio
          2. Botticelli
          3. Leonardo
      C. The Venetian school and the appeal to the senses
      D. The late Renaissance
          1. Raphael and humanism
          2. Michelangelo and idealism
      E. Renaissance sculpture
          1. Donatello and the secular hero
          2. Michelangelo: Classicism to anticlassicism
      F. Renaissance architecture
  IV. The waning of the Italian Renaissance
      A. The French invasion of 1494 and its aftermath
      B. Loss of economic prosperity
      C. The Counter-Reformation
  V. The Renaissance in the North
      A. Spread of the Renaissance outside Italy
          B. Contrast between the Italian and northern Renaissance
      C. Christian Humanism
          1. Erasmus
          2. Thomas More and *Utopia*

       3. Ulrich von Hutten and the *Letters of Obscure Men*

       4. The impact of the Reformation

  D. Northern Renaissance poetry: Rabelais

  E. Northern Renaissance architecture

  F. Northern Renaissance painting

       1. Albrecht Dürer

       2. Hans Holbein the Younger

VI. Renaissance developments in music

  A. Secularization of music

  B. The Ars Nova

  C. The synthesis of national elements

VII. The scientific accomplishments of the Renaissance period

  A. Renaissance foundations of modern science

  B. The heliocentric theory of the universe

  C. Physics

  D. Medicine and anatomy

MULTIPLE CHOICE

Choose the best response.

1. According to your textbook writer, the term "Renaissance" is best understood to identify

    (a) the period when art and literature were reborn in Europe after the Dark Ages.

  *(b) intellectual and cultural developments that emerged in Italy around the mid-fourteenth century and then spread northward.

    (c) the rejection of Christianity that occurred in early-modern Italy.

    (d) a program of studies that emphasized language, literature, history, and ethics.

2. Explanations for why the Renaissance began in Italy do NOT include which of the following?

    (a) Italian aristocrats lived in and focused their wealth on the urban centers.

    (b) The classical past provided Italy with a unique cultural heritage and an alternative to French ideas and art.

    (c) The lines between the aristocracy and the upper bourgeoisie in Italy blended to a much greater degree than in northern Europe.

  *(d) The presence of the papacy made Italy a much more religiously oriented region than the rest of Europe.

3.   Which of the following is NOT included in the definition of humanism?
    *(a)   a rejection of belief in God
    (b)   the preference for the study of the humanities over Scholastic logic and metaphysics
    (c)   a stress on the dignity of humanity
    (d)   optimism about the possibilities of the human race

4.   Petrarch
    (a)   taught that humanity reached fulfillment through civic service and political action.
    (b)   sought to rediscover true Christianity through a new translation of the New Testament.
    *(c)   cultivated literary eloquence in order to inspire readers to live as good Christians.
    (d)   believed that the realities of power, not ideals, should govern politics.

5.   In *The Prince*, Machiavelli
    (a)   portrayed a utopian world in which neither war nor religious persecution existed.
    *(b)   argued that the head of state must maintain his country's power and safety by any means at hand.
    (c)   sought to blend the teachings of Plato with the principles of Christianity.
    (d)   aimed to teach rulers how to behave in accordance with the ideal of the Renaissance Man.

6.   Which of the following is INCORRECT concerning fifteenth-century Italian painting?
    (a)   The laws of linear perspective were discovered.
    (b)   Painting in oils was introduced.
    (c)   Some paintings appealed to the intellect while others aimed to delight the viewer.
    *(d)   Religious themes disappeared.

7.   Each of the following characterized Leonardo da Vinci EXCEPT
    *(a)   the subordination of form to idea in order to express abstract truths in painting.
    (b)   the belief in the artist as inspired creator rather than hired craftsman.
    (c)   worship of nature.
    (d)   perception of the universe as well ordered, even mathematically proportioned.

8. The Sistine Chapel does NOT bear witness to
   (a) Michelangelo's early affirmation of the good of Creation and the heroism of humanity.
   (b) the continuing importance of papal patronage in artistic development.
   *(c) Michelangelo's commitment to realism and a naturalistic style.
   (d) the Renaissance fascination with the human figure.

9. Michelangelo believed that sculpture
   *(a) was the highest of the human arts because it allowed the artist to imitate God and create human forms.
   (b) should imitate nature down to the tiniest detail.
   (c) was blasphemous because it allowed the artist to distort the human figure created by God.
   (d) was an insignificant form of decoration.

10. Factors in the waning of the Italian Renaissance do NOT include
    (a) the devastation resulting from three decades of invasions and wars.
    (b) the shift in trade routes from the Mediterranean to the Atlantic.
    (c) cultural and intellectual censorship by the Church.
    *(d) the loss of religious feeling that accompanied the rise of modern science.

11. Galileo was brought before the Inquisition because he
    (a) argued that humanity had evolved from apes.
    (b) believed that art, not religion, should inspire humanity.
    (c) mocked the clergy in a series of witty satires.
    *(d) defended the idea of a heliocentric universe.

12. The Renaissance spread to other European countries for all of the following reasons EXCEPT
    (a) the attraction of European students to Italian universities.
    *(b) the urbanization of northern Europe.
    (c) French and Spanish invasions of the Italian peninsula.
    (d) the migration of Italian intellectuals and artists to northern European courts.

13. In the *Praise of Folly*, Erasmus
    (a) described an ideal island community to point out the abuses of his day.
    *(b) satirized Scholasticism and superstition as part of his plea for religious reform.
    (c) declared his conviction that humanity should live by the single rule "do what thou wouldst."
    (d) argued in favor of the Protestant Reformation.

14. At the core of Erasmus's Christian humanism was his belief that
  *(a) society was corrupt because it had lost sight of the simple teachings of the Gospels.
   (b) the Roman Catholic Church had to be destroyed.
   (c) the material world was only an illusion.
   (d) society was so corrupt that only an elite minority could redeem itself through the cultivation of the mind.

15. Which of the following wrote *Utopia*?
   (a) Erasmus
   (b) Leonardo da Vinci
   (c) Machiavelli
  *(d) Thomas More

16. The common theme in Rabelais's works was
   (a) the need to look to the Bible for practical guidance.
   (b) the ideal of the Renaissance Man.
   (c) the idea that men are prompted exclusively by motives of self-interest.
  *(d) glorification of the human and the natural.

17. Which of the following is TRUE concerning the Renaissance in music?
   (a) It broke sharply from medieval developments.
   (b) It was unable to attract princely patronage.
  *(c) The distinction between secular and sacred music blurred.
   (d) While Italian music changed, the music of northern Europe remained tied to medieval traditions.

18. Neoplatonism
   (a) emphasized mysticism and therefore slowed scientific development.
   (b) stressed observation and measurement of causes and effects in nature.
  *(c) introduced important ideas to science such as the central position of the sun.
   (c) revived the work of the Greek mathematician Archimedes.

19. Which of the following did NOT contribute to the scientific advances of the sixteenth and seventeenth centuries?
   (a) The philosophical system of Neoplatonism
   (b) The mechanistic interpretation of the universe
  *(c) The spread of humanistic education
   (d) The breakdown of the medieval separation between theory and practice

20. The Copernican revolution
    (a) allowed human bodies to be dissected for the first time.
    (b) resulted from a rejection of a magical, mystical, or spiritual view of the world.
    (c) overturned the mechanistic interpretation of the universe.
    *(d) removed humanity from its medieval position in the center of the universe.

IDENTIFICATIONS

Medici	Thomas More
civic humanism	Ulrich von Hutten
Pico della Mirandola	Rabelais
Masaccio	Albrecht Dürer
Venetian School	mechanism
Botticelli	Paracelsus
Donatello	Andreas Vesalius

TRUE OR FALSE

T 1. The environment of the Italian city-states fostered a secular outlook that valued political success and the attainment of wealth.

T 2. In the broad sense of the term, humanism stressed the nobility and dignity of the human race as the highest of God's creations.

F 3. The civic humanists embraced Neoplatonism and taught that the individual should focus his efforts on the supernatural world.

F 4. Unlike Leonardo da Vinci, Raphael displayed extreme naturalism in his artistic works.

T 5. Like the literary efforts of the Italian Renaissance, the architectural achievements rejected styles dominant in France in favor of those traditions more in keeping with Italy's heritage.

F 6. Like their Italian counterparts, the Christian humanists rejected Scholasticism and turned to classical Greek and Roman literature for moral guidance.

T 7. Both More's *Utopia* and Rabelais's "abbey of Thélème" depict ideal societies in order to indict northern Renaissance society for its abuse of the human spirit.

T   8.   Northern Renaissance painting is more restrained yet more religiously passionate than that of the Italian Renaissance.
F   9.   Unlike literature, painting, and architecture, music during the Renaissance period remained completely religious.
F   10. The upper classes' interest in alchemy and astrology erected barriers of irrationalism and superstition in the path of scientific development.

DISCUSSION AND/OR ESSAY QUESTIONS

1.   Examine the following paintings: *The Birth of Venus* by Botticelli (p. 426), *The Virgin of the Rocks* by Leonardo (p. 428), *The Madonna of the Dawn* by Raphael (p. 431), and *Descent from the Cross* by Michelangelo (p. 435). Using these paintings and sculpture to illustrate your argument, describe and explain the principal characteristics of the Italian Renaissance.
2.   With the following pairs as your focus, compare and contrast the Italian and Northern Renaissance:
         Petrarch and Erasmus
         Machiavelli and More
         Castiglione and Rabelais
3.   Defend or refute, in whole or in part: "Although the common perception of scientific development consists of a picture of 'Truth' gradually emerging out of the mire of religion and superstition, the story of Renaissance science shows that religious beliefs aided rather than obstructed scientific discovery."
4.   Review Chapter 12 and recollect such achievements as Thomas à Kempis's *Imitation of Christ*, William of Ockham's nominalism, Boccaccio and Chaucer's literary works, and Giotto's painting. Did the Renaissance constitute a break with the medieval period?
5.   Agree or disagree with this statement: "Economic and political factors, rather than individual genius, determined the course of the Renaissance in Europe."

SUGGESTED FEATURE FILMS

The Agony and the Ecstasy. 140 min. Color. 1965. Twentieth-Century Fox. Based on Irving Stone's novel about Michelangelo.

Andrei Rublev. 181 min. Color. 1966. Mosfilm. Russian recreation of the life of a fifteenth-century painter.

Rembrandt. 85 min. B/W. 1936. London Films. Dramatization of the last years of Rembrandt's life, with Charles Laughton.

Romeo and Juliet. 152 min. Color. 1968. Paramount. Franco Zeffirelli set his version of Shakespeare's tragedy in Renaissance Italy—a beautiful film.

SUGGESTED CLASSROOM FILMS

Civilisation: A Personal View by Kenneth Clark. No. 4—Man: The Measure of All Things. 52 min. Color. 1970. BBC/Time-Life Films. Presents the early fifteenth century as the period when modern man emerges. Focuses on the courts of Ferrara, Mantua, and Urbino. *No. 5—The Hero as Artist*. Focuses on the Renaissance in art.

François I. 22 min. Color. Films for the Humanities. A biography of the patron of the French Renaissance.

Galileo, the Challenge of Reason. 26 min. Color. 1969. Learning Corporation of America. Centers on Galileo's conflict with the Church.

I, Leonardo da Vinci. 52 min. Color. 1965. McGraw-Hill. Uses his journals and writings.

The Medieval Universe: The Planets. 27 min. Color. 1975. Insight Media. Explores medieval cosmology.

The Medieval Universe: The Stars. 24 min. Color. 1976. Insight Media. Examines the role of astrology in medieval culture.

Michelangelo: The Last Giant. 68 min. Color. 1967. McGraw-Hill. Focuses on both Michelangelo's art and Renaissance politics.

Michelangelo: The Medici Chapel. 22 min. Color. 1964. West. With Michelangelo's sonnets read as commentary.

Nicholas Copernicus. 10 min. Color. 1973. Pyramid Film Production. Examines the background to Copernicus's life and work, using collected documents and artifacts from his five-hundred-year birthday celebration.

Paracelsus. 30 min. B/W. 1965. Indiana University. Uses Paracelsus to illustrate the Renaissance spirit of inquiry.

Renaissance Art and Music. 54 min. Color. 1984. Insight Media. Examines the interactions of artistic production and humanist philosophy.

Science Revises the Heavens. 55 min. Color. 1986. Insight Media. Scientific developments from Copernicus to Newton. Hosted by James Burke.

Scientific Imagination in the Renaissance. 55 min. Color. 1986. Insight Media. From the series *The Day the Universe Changed*.

Vesalius: Founder of Modern Anatomy. 13 min. Color. 1972. Yale Medical School. With illustrations from Yale's collection of ancient medical books.

CHAPTER 14. EUROPE EXPANDS AND DIVIDES: OVERSEAS DISCOVERIES AND PROTESTANT REFORMATION

Outline

I. The overseas discoveries and conquests of Portugal and Spain
   A. Sudden overseas expansion: the medieval explanation
   B. Portuguese voyages and discoveries
   C. Spanish voyages and discoveries
     1. Columbus's journey
     2. The search for a southwest passage to Asia
     3. The *conquistadores*
     4. Spanish South America
   D. Results of European overseas expansion
II. The Lutheran upheaval
   A. The role of Luther: Lutheranism as religious faith
     1. Background: contemporary religious abuses and Catholic doctrine
     2. Luther's biography
     3. The Lutheran break
   B. The role of the people: Lutheranism as national religious revolt
     1. The readiness of Germany for revolt
     2. Luther's pamphlets and trial
   C. The role of the princes: Lutheranism as the search for sovereignty
     1. Economic motives
     2. Political motives
III. The spread of Protestantism
   A. The English break with Rome
     1. The Henrician reformation
     2. The Edwardian reformation
     3. Mary's attempt at Counter-Reformation
     4. The Elizabethan compromise
   B. Swiss Radicalism
     1. Zwinglianism
     2. Anabaptism
     3. Calvinism
       a. Calvin's theology
       b. Calvinism versus Lutheranism
       c. Calvinist theocracy in Geneva
IV. The Protestant heritage
   A. Relationship between the Renaissance and the Reformation
   B. Relationship between Protestantism and "progress"
     1. The nation-state
     2. Capitalism
     3. The role of women

V. Catholic reform
   A. The Catholic Reformation
   B. The Counter-Reformation
      1. The reforming popes
      2. The Council of Trent
      3. Loyola and the Jesuits
   C. The Counter-Reformation heritage
      1. Defense and revitalization of Catholicism
      2. The role of women
      3. The role of reason

MULTIPLE CHOICE
Choose the best response.

1.   Europe began its sudden overseas expansion in the late fifteenth century because
   (a) Renaissance curiosity and self-reliance had overcome medieval inertia.
   (b) the threat of Protestantism sparked the missionary spirit of Catholic Spain.
 *(c) the Portuguese explorations of coastal West Africa led to the discovery of the Cape of Good Hope and the Spanish hunt for an alternate route to India.
   (d) both the necessary technology and geographical knowledge became available after 1450.

2.   By the early sixteenth century, the _____ controlled the sea routes leading to India and Asia around Africa.
   (a) Spanish
 *(b) Portuguese
   (c) Italians
   (d) Dutch

3.   All of the following statements concerning Columbus are INCORRECT EXCEPT:
   (a) Columbus had to fight against the commonly held assumption that the world was flat.
 *(b) Columbus never realized that the lands he encountered were not part of Asia.
   (c) Columbus's voyages were financed by the princes of the Italian city-states.
   (d) Columbus discovered that the Inca people possessed vast amounts of gold.

4. The results of the Spanish colonization of the New World included all of the following EXCEPT
   (a) a shift of Europe's economic focus from the Mediterranean to the Atlantic.
   *(b) the opening of an important and long-lasting gold supply for Europe.
   (c) economic growth in western Europe in the sixteenth century.
   (d) near-extermination of the Indian population of the colonized territories.

5. To explain adequately the success of the Lutheran revolt in Germany, the historian must include all of the following EXCEPT
   (a) Luther's rejection of the Thomistic doctrine of free will.
   (b) the religious nationalism of the German people.
   *(c) the appeal of Luther's social and political radicalism to the poor.
   (d) the German princes' desire for absolute sovereignty in their territories.

6. In Catholic theology, a remission by papal authority of all or part of the temporal punishment due for sin is called
   *(a) an indulgence.
   (b) simony.
   (c) a dispensation.
   (d) penance.

7. The Thomistic theology of the Catholic Church taught that
   (a) God decided whom to save and whom to damn without any regard for human merit.
   (b) the true church is made up of individuals convinced of the truth of Christianity by their own "inner light."
   *(c) human beings can improve their chances of salvation by participating in the Church's sacraments.
   (d) the Eucharist or Lord's Supper is simply a memorial service to honor Christ's death on the cross.

8. Practical consequences of Luther's theology did NOT include
   (a) rejection of all sacraments except baptism and the Eucharist.
   (b) substitution of German for Latin in church services.
   (c) permission for ministers to marry.
   *(d) rejection of the doctrine of Christ's actual presence in the elements of the Lord's Supper.

9. Luther's theology and teachings included all of the following EXCEPT
   (a) the doctrine of justification by faith.
   (b) preference for the literal meaning of the Bible over traditional teachings.
   (c) rejection of the ecclesiastical hierarchy and monasticism.
   *(d) insistence on the barest simplicity in Church worship services.

10. As with the Lutheran Reformation in Germany, the English Reformation
    (a) succeeded because of the support of influential Christian humanists for a break with Rome.
    (b) was instituted from the top down and had little support from ordinary people.
  *(c) occurred against a backdrop of religious nationalism and widening protest against religious abuses.
    (d) was seen as a way to bring unity to a politically divided land.

11. Mary failed to restore Roman Catholicism to England for all of the following reasons EXCEPT:
    (a) The dissolution of the monasteries and distribution of their lands gave powerful families an important economic stake in the success of Protestantism.
    (b) Protestant propaganda against Mary succeeded in strengthening resistance to her.
    (c) Mary's marriage to the Catholic Philip of Spain offended English nationalism and seemed to threaten English independence.
  *(d) Parliament refused to vote to return England to papal allegiance.

12. Which group taught that individuals were not born into any church and that each man and woman had to follow his or her own "inner light"?
    (a) Lutherans
    (b) Zwinglians
  *(c) Anabaptists
    (d) Calvinists

13. Unlike Luther, John Calvin taught that
  *(a) the Christian's role on earth is to remake the world for God's sake.
    (b) good works please God and so ensure salvation.
    (c) while Catholic theology must be abandoned, much of Catholic ritual could be preserved.
    (d) since God chooses who will be saved, an individual can act without regard for morality or goodness.

14. Under Calvin, Geneva
    (a) demonstrated the Protestant Reformers' commitment to the separation of Church and state.
    (b) attempted to build the new Jerusalem but was defeated in military battle by Catholic forces.
  *(c) served as the place where Calvin put into practice his theocratic ideas.
    (d) demonstrated that Protestantism granted to women not only religious but also political equality.

15. Both the Protestant Reformation and the Renaissance
    (a) advocated religious toleration.
    *(b) turned to the past, of either classical or Biblical times, to revitalize the present.
    (c) viewed human nature as inherently corrupt and in need of God's mercy.
    (d) argued that truth lay within each individual and therefore could not be dictated by Church or state.

16. Protestantism contributed to the growth of the power of the state in all of the following ways EXCEPT
    (a) the state in Protestant countries assumed direct control of the Church.
    (b) Protestantism enhanced a sense of national identity in countries where Protestants fought Catholic overlords.
    *(c) Protestantism gave the German kingdoms a common bond and so led to the political unification of Germany.
    (d) Protestant leaders such as Luther and Calvin preached absolute obedience to godly rulers.

17. The sociologist Max Weber argued that
    (a) Catholic women were more emancipated than their Protestant sisters.
    (b) Columbus, Magellan, and the other explorers should be viewed as "Renaissance Men."
    *(c) Calvinism favored modern commercial and industrial development.
    (d) the Reformation is the logical result of the Renaissance.

18. The Counter-Reformation
    (a) is the label given to Calvin's government in Geneva.
    *(b) both defended Roman Catholic doctrine and reformed certain Catholic practices.
    (c) is the label given to the Anabaptists' attempt to create a holy city in Münster.
    (d) weakened Roman Catholicism by refusing to acknowledge any weaknesses in Catholic practices.

19. In answer to the Protestant challenge, the _____ reaffirmed basic Catholic doctrines.
    *(a) Council of Trent.
    (b) Diet of Worms.
    (c) Institute of the Christian Religion.
    (d) Council of Münster.

20. Loyola and his followers
    (a) argued that the Church's renewal required a revival of contemplative monasticism.
    (b) argued that God's omnipotence disallowed the possibility of humanity's free will.
    (c) reacted to the horrors of religious strife by urging religious toleration.
   *(d) saw themselves as a company of soldiers battling to defend the true faith.

IDENTIFICATIONS

Henry the Navigator	Edward VI
Bartholomew Dias	Elizabeth I
Isabella of Castile	Act of Supremacy
Ferdinand Magellan	Ulrich Zwingli
Frederick the Wise	Münster
Treasury of Merits	*Institutes of the Christian Religion*
Leo X	Max Weber
justification by faith	Cardinal Francisco Ximénes
Diet of Worms	Index of Prohibited Books
Anne Boleyn	Society of Jesus

TRUE OR FALSE

T 1. During the fifteenth century a series of heroic sea voyages gave the Portuguese dominance over the sea routes to Asia and thus preeminence in the profitable spice trade.

F 2. The Renaissance belief in the limitless potential of the individual inspired Columbus's search for a new world.

T 3. Cruelty, treachery, and smallpox led to the Spanish triumph over the Indian population of South America.

T 4. Luther broke with the Catholic Church because he rejected its basic doctrines.

F 5. The Holy Roman emperor Charles V backed the Protestant break with Rome in an effort to establish himself as absolute sovereign in his territories.

F 6. During the sixteenth century, Lutheranism spread and became the dominant religion in Scandinavia, England, the Netherlands, and Switzerland.

F   7.   In order to divorce Catherine of Aragon and father a son, Henry VIII adopted Protestant theology and practices.

F   8.   The Elizabethan compromise legalized all forms of religious practice in England.

T   9.   Before Luther's break with Rome the Catholic reformers fought to remedy the Church's moral and institutional weaknesses.

T   10.   Jesuits concentrated on education because they believed that revitalizing Catholicism depended in part on the spread of literacy.

DISCUSSION AND/OR ESSAY QUESTIONS

1. Write an essay on the theme "The Fifteenth and Sixteenth Centuries: The Age of Heroism."
2. Why did the overseas explorations occur where and when they did?
3. Agree or disagree: "Without the Renaissance, the Reformation would never have occurred."
4. With Calvin and Loyola as your focus, compare and contrast the Protestant and Catholic Reformations and their influence on the shape of modern European civilization.
5. Imagine that you are a literate woman in sixteenth-century Germany and that you have received some Lutheran propaganda. Are you going to accept this new form of Christianity? Why or why not?

SUGGESTED FEATURE FILMS

Aguirre, the Wrath of God. 95 min. Color. 1972. Werner Herzog. Set in 1560, the story centers on Pizarro's lieutenant.

Black Robe. 101 min. Color. 1991. Trimark/Samuel Goldwyn. A brutally honest examination of the impact of Christianity on Native American society.

Henry VIII and His Six Wives. 125 min. Color. 1972. EMI. Inspired by the six-part BBC series.

A Man for All Seasons. 120 min. Color. 1966. Columbia. Academy Award–winning film of Robert Bolt's play about Sir Thomas More. With Paul Scofield and Orson Welles.

The Royal Hunt of the Sun. 121 min. Color. 1969. Security Pictures. Pizarro versus the Incas.

SUGGESTED CLASSROOM FILMS

Age of Exploration and Expansion. 16 min. Color. 1970. Centron Films. Covers the fifteenth and sixteenth centuries.

Civilisation: A Personal View by Kenneth Clark. No. 6—Protest and Communication. 52 min. Color. 1970. BBC/Time-Life Films. Focuses on the Christian humanists, Luther, and Shakespeare.

Christopher Columbus: The Americas, 1492; Francisco Pizarro: The Incas, 1532. 30 min. each. Color. 1977. Time-Life Films. These docudramas from the *Ten Who Dared* series come with teachers' guides.

Columbus and the Age of Discovery. 7 parts. 58 min. each. Color. Films for the Humanities. A BBC/WGBH (Boston) production. Programs look not only at Columbus but at the political and economic context and consequences of his voyages.

Conquest of Souls. 45 min. Color. 1978. McGraw-Hill. Examines Catholic missionary efforts in the New World and in Protestant Europe.

A Matter of Conscience: Henry VIII and Thomas More. 30 min. Color. 1972. Learning Corporation of America. From *A Man for All Seasons.*

Reformation: Age of Revolt. 24 min. Color. 1973. Encyclopaedia Britannica Educational Corporation. Portrays the sixteenth century as an era of revolt with Luther as the detonator.

The Reformation and the Rise of the Middle Class. 2 parts. 30 min. each. Color. 1989. Insight Media. Explores the relationship among the centralization of political power, the Protestant Reformation, and the emergence of urbanized middle classes.

CHAPTER 15. A CENTURY OF CRISIS FOR EARLY-MODERN EUROPE (c. 1560–c. 1660)

Outline

I. Economic, religious, and political tests
   A. Price inflation
   B. Economic stagnation
   C. Religious wars
   D. Governmental crises
II. A half-century of religious wars
   A. Religious warfare before 1560
   B. Civil war in France
      1. Increase in Huguenot strength
      2. The St. Bartholomew's Day Massacre
      3. Henry IV and the Edict of Nantes
   C. War of national liberation in the Netherlands
      1. The accession of Philip II
      2. The role of William the Silent
   D. Warfare between sovereign states: England and Spain
      1. Anglo-Spanish rivalries
      2. Philip II and the Armada
III. Years of trembling
   A. The Thirty Years' War
      1. Religious causes
      2. Political and constitutional factors
      3. International rivalries
      4. Results of the Peace of Westphalia
   B. The decline of Spain
   C. The rise of France
      1. The reign of Henry IV
      2. The policies of Richelieu
      3. The *Fronde*
      4. The triumph of absolutism
   D. The English exception
      1. The Tudors
      2. The reigns of James I and Charles I
      3. Civil war and Cromwell
      4. The Stuart Restoration
IV. Quests for light out of darkness
   A. Witchcraft hysteria
   B. Moral and political philosophy
      1. Montaigne
      2. Bodin

3. Milton, the Levellers, and the Diggers
4. Hobbes
5. Pascal
V. Literature and the arts
   A. Literature
      1. Cervantes's *Don Quixote*
      2. The Elizabethan Dramatists: Shakespeare
      3. Milton's *Paradise Lost*
   B. The visual arts
      1. Differing styles of Mannerism
      2. The Baroque
      3. The Dutch painters

MULTIPLE CHOICE
Choose the best response.

1. The turbulence of the iron century rested on all of the following EXCEPT
   (a) an increasingly desperate and hungry class of poor faced with escalating taxes.
   (b) continuous warfare and its resulting devastation.
   (c) moves toward governmental centralization and the suppression of provincial autonomy.
   *(d) the efforts of governments to force their populations to accept the idea of religious diversity and tolerance.

2. Which of the following benefited from the sixteenth-century price revolution?
   (a) peasants
   (b) governments
   (c) the urban poor
   *(d) landlords

3. The single greatest cause of warfare between 1550 and 1600 was
   (a) economic competition.
   (b) disputes over constitutional issues.
   *(c) religious rivalries.
   (d) international disputes over territory.

4. Which of the following is NOT true regarding Calvinism's expansion in France?
   (a) The conversion of many aristocratic women was pivotal.
   (b) By the 1560s, Calvinists comprised 10 to 20 percent of the population.
   *(c) Calvinism was supported by the French monarchy as the official religion.
   (d) Missionaries from Geneva helped spread the Calvinist message.

5. Catholicism was recognized as the official religion of France but limited toleration was extended to Protestantism by the
   (a) Religious Peace of Augsburg.
   *(b) Edict of Nantes.
   (c) Peace of Westphalia.
   (d) St. Bartholomew's Day Settlement.

6. The revolt of the Netherlands against Habsburg rule
   *(a) led to the establishment of an independent and Protestant northern Dutch republic.
   (b) was put down by William the Silent.
   (c) used the Duke of Alva's Council of Blood to torture Catholics.
   (d) restored Spain to the position of the leading power on the Continent.

7. Which of the following was NOT a factor in the struggle between Spain and England?
   (a) the religious hostility between a Catholic country and a Protestant nation
   (b) trading conflicts
   (c) piracy on the Atlantic
   *(d) Swedish support for Spanish troops against England

8. Which of the following is NOT a factor in the Thirty Years' War?
   (a) the Bohemian Protestant revolt against Catholic rule
   (b) French efforts to avoid being encircled by the Habsburgs
   *(c) England's fear of Spanish supremacy in Europe
   (d) the German princes' desire to retain their autonomy

9. All of the following resulted from the Peace of Westphalia EXCEPT
   (a) France became the predominant continental power.
   (b) the Austrian Habsburgs gave up hope of dominating central Europe.
   (c) Germany was left religiously and politically divided.
   *(d) Spain gained control of Catalonia and Portugal.

10. Which of the following played a central role in Spain's failure to build a sound economic base?
   *(a) a militaristic culture
   (b) a rebellious peasantry
   (c) an overly urbanized nobility
   (d) Protestant contempt for business success

11. The *Fronde*
     (a) pitted the Huguenots against the Catholic forces backed by the French monarchy.
     (b) paralleled the English Civil War and resulted in the establishment of a limited monarchy in France.
     (c) established the principle of religious toleration.
     *(d) involved both commoners and aristocrats in a series of uncoordinated revolts.

12. Which of the following did NOT contribute to the defeat of absolutism in England?
     (a) the blundering of the Stuarts
     *(b) the presence of a strong rival for the throne
     (c) traditions of Parliamentary controls on the Crown
     (d) religious resentments and disagreements

13. Under Cromwell, England
     (a) achieved religious uniformity and religious peace.
     (b) became the first nation-state to be ruled by an elected Parliament.
     *(c) grew impatient with the austerities and authoritarianism of Puritan rule.
     (d) lost its continental empire.

14. Witchcraft hysteria
     *(a) resulted from the attempt of ordinary people to make sense out of the horrors they experienced during the iron century.
     (b) occurred only in areas which were predominantly or exclusively Catholic.
     (c) was one way that ordinary people could demand a change in government.
     (d) contributed to Spain's swift fall from its position of power in Europe.

15. Montaigne
     (a) believed that Protestants should be exterminated.
     *(b) viewed his world with both skepticism and tolerance.
     (c) promoted a high view of humanity based on his belief in the limitless capacity of human reason.
     (d) sought to counteract the religious violence of his day by demanding the separation of church and state.

16. Who wrote that human life is "solitary, poor, nasty, brutish, and short?"
     (a) Ben Jonson
     (b) Cardinal Richelieu
     (c) Peter Paul Rubens
     *(d) Thomas Hobbes

17. Shakespeare
      (a) represented the only bright spot in an otherwise dull period of English drama.
   *(b) ended his dramatic career with a series of romances that stressed the final justice of the divine plan for the universe.
      (c) achieved little recognition in his own time.
      (d) argued that human reason and Divine Revelation must always conflict.

18. The epic poem that links the classical tradition to Christianity and explores the moral responsibility and suffering of humanity is
      (a) Pascal's *Pensées*.
      (b) Shakespeare's *The Tempest*.
      (c) Marlowe's *Doctor Faustus*.
   *(d) Milton's *Paradise Lost*.

19. Both Tintoretto and El Greco
   *(a) emphasized contrasts, distortion, and restlessness in their paintings.
      (b) sought in their poetry to defend Roman Catholicism from the Puritan onslaught.
      (c) argued that in a world of chaos, one must live a life of cultivated detachment.
      (d) used color and composition in their paintings to depict an ideal of tranquility.

20. The Baroque style of painting was an artistic expression of the ideals of the
      (a) Dutch revolt against Spanish control.
   *(b) Counter-Reformation.
      (c) English Civil War.
      (d) humanist rejection of religious war.

IDENTIFICATIONS

St. Bartholomew's Day Massacre	Roundheads
Charles V	Rump Parliament
William the Silent	Levellers
Armada	Blaise Pascal
Peace of Augsburg	*Don Quixote*
Cardinal Richelieu	Christopher Marlowe
intendants	Baroque
Puritans	Rembrandt

TRUE OR FALSE

T   1.   The inpouring of silver from the New World increased the volume of money in circulation and thus contributed to the price revolution of the sixteenth century.

F   2.   The Peace of Augsburg established religious toleration within the German states.

T   3.   Philip II's Spanish nationalism and ardent Catholicism worked together to encourage the Dutch revolt against Habsburg rule.

T   4.   Cardinal Richelieu's policies contributed to the centralization of the French state.

F   5.   Sweden and France allied together against Austria and Spain in the Thirty Years' War to defend the Protestant cause in the Holy Roman Empire.

T   6.   Although Spain's decline stemmed from economic weaknesses, cultural factors such as the nobility's continued belief in chivalry played an important role in contributing to her economic frailty.

T   7.   James I succeeded in alienating large numbers of his subjects by his insistence that he ruled by divine right, by his interference with business freedoms, and by his commitment to peace.

F   8.   The religious belief that black magic required alliance with Satan stemmed from the Middle Ages and caused the greater tendency toward witchcraft hysteria in Catholic over Protestant countries.

T   9.   Jean Bodin defended governmental absolutism as the solution to political turmoil.

T   10.   The plays that Shakespeare wrote in his early years are characterized by a sense of confidence.

DISCUSSION AND/OR ESSAY QUESTIONS

1.   The chapter opens with a quotation from the *History of the Troubles in Great Britain* (1649): "I do not wish to say much about the customs of the age in which we live. I can only state that this age is not one of the best, being a century of iron" (p. 501). Write an essay in which you explain this quotation to a fellow student who has never studied the history of Europe between 1560 and 1660.

2.   Examine the color images on pages 534–45 in your textbook. How do these artistic products of the iron century explore the twin themes of humanity's wretchedness and greatness?

110

3. Examine the interrelationships among religious hostilities, provincial and constitutional disputes, and economic conflicts in two of the following: the Huguenot Wars, the Dutch Revolt, the *Fronde*, the English Civil War.
4. Agree or disagree: "The Thirty Years' War bears witness to the primacy of politics—the struggle for power—in determining the course of the iron century."
5. What are the central themes in the writings of Pascal, Montaigne, and Bodin? What do these writings have in common?

SUGGESTED FEATURE FILMS

Cromwell. 141 min. Color. 1970. Columbia. Richard Harris as Cromwell, Alec Guinness as Charles I. The AHA publishes a study guide for use with this film.

Day of Wrath. 105 min. B/W. 1943. Palladium Films. Carl Dreyer's look at witch hunting and religious persecution in a seventeenth-century Danish community.

Don Quixote. 105 min. Color. 1957. Lenfilm. Soviet version of Cervantes's masterpiece.

Mary of Scotland. 123 min. B/W. 1936. RKO. John Ford's depiction of the life of Elizabeth's rival. With Katharine Hepburn.

Queen Margot. 144 min. Color. 1994. Buena Vista Home Video. Unforgettable portrayal of Marguerite of Valois's arranged marriage to Henri of Navarre, and the subsequent Huguenot massacre. Controversial in its deliberate use of Holocaust imagery.

SUGGESTED CLASSROOM FILMS

Babel: Brueghel and the Follies of Men. 18 min. Color. 1970. Contemporary Films. With commentary drawn from contemporary proverbs.

Brueghel's People. 19 min. Color. 1974. International Film Bureau. Examination of sixteenth-century Flanders.

The Civil War in England 1645–1649. 37 min. Color. Films for the Humanities. Examines the English Civil War as a model for subsequent revolutions.

Civilisation: A Personal View by Kenneth Clark. No. 7—Grandeur and Obedience. 52 min. Color. 1970. BBC/Time-Life Films. The Baroque in art and religious literature.

El Greco. 30 min. Color. 1970. Graphic Curriculum. Uses both dramatization and photography to tell the story of the painter's life and work.

The Puritan Revolution: Cromwell and the Rise of Parliamentary Democracy. 33 min. Color. 1972. Learning Corporation of America. Edited version of the feature film *Cromwell.*

Rubens. 27 min. Color. 1974. International Film Bureau. Contrasts Rubens as court painter with Rubens after 1630.

Seven Ages of Fashion: The Stuarts. 26 min. Color. 1992. Films for the Humanities. Part of a series that explores changes in fashion as a means of opening up cultural history.

'Tis Pity She's a Whore: The First Women on the London Stage. 26 min. Color. 1994. Films for the Humanities. Explores the lives and careers of Moll Davis and Nell Gwynn as a means of looking at attitudes toward gender and sexuality in the seventeenth century.

CHAPTER 16. THE ECONOMY AND SOCIETY OF EARLY-MODERN EUROPE

Outline

I. Life and death: patterns of population
    A. Population rhythms
        1. The centrality of the harvest
        2. Health and sanitation
        3. Marriage patterns
    B. Population increase
    C. Shifts in urban population
II. The dynamics of agriculture and industry
    A. Traditional agricultural techniques
    B. Agricultural improvements
        1. Enclosure and its consequences
        2. New crops
    C. Proto-industrialization
    D. Transportation improvements
    E. Technological change and human response
III. The commercial revolution
    A. Capitalism and mercantilism
    B. Aspects and consequences of the commercial revolution
IV. Colonization and overseas trade
    A. Early Spanish predominance
    B. English, French, and Dutch efforts
    C. The slave trade
V. Life within a society of orders
    A. Intricacies of rank
    B. Rural society: the nobility and the peasants
    C. Urban society: the bourgeoisie, shopkeepers and artisans, and the poor
    D. Attitudes toward poverty
    E. Education and literacy
    F. Popular culture

MULTIPLE CHOICE
Choose the best response.

1. What played the most important role in determining the rise and fall of local populations in early-modern Europe?
    (a) frequency of civil war
  *(b) the fortunes of the harvest
    (c) the stability of the monarchy
    (d) religious beliefs concerning marriage and childbirth

2. The most spectacular urban population growth occurred in the
   * (a) administrative capitals.
   (b) new manufacturing centers.
   (c) port towns.
   (d) university towns.

3. Which of the following is INCORRECT regarding early-modern birth and parenting trends?
   (a) Illegitimacy apparently increased.
   (b) The population of unwanted babies grew.
   * (c) Poor sanitation meant the rates of infant mortality remained unchanged.
   (d) Parents began to invest emotion in their relationships with their children.

4. Enclosure was carried through most thoroughly and effectively in England because
   (a) the English government did not embrace mercantilism.
   (b) English peasants, unlike their continental counterparts, had no protection before the law.
   (c) England had never adopted the manorial system.
   * (d) English agriculture was characterized by a system of absolute property rights and wage labor.

5. Scientific farming did NOT include
   (a) new crops that improved the quality of the soil.
   * (b) placing farmers rather than aristocrats in control of the land.
   (c) intensive manuring.
   (d) elimination of common land.

6. Manufactured goods were increasingly produced in the countryside because
   (a) agricultural prosperity gave farming families the freedom to turn to other occupations.
   (b) wealthy peasants demanded luxury goods.
   * (c) guild regulations limited production in urban centers.
   (d) proto-industrialization requires large amounts of space.

7. As a result of rural proto-industrialization,
   (a) the growth of urban manufacturing centers was halted.
   (b) workers were forced to move to the new industrial cities.
   (c) laborers' wives were no longer expected to work.
   * (d) workers could stave off starvation in years of bad harvests.

8. One result of the changes in commerce and manufacturing of the seventeenth and eighteenth centuries was the
   * (a) violation of customary rights.
   (b) decline of cities and urban life.
   (c) rapid industrialization of eastern Europe.
   (d) rise of workers' enthusiasm for the mechanization of labor.

9. Which of the following is INCORRECT regarding mercantilism?
   (a) It emphasized direct government intervention in economic affairs.
   (b) It led to the establishment and development of overseas colonies.
   (c) It held that a state's power depended on the amount of gold and silver it possessed.
   * (d) It represented a rejection of economic ideas prevalent in the Middle Ages.

10. Throughout the seventeenth and eighteenth centuries, the Dutch
    (a) successfully resisted the changes imposed by the commercial revolution on the rest of Europe.
    * (b) remained dedicated in both theory and practice to free trade.
    (c) embraced mercantilism as the path to economic self-sufficiency.
    (d) fell increasingly behind Spain in economic production.

11. The commercial revolution resulted in
    (a) the shift from capitalism to mercantilism.
    * (b) larger units of business organization.
    (c) the rapid mechanization of industry.
    (d) the depopulation of the European countryside.

12. As a result of the commercial revolution
    * (a) speculation and alternating booms and recessions impoverished many people.
    (b) economies became more stable and predictable.
    (c) agriculture dwindled in economic importance.
    (d) the lower classes no longer had to struggle for subsistence.

13. England's overseas colonization was NOT
    * (a) focused on quick profit through gold and silver mining.
    (b) motivated to a great degree by religious factors.
    (c) centered around agricultural settlements in North America and the Caribbean.
    (d) oriented toward the production of tobacco and sugar.

14. The three key cargoes in the western triangular trade were
    (a) tobacco, textiles, and coal.
    (b) steel, spices, and silk.
    (c) coal, iron, and lumber.
    *(d) sugar, slaves, and rum.

15. Spain predominated in the colonization of
    (a) India.
    *(b) Central and South America.
    (c) China.
    (d) the North American interior.

16. Many early-modern members of the nobility
    *(a) involved themselves in a variety of commercial enterprises.
    (b) rejected the concept of society as an ordered hierarchy.
    (c) aspired to enter the ranks of the bourgeoisie.
    (d) forced their peasantry to accept more scientific methods of farming, such as the open-field system.

17. In western Europe by the sixteenth century, unlike in eastern Europe,
    (a) noblemen owned most of the land.
    *(b) serfdom had almost completely disappeared.
    (c) the commercial revolution had brought great prosperity to rural laborers.
    (d) proto-industrialization resulted in depopulation of the countryside.

18. The bourgeoisie
    (a) replaced the nobility as the highest social order in capital cities.
    (b) earned its income primarily from industry.
    *(c) flourished as a result of the growth in administration and bureaucracy.
    (d) possessed economic power but was excluded from state and city government.

19. Which of the following is INCORRECT concerning education in early-modern Europe?
    *(a) Mercantilist governments provided free elementary education for their subjects.
    (b) The "grand tour" was seen as a vital part of a nobleman's education.
    (c) Female children were educated at home, if at all.
    (d) Bourgeois males received a "useful" education at private schools.

20. The popular culture of the early-modern period
   (a) was shaped by the new literacy.
   (b) had completely lost touch with medieval religious traditions.
   (c) provided opportunities for revolution and so threatened the social order.
   *(d) tended to reinforce the traditions of order and hierarchy.

IDENTIFICATIONS

open-field system	South Sea Bubble
enclosure	Jean Baptiste Colbert
putting-out system	middle passage
commercial revolution	sumptuary laws
mercantilism	bourgeoisie
joint-stock company	the "world turned upside down"

TRUE OF FALSE

F   1. The precariousness of life led most European men and women to wed much earlier than in traditional Asian and African societies.

T   2. Enclosure eroded the communal base of agriculture and deprived villagers of not only traditional rights but even important resources for survival.

T   3. The potato was considered a miracle crop because it could be grown on small plots and was highly nutritious, and thus enabled the very poor to survive.

F   4. Proto-industrialization, although known in some regions of Europe in the early seventeenth century, did not flourish until the improvement of roads and transport systems.

F   5. Although workers feared new technologies, governments welcomed new machinery as the route to increased production and so enforced their use.

T   6. Although capitalism and mercantilism differed as to ends, they worked together well enough to create the institutions that propelled the commercial revolution in Europe.

T   7. The surplus capital needed to fuel the commercial revolution came from gradually increasing agricultural prices.

F   8. The regulated company was granted by the government a monopoly of the trade in a certain colony, along with extensive authority over the local inhabitants.

F   9. North America received the highest percentage of black slaves shipped across the Atlantic in the eighteenth century.

T   10. Educational differences reflected and reinforced the social hierarchy in early-modern Europe.

DISCUSSION AND/OR ESSAY QUESTIONS

1. Imagine you are a villager in rural England in 1725. What changes do you
    see occurring around you? How do these changes affect you? In what ways
    do you live the same as your grandfather did?
2. Capitalism emphasizes private enterprise while mercantilism stresses the role
    of the state. Why did the two systems not work against each other in the
    early-modern era? How could these two apparently opposing systems
    together foster and benefit from the commercial revolution?
3. Agree or disagree, in whole or in part: "Slavery undergirded Europe's
    commercial revolution. Europe's prosperity rests on Africa's tragedy."
4. Why did European governments encourage colonization during the early-
    modern period? What was the relationship between the establishment of
    overseas colonies and the economic changes that were occurring in Europe
    in this period?
5. Early-modern European society can be described as a "theater" in which all
    members of society had roles to perform. Which characters on stage in the
    early-modern period posed the greatest threat to the stability of traditional
    society?

SUGGESTED FEATURE FILMS

Mutiny on the Bounty. 135 min. B/W. 1935. With Charles Laughton and Clark
    Gable. Or *Mutiny on the Bounty.* 185 min. Color. 1962. MGM. With Marlon
    Brando. Tale of an ill-fated eighteenth-century commercial venture.

Tom Jones. 129 min. Color. 1963. Universal. A delightful version of Fielding's
    novel. With Albert Finney and Susannah York.

SUGGESTED CLASSROOM FILMS

The London of William Hogarth. 27 min. B/W. 1957. International Film Bureau.
    Looks at eighteenth-century London through Hogarth's engravings.

CHAPTER 17. THE AGE OF ABSOLUTISM (1660–1789)

Outline

Introduction: the definition, limitations, and context of absolutism

I. The appeal and justification of absolutism
    A. The appeal of domestic order
    B. The goals of absolutism
        1. Army, administration, and revenue
        2. Control of the Church and nobility
        3. Apologies for absolutism

II. The absolutism of Louis XIV
    A. The theater of Versailles
    B. The policies of Louis XIV
        1. Absolutist responsibility
        2. *Intendants* and revenue
        3. Struggle against regionalism
        4. Imposition of religious unity
    C. The financial policies of Colbert

III. Absolutism in central and eastern Europe, 1660–1720
    A. Absolutism in the German states
        1. Imitations of Louis XIV
        2. The absolutism of Frederick William
    B. Absolutism in the Habsburg Empire
    C. Absolutism in Russia
        1. The rule of the Romanovs
        2. The Westernizing policies of Peter the Great
        3. Peter's Eastern-style absolutism
        4. Peter's successors

IV. The English exception
    A. The policies of Charles II
    B. The reign of James II
    C. The Glorious Revolution
    D. John Locke's anti-absolutism

V. Warfare and diplomacy: The emergence of a state system
    A. The new international order
        1. The idea of state interests
        2. Diplomacy and armies
    B. Europe at war
        1. The foreign policies of Louis XIV
        2. The War of the League of Augsburg
        3. The War of the Spanish Succession
        4. The Treaty of Utrecht

MULTIPLE CHOICE
Choose the best response.

1. As practiced by European eighteenth-century rulers, absolutism
   (a) was understood as a license for unlimited and arbitrary rule.
   (b) meant that monarchs freely ignored the processes of law.
 *(c) consisted of the conscious extension of the monarch's legal and administrative powers over their subjects.
   (d) allowed the monarchs to interfere with great consistency and efficiency in the daily lives of their subjects.

2. The goals of absolute monarchs did NOT include
 *(a) the establishment of a free-market economy.
   (b) the establishment of a state-controlled professional army.
   (c) an effective and state-controlled legal administration.
   (d) an efficient system for the collection and distribution of tax revenues.

3. All of the following were obstacles to the achievement of strong, centralized monarchical government EXCEPT
   (a) the Church.
 *(b) standing armies.
   (c) the nobility.
   (d) representative bodies.

4.   Bossuet argued that
     (a) since citizens gave the state its sovereignty, citizens could reclaim this
          sovereignty.
     (b) monarchs had absolute power as the first servants of the state.
     (c) "one king, one faith" was a necessary prerequisite of social stability.
   *(d) the king was answerable to God alone.

5.   In order to strengthen his hold on France, Louis XIV did NOT
   *(a) carefully limit his military expenditures.
     (b) utilize the upper-middle classes in administration.
     (c) declare that members of regional *parlements* who vetoed his legislation
          would be exiled.
     (d) persecute the Huguenots, Quietists, and Jansenists.

6.   The basic achievements of Frederick William, the Great Elector, did NOT
     include
     (a) a foreign policy that enabled him to establish effective sovereignty
          over his territories.
     (b) the establishment of a large standing army.
     (c) the creation of an effective system of taxation and efficient bureaucracy.
   *(d) enhancement of the cultural life and architecture of St. Petersburg to
          make it a great capital city.

7.   Seventeenth-century Habsburg emperors faced the problem of
     (a) trying to make Russia conform to Western models of government.
     (b) teaching former serfs to become rational and productive citizens.
     (c) defeating the "Glorious Revolution" of the nobility.
   *(d) blending ethnically and linguistically diverse regions into a single state.

8.   Unlike absolutist monarchs in the West, Peter the Great
     (a) sought to develop policies that would enhance his nation's economic
          prosperity.
     (b) created a large standing army.
     (c) developed a large and efficient bureaucracy.
   *(d) considered himself above the law, with arbitrary power.

9.   Peter the Great is associated with policies of
   *(a) Westernization.
     (b) democratization.
     (c) enlightened absolutism.
     (d) free-market capitalism.

10. Which of the following is NOT one of the "great" seventeenth-century absolutists?
     (a) Peter the Great
    *(b) Louis XVI
     (c) Leopold I
     (d) Frederick William

11. During the reign of Charles II in England
    *(a) the social and moral restraints of the Puritan past were forgotten.
     (b) religion ceased to be a divisive national issue.
     (c) Whig leaders appealed to William of Orange to help restore English freedom.
     (d) Parliament met annually.

12. Factors leading up to the Glorious Revolution did NOT include
     (a) James II's obstinate and arrogant personality.
    *(b) the royal declaration of war against absolutist France.
     (c) the trial of the bishops.
     (d) the birth of a male and Catholic heir.

13. The real winners of the Glorious Revolution were the
    *(a) large property holders.
     (b) English working classes.
     (c) Irish Catholics.
     (d) theorists of absolutism.

14. John Locke argued that
    *(a) the people had the right to overthrow a government that exceeded or abused its authority.
     (b) the king is God's representative on earth and therefore, sovereign.
     (c) only an absolute ruler can assure social stability.
     (d) elected bodies, such as Parliament, rather than the king, possess absolute sovereignty.

15. During the late seventeenth and eighteenth centuries
     (a) mercenary armies did most of the fighting.
     (b) absolute monarchs deprived the nobility of their military functions.
    *(c) professional armies came under the direct control of the state.
     (d) the cavalry came to dominate early-modern warfare.

16. The War of the League of Augsburg
    (a) was begun by Peter the Great.
    (b) resulted in the partition of Poland.
    (c) gave the English overseas territories that served as the foundation of their empire.
    *(d) preserved the balance of power in Europe by restricting Louis XIV's expansionism.

17. Like their seventeenth-century forebears, Enlightened absolutists
    (a) justified their sovereignty on the basis of their position as "first servant of the state."
    (b) aimed to reform legislation and administration to fit rational patterns.
    *(c) insisted that state sovereignty rested with the monarchy.
    (d) often supported Enlightenment thinkers.

18. Under Louis XV and Louis XVI
    (a) France moved even further in the direction of strong, centralized state control than in the reign of the Sun King.
    (b) the *parlements* established themselves as protectors of absolute authority.
    (c) France became an efficient military machine.
    *(d) regional and aristocratic obstacles to absolutist power grew larger and stronger than in the reign of the Sun King.

19. Frederick the Great
    (a) developed the military might of Prussia by excluding the nobility from the army.
    (b) backed away from the militarism of his father in favor of more enlightened ideals.
    *(c) used warfare to make Prussia one of the leading nations in Europe.
    (d) established himself as uncontested leader of Prussia through the Glorious Revolution.

20. Enlightened policies of Maria Theresa and/or Joseph II did NOT include
    *(a) widening the opportunities for political participation for the common people.
    (b) assertion of state control over the Church.
    (c) establishment of a state-wide system of primary education.
    (d) relaxation of censorship.

21. The enlightened absolutist who tightened aristocratic control over the peasantry after Pugachev's rebellion was
    (a) Peter the Great.
    (b) Frederick the Great.
    *(c) Catherine the Great.
    (d) Maria Theresa.

22. In Britain in the first half of the eighteenth century, _____ played the political game of "interest and influence" to perfection.
    (a) James II
    *(b) Robert Walpole
    (c) Maria Theresa
    (d) John Colbert

23. In the eighteenth century the European balance of power was threatened by the increasing strength of
    *(a) Prussia and Britain.
    (b) Poland and Russia.
    (c) Italy and France.
    (d) the Netherlands and the Habsburg monarchy.

24. Britain's success in _____ was one of the causes of the American Revolution.
    (a) the War of the Spanish Succession
    *(b) the Seven Years' War
    (c) the War of the League of Augsburg
    (d) the Habsburg Wars

25. All of the following contributed to the partitions of Poland EXCEPT
    *(a) Britain's desire to expand its empire in eastern Europe.
    (b) Russian expansionism.
    (c) a constitution that guaranteed political disorder and division.
    (d) a geographical position between powerful absolutist states.

IDENTIFICATIONS

Jacques Bossuet
"*L'état, c'est moi*"
Jansenists
Junkers
Leopold I
St. Petersburg
Tories
Clarendon Code
William of Orange
Act of Succession

Hanover
John Churchill (Marlborough)
Treaty of Utrecht
Louis XVI
Frederick William I
pragmatic sanction
War of the Spanish Succession
Catherine the Great
cabinet
diplomatic revolution

TRUE OR FALSE

T 1. Louis XIV constructed Versailles to serve as the strategic theater for his absolutist performance.

F 2. Although forms of absolutism varied, one common feature of absolutist rule throughout Europe was a strong alliance between monarchy and nobility.

F 3. In order to put France's fiscal house in order, Colbert reformed the state bureaucracy and stopped the sale of government positions.

T 4. The Hungarian nobility prevented the Habsburg rulers from achieving fully their goal of a unified, centrally controlled and administered state.

T 5. William of Orange welcomed the chance to gain control of England in order to use the nation's resources in his fight against the French.

F 6. After 1700, dynasty and religion ceased to be factors in European warfare and diplomacy.

T 7. The Treaty of Utrecht is an example of the importance of the balance of power in eighteenth-century international relations.

F 8. Louis XIV, Frederick the Great, and Maria Theresa are all examples of enlightened absolutists.

F 9. Catherine the Great deserves the title of "enlightened" absolutist because of her abolition of serfdom and establishment of a national system of primary education.

F 10. George III's effort to reimpose absolutist rule on Britain, and his battle with Parliament, threatened to destroy the political stability established in Britain by the Glorious Revolution.

DISCUSSION AND/OR ESSAY QUESTIONS

1. Discuss the ways in which mercantilism, absolutism, and the new stress on a European balance of power were responses to the chaos and violence of the seventeenth century.
2. Defend or refute this statement: "To view the opponents of absolutist rule, such as the French *parlements*, as modern and progressive is to misunderstand European history in the seventeenth and eighteenth centuries. Such opponents were actually backward-looking and self-interested."
3. "There are four essential characteristics or qualities of royal authority. First, royal authority is sacred. Second, it is paternal. Third, it is absolute. Fourth, it is subject to reason." Discuss Bossuet's description of royal authority with the reign of Louis XIV as your focus.
4. "'Enlightened absolutism' is a contradiction in terms. No monarch could be both truly 'enlightened' and possess absolute power." Do you agree? Consider in your argument the reigns of Frederick the Great, Joseph II and Maria Theresa, and Catherine the Great.
5. Imagine you have been asked to deliver a lecture on "Changing Patterns of Warfare and the New State System in Early-Modern Europe." Outline your main points.

SUGGESTED FEATURE FILMS

Barry Lyndon. 187 min. Color. 1975. Warner. Production of Thackeray's novel about an eighteenth-century rogue.

The Madness of King George. 103 min. Color. 1994. Goldwyn. With a screenplay by Alan Bennett, this film explores the clash between madness and sanity, modernity and tradition, in late eighteenth-century England.

Rob Roy. 139 min. Color. 1995. United Artists. Set around 1715, a depiction of Scottish hero Rob Roy MacGregor's revolt.

SUGGESTED CLASSROOM FILMS

Absolutism and the Social Contract. 2 parts. 30 min. each. 1989. Insight Media. Looks at the development of political absolutism, and the theories of Grotius, Locke, and Hobbes.

The Age of Charles II. 50 min. Color. Films for the Humanities. Covers both Charles' life and times, with special focus on intellectual and artistic developments.

The Battle of Culloden. 72 min. B/W. BBC/Time-Life Films. Recreation of the 1746 battle between Bonnie Prince Charlie and the British army.

John Locke. 52 min. Color. Films for the Humanities. Uses dramatized conversations to explore the character and ideas of Locke.

Peter the Great. 30 min. Color. Films for the Humanities. An exploration into Peter's contradictions and character.

Seven Ages of Fashion: The Stuarts. 26 min. Color. 1992. Films for the Humanities. Part of a series that explores changes in fashion as a means of opening up cultural history.

'Tis Pity She's a Whore: The First Women on the London Stage. 26 min. Color. 1994. Films for the Humanities. Explores the lives and careers of Moll Davis and Nell Gwynn as a means of looking at attitudes toward gender and sexuality in the seventeenth century.

CHAPTER 18. THE SCIENTIFIC REVOLUTION AND THE ENLIGHTENMENT

Outline

I. The scientific revolution
   A. New attitudes toward learning and the universe
      1. Bacon, empiricism, and England
      2. Descartes, rationalism, and France
   B. Newton's synthesis
II. The foundations of the Enlightenment
   A. The triumph of naturalism over supernaturalism
   B. The scientific method
   C. The perfectibility of humanity
III. The world of the philosophes
   A. France as center stage
      1. Voltaire: prince of the philosophes
      2. Montesquieu, Diderot, Condorcet
   B. The Enlightenment in Europe
      1. England: Gibbon, Hume, Smith
      2. Italy: Becarria
      3. Germany: Lessing, Kant
   C. Elitism and utopianism
IV. The onward march of science
   A. Classification and steps toward evolutionism in biology
   B. Advances in electricity
   C. The demise of the phlogiston theory in chemistry
   D. Lack of progress in medicine
V. Classicism and innovation in art and literature
   A. Resistance to the Baroque
      1. French classicism in art and literature
      2. Dutch art: Rembrandt and Vermeer
      3. English architecture: Wren and the Palladians
      4. The English Augustans
   B. The development of the Rococo
   C. The emergence of the English novel
VI. Baroque and classical music
   A. The flowering of Baroque music
      1. Monteverdi and opera
      2. Bach and Handel
   B. The emergence of classical music
      1. Mozart and Haydn
      2. The secularization of music

MULTIPLE CHOICE
Choose the best response.

1. The climate of opinion of late-seventeenth-century and eighteenth-century Europe differed from that of earlier centuries in what way?
   * (a) The great thinkers refused to bow to authority and advocated freewheeling scientific and intellectual exploration.
   (b) The Church's patronage of art, music, and literature contributed to a religious resurgence notable for its aesthetic concerns.
   (c) Abstract knowledge was valued most highly.
   (d) Secularization had progressed to such a degree that most educated men and women were atheists.

2. Explanations for the intellectual shift in early-modern Europe do NOT include
   (a) rediscovery of classical Greek texts in the fifteenth and sixteenth centuries.
   (b) the widening of the world through geographical discoveries.
   (c) the acceptance of Copernican cosmology.
   * (d) confidence in the ability of humanity to progress due to advances in medicine.

3. Both Descartes and Bacon
   * (a) argued that science needed to free itself from the learning of past ages.
   (b) were important philosophes.
   (c) viewed man as a machine.
   (d) believed light to be a subjective impression of the human mind.

4. In the Cartesian universe
   (a) God was rigorously excluded.
   (b) mutual attractions among the solar bodies accounted for planetary motion.
   * (c) physical causes accounted for all phenomena.
   (d) much of the Greek worldview remained intact.

5. In _____, Newton formulated the law of gravity
   (a) the *Discourse on Method*
   (b) the *Encyclopedia*
   * (c) the *Principia Mathematica*
   (d) *Candide*

6. Enlightenment confidence rested on all of the following EXCEPT
    (a) the belief that the universe was governed by natural and understandable laws.
    *(b) the belief that a loving God would not allow bad things to happen to the created world.
    (c) faith in the scientific method.
    (d) faith in education.

7. The belief system that assumes that although God exists and created the universe, he no longer takes any interest in this world is called
    *(a) deism.
    (b) agnosticism.
    (c) supernaturalism.
    (d) idealism.

8. The philosophes
    (a) have been dismissed as utopians because of their tendency toward highly abstract thought.
    (b) were centered in England where the defeat of absolutism allowed for free thinking.
    (c) believed that human conduct could not be changed.
    *(d) championed the ideas and methodologies of the scientific revolution.

9. In *Candide*, Voltaire
    (a) expressed the typical Enlightenment faith in the perfectibility of humanity.
    *(b) demonstrated the philosophes' advocacy of gradual social reform.
    (c) systematically outlined the steps that humanity needed to take in order to reach "Eldorado" (a more just and humane world).
    (d) expressed his democratic beliefs by identifying with the laboring classes.

10. Which philosophe wrote *The Spirit of the Laws*, an exploration of the ways different environments and tradition influence political institutions?
    (a) Voltaire
    *(b) Montesquieu
    (c) Condorcet
    (d) Beccaria

11. Which philosophe wrote the *Outline of the Progress of the Human Mind*, which argued that indefinite and uninterrupted progress would characterize the future?
    (a) Voltaire
    (b) Montesquieu
    *(c) Condorcet
    (d) Beccaria

12. Rousseau did NOT teach that
    (a) children should learn by doing.
    (b) women are naturally inferior to men.
    (c) the roots of repression can be traced to the institution of private property.
    *(d) an individual has the right and the duty to resist the general will.

13. Adam Smith is associated with
    *(a) the theories of laissez-faire economics.
    (b) limitations on the use of capital punishment.
    (c) the belief that the rise of Christianity was a great calamity in Western history.
    (d) the triumph of rationalism over empiricism.

14. The philosopher who insisted on the existence of a realm of absolute reality beyond human knowledge was
    (a) David Hume.
    (b) Denis Diderot.
    (c) Gotthold Lessing.
    *(d) Immanuel Kant.

15. The "Linnean Order"
    (a) describes a style of architecture that emphasized proportion and straight lines.
    (b) was formed in England in the early eighteenth century as one of the first royal scientific associations.
    *(c) divided physical bodies into three realms: animal, vegetable, mineral.
    (d) was one of the few noteworthy medical advances in Enlightenment Europe.

16. Medicine and physiology progressed quite slowly in the eighteenth century for all of the following reasons EXCEPT
    (a) the inadequate preparation of physicians.
    *(b) lack of significant progress in the related field of chemistry.
    (c) the low status of the surgical profession.
    (d) prejudice against dissection of human bodies.

17. Classicism characterized Louis XIV's France because of
    *(a) Louis's own preferences for the grand and sober.
    (b) Louis's desire to imitate his Spanish rivals.
    (c) the rise of a wealthy but nonaristocratic class.
    (d) French hostility toward England and therefore the English Baroque.

18. The artistic style marked by cheerful abandonment and the architectural style characterized by delicacy and playfulness are called
    (a) Baroque.
    (b) Classical.
    *(c) Rococo.
    (d) Palladian.

19. The emergence of the novel in the eighteenth century
    (a) occurred in France, in connection with the writings and interests of the philosophes.
    (b) points to the triumph of the Baroque in literature as well as art.
    (c) is best understood as a reflection of early feminism.
    *(d) owes much to the growth of nonaristocratic but wealthy classes in England.

20. Haydn's career illustrates all of the following EXCEPT the
    (a) eighteenth-century transition between aristocratic patronage and public support.
    (b) rise of the symphony as the dominant classical musical form.
    (c) secularization of musical writing.
    *(d) failure of the men now regarded as musical geniuses to gain recognition in their own day.

IDENTIFICATIONS

dualism	laissez-faire
Baruch Spinoza	categorical imperative
Principia Mathematica	Georges Buffon
The Social Contract	phlogiston theory
inductive method	Pierre Corneille
John Locke	Palladianism
tabula rasa	Augustans
Denis Diderot	Alexander Pope
Edward Gibbon	Henry Fielding
The Wealth of Nations	Claudio Monteverdi

TRUE OF FALSE

T   1.   Eighteenth-century Europe witnessed a shift in the religious beliefs of many in the educated classes away from a personal God active in the affairs of the world.

F   2.   In his battle cry *Ecrasez l'infâme*, Voltaire called for violent revolution to overthrow the political order based on repression, fanaticism, and bigotry.

T   3.   Montesquieu's study of the effects of climate and geography on governmental forms illustrates the philosophes' belief in the importance of environment in determining human behavior.

T   4.   Rousseau advocated government by the "general will," in which authority is held by all the people, acting in collective assemblies.

F   5.   Beccaria's *On Crimes and Punishments* illustrates the elitism of the philosophes in their support for swift and severe retribution as the basis of judicial law.

F   6.   The development of the smallpox vaccine demonstrates how medical advances led the field in eighteenth-century scientific progress.

T   7.   In works like *Tartuffe*, *The Bourgeois Gentleman*, and *The Misanthrope*, Molière satirized the French society of his day.

T   8.   Literary classicism flourished in eighteenth-century England at least in part because of its resemblance to the clarity and symmetry of Newtonian science.

F   9.   In her success as a novelist, Jane Austen opened up an important cultural field for women.

T   10.   Bach and Handel were among the last composers of Baroque music.

DISCUSSION AND/OR ESSAY QUESTIONS

1. The seventeenth century witnessed a long-running battle between the Baconians and the Cartesians. What was the battle about? Which side triumphed? What was Newton's role?
2. Defend or refute this statement: "The Enlightenment is best seen as an expansion of the scientific revolution into new arenas."
3. The Scottish philosopher David Hume preferred "to voyage amidst a sea of uncertainties than to dwell in a forest of supernatural shadows" (p. 649). Why would Hume have preferred such a risky voyage? Did the "sea of uncertainties" engulf most of the philosophes or did they find a shore of safety? Defend your answer.
4. Compare and contrast the Rococo and Palladian styles of architecture. What is the relationship between the development of these styles and the religious, political, and economic context in which they occurred?
5. Discuss this statement: "The novel could have emerged as a cultural form only in Britain."

SUGGESTED FEATURE FILMS

Sense and Sensibility. Approx. 2 hrs. Color. 1995. Columbia. Emma Thompson wrote and starred in this brilliant dramatization of Austen's novel.

Voltaire. 72 min. B/W. 1933. Warner. With George Arliss as the philosophe.

SUGGESTED CLASSROOM FILMS

The Christians: Politeness and Enthusiasm (1689–1791). 45 min. Color. 1978. McGraw-Hill. Compares and contrasts the Church of England of the eighteenth century with the revivalist faith of Methodism.

Civilisation: A Personal View by Kenneth Clark. No. 8—The Light of Experience. 52 min. Color. 1970. BBC/Time-Life Films. Seventeenth-century Dutch painters, Christopher Wren, and Isaac Newton demonstrate a shift in worldview. *No. 9—The Pursuit of Happiness.* Eighteenth-century music and architecture. *No. 10—The Smile of Reason.* The Enlightenment.

The Comedy of Manners. Molière: The Misanthrope. 49 min. Color. 1975. Films for the Humanities. A dramatization.

The Enlightenment. 2 parts. 30 min. each. Color. 1989. Insight Media. Focuses on the unlikely alliances between the philosophes and absolutist rulers.

The Enlightenment and the Age of Louis XIV. 30 min. Color. 1985. Insight Media. Interprets the Enlightenment as a clash between old ideas of hierarchy and the new ideas of liberty, equality, and fraternity.

Johann Sebastian Bach. 27 min. Color. 1974. International Film Bureau. Examination of his music.

Science Revises the Heavens. 55 min. Color. 1986. Insight Media. Scientific developments from Copernicus to Newton.

Scientific Imagination in the Renaissance. 55 min. Color. 1986. Insight Media. From the series *The Day the Universe Changed.*

PART FIVE. THE FRENCH AND INDUSTRIAL REVOLUTIONS AND THEIR CONSEQUENCES

CHAPTER 19. THE FRENCH REVOLUTION

Outline

I. The coming of the Revolution
   A. The old interpretation: revolution as class conflict
   B. The open nobility
   C. The role of ideas
   D. Administrative weaknesses
   E. Financial chaos

II. The destruction of the Ancien Régime
   A. Economic crisis and the summoning of the Estates-General
   B. Formation of the National Assembly
   C. Spread of the Revolution
      1. The fall of the Bastille
      2. The Great Fear
      3. The October Days
   D. Achievements of the first stage
      1. The *Declaration of the Rights of Man*
      2. The Civil Constitution
      3. The Constitution of 1791

III. A new stage: popular revolution
   A. Causes of the radicalization
      1. Lower-class disillusionment
      2. Lack of national leadership
      3. The war
   B. The Jacobins
      1. The September massacres and the death of the king
      2. Domestic reforms
      3. The revolutionary wars
      4. The Committee of Public Safety
   C. The results of the Terror
      1. A new popular culture
      2. Centralization of power
      3. Slowing of industrialization
      4. The new nationalism
   D. The Thermidorian reaction
   E. The Constitution of 1795 and the Directory
   F. Bonaparte's coup d'état

136

IV. Napoleon and Europe
   A. The success of the Napoleonic myth
   B. The reality
      1. Napoleonic reforms
      2. Napoleon the Emperor
      3. The European wars
      4. Napoleonic reforms in Europe
   C. Napoleon's decline and fall
      1. Personal ambition
      2. The invasion of Spain
      3. The invasion of Russia
      4. Napoleon's fall
   D. The legacy of the French Revolution and Napoleon
 V. The Vienna Settlement
   A. The Congress of Vienna
   B. The triumph of legitimacy

MULTIPLE CHOICE
Choose the best response.

1. Which of the following statements is INCORRECT regarding the eighteenth-century French nobility?
    (a) Noble status was available to those who could pay the price of an ennobling office.
    (b) The nobility received a constant infusion of talent and economic resources from the ranks of the non-nobles.
    (c) The distinction between the nobility of the robe and the nobility of the sword was often meaningless.
    *(d) Noble families avoided investments in trade and commerce.

2. Wealthy members of the Third Estate
    (a) could not acquire political power and social prestige to match their economic might.
    (b) avoided tying up their wealth in land.
    (c) possessed a strong sense of class consciousness.
    *(d) aspired to become members of the nobility.

3. Which of the following was NOT a contributing factor in France's administrative weakness before the Revolution?
    *(a) Louis XVI's ruthlessness in imposing centralization and rationalization on traditional political structures
    (b) conflict between traditionalist and reforming factions within the Court
    (c) rivalry between the *intendants* and provincial authorities
    (d) the battle between central government and provincial *parlements*

4. All of the following statements describe the French economy in the spring of 1789 EXCEPT which one?
    (a) Unemployment levels escalated.
    (b) Poor harvests led landlords to demand larger rents from the peasants.
    (c) The collapse in manufacturing deprived peasants of a crucial part of their income.
    *(d) The peasants grew increasingly worse off at the same time that the urban poor found their incomes rising.

5. In 1788, in hopes of finding a solution to France's financial crisis, noblemen and other politically conscious persons demanded that the king call the
    *(a) Estates-General.
    (b) National Assembly.
    (c) Constitutional Convention.
    (d) *Parlement.*

6. The delegates of the Third Estate
    *(a) represented the interests of the dominant order.
    (b) were largely from noble families.
    (c) saw themselves as champions of capitalism.
    (d) believed that aristocrats should be beheaded and Catholicism outlawed.

7. The real beginning of the French Revolution was marked by the
    *(a) Oath of the Tennis Court.
    (b) accession of Napoleon.
    (c) beheading of the Jacobins.
    (d) Civil Constitution of the Clergy.

8. The formation of the National Assembly
    (a) was engineered by the king to gain approval for a new stamp tax.
    *(b) challenged Louis XVI's claim to absolute sovereignty.
    (c) marked the end of Jacobin rule.
    (d) marked the first time that the lower classes participated in the government of France.

9. The first stage of the French Revolution is best described as
    (a) atheistic.
    (b) democratic.
    *(c) moderate.
    (d) reactionary.

10. The fall of the Bastille
    (a) signified that France had declared itself a republic.
    (b) preceded the moderates' reassertion of control over the course of the Revolution.
    *(c) demonstrated the commitment of the lower classes to revolutionary change.
    (d) was the first sign of Napoleon's decline.

11. In the summer of 1789 peasants attacked and burned manor houses. Historians called this event
    *(a) the Great Fear.
    (b) the fall of the Bastille.
    (c) Thermidor.
    (d) the Declaration of the Rights of Man and of the Citizen.

12. The Constitution of 1791
    (a) granted the suffrage to all adult males in France.
    (b) demonstrated the Jacobins' commitment to the Enlightenment ideal of equality.
    (c) abolished Christianity and declared France a republic.
    *(d) converted the French government to a limited monarchy.

13. In the summer of 1792 radical republicans replaced the moderate revolutionary leaders, in part because
    (a) the people feared Napoleon's power.
    *(b) the poor and lower classes had failed to benefit from the moderate revolution.
    (c) violence escalated after the beheading of Louis XVI.
    (d) military victories over the Revolution's European enemies made the revolutionaries more daring.

14. An influential case against the French Revolution was made by _____ in his *Reflections on the Revolution in France.*
    (a) William Wordsworth
    (b) Johann von Herder
    *(c) Edmund Burke
    (d) Tom Paine

15. The declaration of war in 1792
    (a) resulted from the failure of Napoleon's Continental System.
    (b) enriched the pockets of the members of the Directory.
    (c) resulted in the Girondist seizure of power from the Jacobins.
    *(d) resulted in the radicalization of the Revolution and the rise of the Commune in Paris.

16. The group that came to dominate the National Assembly during the popular phase of the Revolution was called
     (a) Thermidor.
     *(b) the Mountain.
     (c) the Directory.
     (d) the *Cahiers des Doléances*.

17. Jean Paul Marat
     (a) led the Thermidorian reaction.
     *(b) stood as a champion of the common people.
     (c) was sent to the guillotine by radicals who opposed his moderate policies.
     (d) sought to restore absolutism to France.

18. Which of the following is NOT associated with the popular stage of the Revolution?
     (a) astonishing military victories
     *(b) the Declaration of the Rights of Man and of the Citizen
     (c) the execution of Louis XVI
     (d) a short-lived attempt to abolish Christianity

19. Robespierre advocated all of the following EXCEPT
     (a) the philosophy of Rousseau.
     *(b) multi-party democracy.
     (c) exaltation of the masses.
     (d) ruthlessness as a necessary means to revolutionary victory.

20. The rule of the Committee of Public Safety did NOT result in
     (a) a new popular culture.
     (b) political centralization.
     *(c) accelerated industrialization.
     (d) a new sense of French national identity.

21. As a result of the Thermidorian reaction, political power was placed in the hands of
     (a) the dictator Robespierre.
     (b) the sans-culottes.
     (c) the peasants.
     *(d) wealthy citizens.

22. As a result of the Thermidorian reaction and the constitution of 1795, executive authority was vested in
     (a) the Committee of Public Safety.
     (b) Napoleon.
     *(c) the Directory.
     (d) the First Consul.

23. The durability of the Napoleonic myth is NOT due to Napoleon's
    (a) military and political successes.
    (b) embodiment of the ideal of careers open to talent.
    *(c) championship of democracy.
    (d) confidence in France.

24. Napoleon's accomplishments included all of the following EXCEPT the
    *(a) restoration of aristocratic estates and feudal privileges.
    (b) construction of an efficient and fair taxation system and budgetary procedure.
    (c) establishment of a nation-wide system of secondary education.
    (d) standardization of the French legal system.

25. The Napoleonic Code did NOT
    (a) make French law uniform.
    *(b) protect labor's rights by legalizing trade unions.
    (c) emphasize the individual's right to property.
    (d) benefit the wealthy members of society.

26. The Continental System failed for all of the following reasons EXCEPT which one?
    (a) Britain retained control of the seas.
    (b) Internal tariffs divided Europe into economic camps.
    (c) Continental trade stagnated and unemployment rose.
    *(d) Napoleon found himself militarily outmatched by the British.

27. Factors in Napoleon's downfall include
    (a) his failure to centralize governmental and financial administration.
    (b) the early success of the European coalition against him.
    *(c) his overconfidence, which led him to invade Russia.
    (d) his refusal to restore their landed estates to the aristocrats.

28. The guiding hand in the Congress of Vienna belonged to
    (a) the duke of Wellington.
    (b) Talleyrand.
    (c) Louis XVIII.
    *(d) Metternich.

29. The Vienna Settlement
    (a) was forced on central Europe by Napoleon.
    (b) returned all of Europe to its pre-Revolutionary political boundaries.
    (c) collapsed when Napoleon re-entered France in 1815.
    *(d) satisfied both the territorial ambitions and the reactionary impulses of Europe's leaders.

30. The basic idea that guided the work of the Congress of Vienna was the principle of
    * (a) legitimacy.
      (b) equality.
      (c) legal parity.
      (d) rationality.

IDENTIFICATIONS

physiocrats	Edmund Burke
Abbé Sieyès	Girondins
Estates-General	Maximilien Robespierre
Mirabeau	the Directory
Oath of the Tennis Court	Code Napoleon
sans-culottes	Battle of Waterloo
the Great Fear	Congress of Vienna
Declaration of the Rights of Man	Metternich

TRUE OR FALSE

T   1. Until fairly recently, many historians argued that the French Revolution broke out because of class conflict between the rising bourgeoisie and the politically powerful aristocracy.

T   2. The grievances listed in the *cahiers des doléances* underlay the reforms of the National Assembly.

F   3. Until the Jacobins seized power, Louis XVI remained at the head of the reforming party of the Revolution.

F   4. Both the National Assembly and the Committee of Public Safety were dominated by middle-class factory owners who sought to liberalize French politics and economics and thus move France toward industrial capitalism.

F   5. The ideas and actions of the French Revolution met with immediate condemnation by the literate classes of Europe.

F   6. During the Terror, only noble men and women were executed.

T   7. The Thermidorian reaction ended the rule of Jacobins and swung the Revolution onto a conservative course.

T   8. Napoleon's political, legal, and economic reorganization of the territories of central Europe worked in favor of the business and professional classes.

F   9. Napoleon's Continental System redrew the map of Germany and instituted a uniform legal system in Europe.

F   10. Tsar Alexander I regarded all political and social innovation as an act of contempt against God.

DISCUSSION AND/OR ESSAY QUESTIONS

1. Write an essay entitled "The Terror: The End Justifies the Means."
2. Imagine that you are wandering through France in July 1815. You meet up with a peasant, a Catholic priest, a small shopkeeper, the wealthy owner of a textile manufacturing firm, and an aristocrat. How would these individuals evaluate the achievements of the Revolution?
3. "Although political ideas appeared to dominate the French Revolution, economic forces actually dictated the Revolution's outbreak, course, and outcome." Do you agree? Why or why not?
4. Defend or refute this statement, in whole or in part: "The French Revolution, from the formation of the National Assembly to Waterloo, can be seen as a struggle between the incompatible Enlightenment ideals of liberty and equality. In the end, liberty triumphed over equality."
5. Compare and contrast Europe on the eve of the French Revolution with the Europe shaped by the Congress of Vienna. What had changed? Who were the winners? Who were the losers?

SUGGESTED FEATURE FILMS

La Marseillaise. 135 min. B/W. 1938. CGT. Jean Renoir's version of the French Revolution.

Marie Antoinette. 160 min. B/W. 1938. MGM. Directed by W. S. Van Dyke. Chosen by the National Board of Review as one of the Ten Best Films of 1938.

A Tale of Two Cities. 121 min. B/W. 1935. MGM. Directed by Jack Conway, with Ronald Coleman.

Waterloo. 132 min. Color. 1971. Mosfilm. With Rod Steiger as Napoleon and Christopher Plummer as Wellington.

SUGGESTED CLASSROOM FILMS

The Age of Revolutions (1776–1848). 26 min. Color. 1989. Insight Media. Looks at the spread of revolutionary ideas and politics.

The Battle of Austerlitz: 1805. 30 min. Color. 1990. Films for the Humanities. A study of the battle of the three emperors.

The Battle of Waterloo: 1815. 30 min. Color. 1990. Films for the Humanities. Looks not only at the battle but at the political and military context.

The Death of the Old Regime and The French Revolution. 2 parts. 30 min. each. Color. 1989. Insight Media. An examination of not only the French but also the American revolutions and the spread of revolutionary ideas throughout Europe.

The French Revolution: The Terror. 29 min. Color. 1971. Learning Corporation of America. Focuses on the role of Robespierre.

The Hundred Days: Napoleon from Elba to Waterloo. 53 min. Color. 1969. Time-Life. Filmed on site.

Napoleon: The End of a Dictator; The Making of a Dictator. 27 min. each. Color. 1970. Learning Corporation of America. From the *Western Civilization: Majesty and Madness* series.

Napoleon Bonaparte. 12 min. Color. 1988. Films for the Humanities. Napoleon as military strategist and empire builder.

CHAPTER 20. THE INDUSTRIAL REVOLUTION

Outline

I. The Industrial Revolution in Britain
  A. Why Britain?
    1. The economy of abundance
    2. Intellectual habits
    3. Expansion of foreign and domestic markets
  B. The cotton industry
    1. Mechanical breakthroughs
    2. Shift from home to factory
    3. The cotton trade
  C. The iron industry
  D. The steam engine
  E. The character and limits of the Industrial Revolution in Britain
II. The Industrial Revolution on the Continent
  A. The delay of continental industrialization
    1. Lack of transport and raw materials
    2. Social divisions and the lack of entrepreneurial spirit
    3. Disruption of war
  B. Increased industrialization after 1815
    1. Population increase
    2. Transportation improvements
    3. Political centralization and state involvement
    4. Lack of technicians
  C. The textile industry
  D. Heavy industry
III. The coming of railways
  A. Origins
  B. Stimulation to industry
  C. The navvies' achievement
IV. Industrialization after 1850
  A. Continued industrial advance
  B. Industrial Europe and the world

MULTIPLE CHOICE
Choose the best response.

1. Europe industrialized before other regions partly because
    * (a) the colonies provided Europe with a dependent market.
    (b) European economies were primarily commercial rather than agricultural.
    (c) the belief in the unpredictability of events made men anxious to get rich as quickly as possible.
    (d) declining population squeezed profit margins and so demanded new industrial techniques.

2. Industrialization depends on all of the following EXCEPT
    (a) sufficient supply of raw materials, capital, and technical ability.
    (b) adequate transport systems.
    * (c) a government devoted to laissez-faire economic policies.
    (d) availability of markets for manufactured goods.

3. Factors in Britain's relative economic abundance include all of the following EXCEPT
    (a) the high standard of living of British laborers relative to their continental counterparts.
    * (b) a working class prosperous enough to support a luxury goods industry.
    (c) change in agricultural patterns and an increased food supply.
    (d) the growth of London as a financial center.

4. The entrepreneurial spirit was far more likely to flourish in Britain than on the Continent because
    (a) Britain had not been at war.
    (b) the British aristocracy had lost their position of political and economic dominance by the end of the eighteenth century.
    * (c) few barriers separated the British rural gentry from the commercial class.
    (d) the British government was much more involved in originating and cultivating business ventures.

5. Britain's Parliament in the eighteenth century
   (a) tried to block industrialization.
   (b) encouraged industrial growth by financing a national railway system.
   (c) tried to protect new industry by erecting a framework of internal tariffs.
   *(d) developed a foreign policy responsive to Britain's commercial needs.

6. Mechanical inventions and improvements in Britain's cotton industry did NOT
   (a) enable British entrepreneurs to take advantage of the tariffs prohibiting the importation of East Indian cottons.
   (b) remove bottlenecks in the manufacturing process and so increase production.
   (c) make production in a large mill more efficient than home manufacture.
   *(d) increase the standard of living for the hand-loom weavers.

7. Which of the following is correct concerning textile production in Britain?
   (a) Cotton was a luxury product bought by the wealthy bourgeoisie as well as the aristocracy.
   *(b) The cotton gin and American slave plantations kept the supply of cotton rising to meet the growing British demand.
   (c) Cotton production was exceeded only by the production of wool, a long-established British industry.
   (d) It was a domestic rather than an export product.

8. The key invention in the manufacturing of iron was the
   (a) water frame.
   (b) spinning mule.
   *(c) steam engine.
   (d) Arkwright engine.

9. The Industrial Revolution in Britain
   (a) demonstrates the link between the scientific revolution and industrialization.
   (b) depended on the high quality of British education relative to that on the Continent.
   *(c) resulted from a climate of opinion that encouraged creative and practical experimentation.
   (d) was limited to the iron and cotton industries.

10. The historian seeking to explain the delay of industrialization on the Continent would point to all of the following EXCEPT the lack of
   *(a) scientific education.
   (b) a developed transportation system.
   (c) internal free trade.
   (d) able technicians.

11. The French Revolution
   (a) encouraged aggressive economic competition in France.
   *(b) strengthened the small peasant landholders and so limited the supply of capital available for investment.
   (c) built up tariff barriers across the Continent.
   (d) encouraged the development of internal commerce with the Continental System.

12. The revolutionary and Napoleonic wars did NOT
   (a) impede industrialization by destroying Continental factories and machinery.
   (b) instill caution in Continental businessmen and thereby impede industrialization.
   (c) destroy French merchant shipping and thereby weaken Continental commerce.
   *(d) strengthen the trade guilds and so slow industrialization.

13. After 1815 industrialization increased on the Continent for all the following reasons EXCEPT
   (a) population growth.
   (b) escalated road-building.
   (c) the coming of the railroad.
   *(d) imitation of British laissez-faire policies.

14. One of the reasons that the pace of Continental industrialization remained slower than in Britain even after 1815 was
   (a) the lack of national educational systems.
   (b) governmental reluctance to intervene in economic affairs.
   (c) lack of a wealthy consumer class.
   *(d) Britain's law against the export of innovative machinery.

15. The growth of the textile industry on the Continent was slowed by
    (a) the pace of British inventions.
    *(b) the circumstances of the Napoleonic Wars.
    (c) the boom and bust cycle of unregulated economies.
    (d) changes in fashion.

16. The railroad played a role in all of the following EXCEPT
    (a) the contrast between state involvement in industrialization in Britain and on the Continent.
    *(b) the start of industrialization in Britain.
    (c) the development of an efficient system for the transportation of heavy goods.
    (d) capital investment and economic growth.

17. The building of the railways
    (a) remained confined to Britain during the first half of the nineteenth century.
    (b) absorbed much capital needed elsewhere.
    (c) resulted from the need to move laborers to the new industrial centers.
    *(d) rested on human rather than mechanical effort.

18. Between 1850 and 1870
    (a) Britain lost its position as industrial leader.
    (b) competition led to an increase in barriers hindering the movement of goods.
    (c) raw materials became scarcer and more expensive.
    *(d) industrialization in eastern Europe proceeded more slowly than in the west.

19. Which of the following is INCORRECT?
    (a) The Industrial Revolution happened at different speeds in different industries in different nations.
    (b) Small workshops and home industries remained important centers of production during the nineteenth century.
    (c) Half of France's laborers remained on the farms in 1870.
    *(d) Eastern Europe remained untouched by industrialization before 1880.

20. Europe's industrial dominance in the nineteenth century resulted in part from
    *(a) the willingness to use military force to deny other areas industrial power.
    (b) superior talent.
    (c) the abolition of the aristocratic class.
    (d) an elaborate system of protective regulations.

IDENTIFICATIONS

Robinson Crusoe	Société Générale
laissez-faire capitalism	William Cockerill
tariff	the Stockton-Darlington line
spinning jenny	George Stephenson
water frame	Thomas Brassey
Richard Arkwright	navvies
James Watt	*Zollverein*
Matthew Boulton	the Ruhr valley

TRUE OR FALSE

T 1. The right of private property and security of contract were prerequisites of the Industrial Revolution.

T 2. Through overseas expansion and development, Europe built a system of foreign markets suitable to its commercial needs.

F 3. Britain, unlike the Continent, was free of the social snobbery and class distinctions that made a career in business unappealing.

F 4. Unlike wool, cotton was a luxury item and so quickened the expansion of the market for luxury goods.

T 5. The story of the hand-loom weavers demonstrated that the human costs of industrialization were frequently very high.

T 6. A ready supply of both cheap manual labor and abundant wood for fuel slowed mechanization on the Continent.

F 7. Industrialization is the inevitable conclusion of a significant increase in population.

T 8. Laws forbidding the emigration of artisans and technicians demonstrate the intermingling of profits and patriotism that partly spurred on industrialization.

F 9. Richard Arkwright was the man responsible for the first steam railway.

F 10. Foreign markets were not important in the origins of industrialization in Britain.

DISCUSSION AND/OR ESSAY QUESTIONS

1. What are the prerequisites of industrialization? Is the history of nineteenth-century European industrialization of any use to administrators and politicians involved in Third World development today?

2. Which was more significant in industrialization: intellectual achievements or social structure?

3. The story of Britain's industrial revolution is often reduced to a list of inventors and inventions. Why is such an account fundamentally inaccurate?
4. Defend or refute this statement from the chapter: "Britain made a revolution every bit as profound and long-lasting as that which occurred simultaneously in France" (p. 734). Did the Industrial Revolution further the French revolutionary ideals of liberty, equality, and brotherhood?
5. Discuss the role of the state in industrialization. Can a nation "catch up" with industrially advanced competitors without government direction?

SUGGESTED CLASSROOM FILMS

The Ascent of Man: The Drive for Power. 52 min. Color. 1974. Time-Life Films. Dr. Jacob Bronowski explores the eighteenth-century economic revolution.

Coal, Blood, and Iron: Industrialization. 55 min. Color. 1991. Insight Media. Examines the technological and social transformations centering on the use of coal as fuel.

The Industrial Revolution. 20 min. each. Color. 1992. Films for the Humanities. This series explores the Industrial Revolution in Britain through the approach of case studies:
I. *Working Lives.*
II. *Evolving Transportation Systems.*
III. *The Railway Age.*
IV. *Harnessing Steam.*
V. *The Growth of Towns and Cities.*

The Industrial Revolution and the Industrial World: Part One. 30 min. Color. 1989. Insight Media. Looks not only at changes in industry but also the related changes in commerce, agriculture, and communications.

The Luddites. 50 min. Color. 1992. Films for the Humanities. A docudrama that looks at the Luddites not simply as opponents of machines but as protesters against dehumanization.

CHAPTER 21. CONSEQUENCES OF INDUSTRIALIZATION: URBANIZATION AND CLASS CONSCIOUSNESS (1800–1850)

Outline

I. People on the land
  A. Population increase and poverty
  B. Agricultural capitalism and poverty
  C. Varying patterns of agricultural development
  D. Impact of industrialization
II. Urbanization and the standard of living
  A. Reasons for the growth of cities
  B. Urban population increases
  C. Urbanization and disease
  D. The standard of living debate
    1. The optimists' case
    2. Unemployment and economic instability
    3. Qualitative versus quantitative evidence
III. The life of the urban middle class
  A. Subcategories of the middle class
  B. Social mobility
  C. The middle-class creed: Samuel Smiles and *Self Help*
  D. Devotion to home and family
    1. Women and Queen Victoria
    2. Sexual attitudes and roles
    3. Middle-class rituals
    4. Material security and seclusion
IV. The life of the urban working class
  A. Subcategories of the working class
  B. Social mobility
  C. Living conditions
  D. The female experience and sexuality
  E. Working conditions
V. The middle-class worldview
  A. Uncertainty and the need for reassurance
  B. Political economics
    1. Classical economic theory
    2. Malthusian doctrine and its application
    3. Ricardo's laws of wages and rents
    4. Benthamite utilitarianism and its appeal
    5. Saint-Simon and Comte

VI. Early critics of the middle-class worldview
   A. Challenges in writing
   B. John Stuart Mill
   C. Challenges in art
      1. The Pre-Raphaelite Brotherhood and Millet
      2. Courbet and Daumier
   D. Radical reformers
      1. Owen and Fourier: utopian radicalism
      2. Blanc and Proudhon: social reorganization

MULTIPLE CHOICE
Choose the best response.

1. The nineteenth-century population explosion
   (a) resulted from the better standard of living brought on by industrialization.
   (b) appears to have occurred only in the expanding cities.
   *(c) apparently resulted from a decline of fatal disease, better nutrition, and earlier marriages.
   (d) was confined to industrializing western Europe.

2. Which of the following is NOT true of agricultural capitalism?
   (a) It freed land ownership from customary obligations.
   *(b) It was most advanced in post-revolutionary France.
   (c) It concentrated land ownership in the hands of the wealthy.
   (d) It often deprived the rural poor of their means of security.

3. Of the following countries, the one least affected by agricultural change in the first half of the nineteenth century was
   (a) Germany.
   (b) Spain.
   (c) Britain.
   *(d) Russia.

4. Cities grew in the first half of the nineteenth century for all of the following reasons EXCEPT which one?
   (a) The steam engine allowed the concentration of production in factories in the cities.
   (b) Efficient and economical transportation was found more easily in urban than rural areas.
   (c) The hope of finding steady work at high wages drew needed laborers into the cities.
   *(d) The "optimists" told workers they would find a higher standard of living in urban areas.

5. In the cities laborers found
    (a) steady work at higher wages than those paid in agriculture.
    *(b) overcrowding, poor sanitation, and high rates of illness.
    (c) profitable opportunities for those willing to work hard.
    (d) a revolutionary consciousness uniting the workers into a powerful political bloc.

6. The "optimists" did NOT argue that
    (a) European workers' standard of living improved as a result of industrialization.
    (b) the hardships of the first generation of factory workers were necessary to provide Europe with the capital needed for sustained economic growth.
    (c) life in pre-industrial regions was very hard for ordinary Europeans.
    *(d) although wages dropped, stability of employment meant an improved working-class standard of living before 1850.

7. Nineteenth-century middle-class Europeans
    (a) scorned the dirty cities and established themselves in the countryside.
    (b) argued that women were sexual beings who should be allowed to choose their sexual partners.
    *(c) were unified in a single class by obedience to a common set of standards and expectations.
    (d) built simple, sparsely furnished homes that reflected the high value they placed on frugality.

8. Middle-class women
    (a) sought to be the intellectual, although not political or economic, partners of their husbands.
    (b) were seen as morally superior to men and thus found themselves on a greater footing of equality with men.
    (c) found industrialization a liberating experience as they began to work in the new factories.
    *(d) sought to create a home that would shelter the man from the competitiveness and confusion of the business world.

9. Prostitution flourished in the nineteenth century for all of the following reasons EXCEPT
    (a) middle-class postponement of marriage.
    (b) the middle-class ideal of the wife as pure and untouched by sexual desires.
    *(c) working-class approval of female sexual promiscuity.
    (d) urbanization and resulting anonymity.

10. Which of the following is NOT true of the European working class in the first half of the nineteenth century?
    (a) Workers moved both up and down the socioeconomic ladder.
    (b) Differences in skill, wages, and work place divided the working class into numerous ranks.
    (c) Education was often considered an unnecessary or impossible luxury.
    *(d) The difficult process of adjustment to the new urban industrial world shaped a common European working-class experience.

11. Unlike middle-class women, working-class wives
    (a) were treated as their husbands' servants.
    *(b) were acknowledged as sexual beings.
    (c) were forced by poverty to limit the number of children they bore.
    (d) found financial and mental independence from men through working outside the home.

12. Adjustment to the factory system was difficult for workers for all of the following reasons EXCEPT which one?
    (a) Factory work stressed uniformity and thus denied craftsmanship.
    (b) They were faced with twelve-to-fourteen-hour workdays and no security of employment.
    (c) Dangerous working conditions and production processes made work a constant hazard.
    *(d) They lost their right to freedom of contract.

13. Both the classical economists and their middle-class followers argued that
    *(a) freedom of contract governed the negotiations between workers and employers for wages and hours.
    (b) economic individualism meant that landlords had the right to profit from the property they had inherited.
    (c) natural laws governed the production of wealth but not its distribution.
    (d) the doctrine of laissez-faire demanded that the state ensure public safety.

14. Who argued that because population growth naturally outstrips the food supply, poverty and pain are inevitable?
    *(a) Thomas Malthus
    (b) Victor Hugo
    (c) Gustave Courbet
    (d) Samuel Smiles

15. Which of the following held as an inescapable law that workers' wages must remain at subsistence level?
    (a) Charles Dickens
    *(b) David Ricardo
    (c) Robert Owen
    (d) John Stuart Mill

16. The principle that every law and institution must be measured according to its social usefulness is called
    (a) the iron law.
    (b) laissez-faire.
    (c) pre-Raphaelitism.
    *(d) utilitarianism.

17. John Stuart Mill argued all of the following EXCEPT that
    (a) the distribution of wealth could be regulated by society for the benefit of all its members.
    *(b) only socialism could right the wrongs of industrialism.
    (c) middle-class conformism threatened individual liberty.
    (d) the state should tax inheritances as a first step toward redistributing wealth.

18. Victorian art demonstrated all of the following EXCEPT the
    (a) middle-class desire to display their wealth and power.
    *(b) growing cultural awareness of the urbanized working class.
    (c) power of sentimentality to mute social protest.
    (d) refusal of some artists to accept and condone the middle-class worldview.

19. Who argued in favor of the abolition of the wage system and complete equality of the sexes?
    (a) Queen Victoria
    (b) David Ricardo
    (c) Thomas Malthus
    *(d) Charles Fourier

20. The radical reformers such as Blanc and Proudhon
    *(a) criticized the middle-class belief that the profit motive would shape a better world for all men and women.
    (b) sought to return society to an idealized, pre-industrial past.
    (c) argued that the threat of state control imperiled the gains Western society had made.
    (d) were working-class men driven to radical ideas by their wretched economic situation.

IDENTIFICATIONS

Captain Swing
the standard-of-living debate
Self Help
the Angel in the House
Queen Victoria
sweatshops
freedom of contract
David Ricardo
law of wages
utilitarianism

Nassau Senior
Claude de Saint-Simon
positivism
Thomas Carlyle
Abbé Felicité Lamennais
John Stuart Mill
Pre-Raphaelite Brotherhood
Honoré Daumier
William Cobbett
Robert Owen

TRUE OR FALSE

T   1. In 1850, the European population was still composed predominantly of peasants.

T   2. In many rural areas of Europe in the first half of the nineteenth century, the standard of living for laborers declined.

F   3. Britain and Russia witnessed the furthest advance of agricultural capitalism in the first half of the nineteenth century.

T   4. Some historians argue that the first generation of industrial workers had to undergo extreme hardship to enable Western society to build a capital base sufficient for sustained economic growth.

F   5. The career of William Gladstone demonstrates that passage from the working to the aristocratic classes was common in industrial Britain.

F   6. Working-class men regarded their wives as their economic, intellectual, and social equals.

T   7. In comparison to factory labor, pre-industrial work rhythms allowed some degree of independence and flexibility.

F   8. Political economic theory of the nineteenth century reflects the self-confidence and intellectual certainty characteristic of the industrial middle class.

T   9. The Victorian middle class advocated both laissez-faire policies and governmental intervention in economic matters.

F   10. Louis Blanc and Pierre Proudhon sought to neutralize the competitiveness of industrial society by establishing worker-organized communities.

DISCUSSION AND/OR ESSAY QUESTIONS

1. If you had to choose, would you prefer life as an agricultural laborer or as a factory worker in early-nineteenth-century Britain? Why?

2. In what ways did middle-class and working-class women share similar experiences in industrializing Europe? In what ways were their experiences different?
3. "Like the nineteenth-century political economists, the optimists in the standard-of-living debate treat the factory workers as numbers, as parts of the productive process, rather than as human beings. The pessimists are right: the standard of living for non-elites declined in the nineteenth century." Do you agree? Why or why not?
4. Compare and contrast the ideas of Jeremy Bentham and John Stuart Mill. Why did the middle class find Bentham's ideas so appealing and Mill's so dangerous?
5. Discuss this statement: "The city halls, stock exchanges, and opera houses were the new cathedrals of the industrial age."

SUGGESTED FEATURE FILMS

Adventures of Robinson Crusoe. 89 min. Color. 1953. Tepeyac. Mexican version of Defoe's novel.

Beau Brummel. 111 min. Color. 1954. MGM. Set in Regency England and starring Stewart Granger, Elizabeth Taylor, and Peter Ustinov.

Becky Sharp. 83 min. Color. 1935. RKO. First feature film made in three-color Technicolor.

David Copperfield. 132 min. B/W. 1935. MGM. With Lionel Barrymore, Basil Rathbone, and W. C. Fields.

Great Expectations. 118 min. B/W. 1947. Rank. Often considered one of the best film versions of a Dickens novel.

Les Miserables. 109 min. B/W. 1935. Twentieth-Century Fox. With Frederic March as Jean Valjean, Charles Laughton as Javert. A very effective film version of Victor Hugo's novel.

Oliver Twist. 116 min. B/W. 1948. GFD-Rank. A David Lean production.

Sense and Sensibility. Approx. 2 hrs. Color. 1995. Columbia. Emma Thompson wrote and starred in this brilliant dramatization of Austen's novel.

SUGGESTED CLASSROOM FILMS

Balzac. 23 min. B/W. 1950. Radim Films. Biography of the novelist, which uses contemporary portraits and sculpture.

Charles Dickens: An Introduction to His Life and Work. 27 min. Color. 1979. International Film Bureau. A magic lantern show tells the story of Dickens's life and dramatizes excerpts from his work.

Early Victorian England and Charles Dickens. 30 min. Color. 1962. Encyclopaedia Britannica Educational Corporation. Excerpts from Dickens's works highlight characteristics of Victorian society.

The Industrial Revolution. I. Working Lives. 20 min. Color. 1992. Films for the Humanities. Studies the human consequences of industrialization.

The Industrial Revolution and the Industrial World: Part Two. 30 min. Color. 1989. Insight Media. Focuses on the political and cultural changes that accompanied industrialization.

Les Miserables. 54 min. B/W. Indiana University Audio-Visual Center. Condensed version of the Frederic March–Charles Laughton film.

London: The Making of a City. Part V: Early Victorian London 1837–1870. 20 min. Color. 1990. Films for the Humanities. A look at economic and social changes in what had become the largest city in the world.

The Luddites. 50 min. Color. 1992. Films for the Humanities. A docudrama that looks at the Luddites not simply as opponents of machines but as protesters against dehumanization.

The Pre-Raphaelite Revolt. 30 min. Color. 1970. Films, Inc. Uses both artistic and literary works to trace the movement's history.

Seven Ages of Fashion: The Victorians. 1837–1901. 26 min. Color. 1992. Films for the Humanities. Uses changes in clothing styles to illuminate social and cultural shifts.

CHAPTER 22. THE RISE OF LIBERALISM (1815–1870)

Outline

I. Conservative reaction, 1815–1830
  A. The conservative restoration and alliance systems
  B. Conservative victories: Naples and Spain
  C. Failure of the congress system: Central and South America, Greece
II. Liberal gains in western Europe, 1815–1832
  A. The case of France
    1. Louis XVIII and the constitutional charter
    2. Charles X and the threat to liberalism
    3. The Revolution of 1830
  B. The case of Britain
    1. "Peterloo" and the Six Acts
    2. The liberalizing Tories: Canning and Peel
    3. The battle over parliamentary reform
  C. Liberal agitation in Russia
  D. Liberal revolts in 1830: Belgium, Poland, and Spain
III. Liberalism in Britain and France, 1830–1848
  A. Slow pace of reform in France under Louis Philippe
    1. The slow pace of industrialization
    2. The character of Louis Philippe
  B. The new poor law in Britain
  C. The repeal of the Corn Laws in Britain
  D. Religion and reform in Britain
    1. Abolition of the slave trade and the Factory Acts
    2. Educational reform
  E. Radical dissatisfaction in Britain and France
    1. Trade unionism in Britain
    2. Chartism
    3. Radical unrest in France
IV. The Revolution of 1848 in France
  A. The provisional government: middle-class republicans versus radical socialists
  B. The April elections
  C. The June Days
  D. The rise of Louis Napoleon
  E. The implications of the Revolution of 1848
V. Liberalism in France and Britain after 1850
  A. France under Napoleon III
    1. The constitution
    2. Economic freedom for the middle class
    3. The appeal of calculated grandeur

    B. Liberalism in Britain
       1. The labor aristocracy
       2. Middle-class dissatisfaction
       3. The Reform Bill of 1867

MULTIPLE CHOICE
Choose the best response.

1. To the middle classes of Britain and France, liberalism meant
    (a) universal male suffrage.
    (b) the construction of a modern republican nation-state.
    *(c) belief in individualism and classical economic doctrines.
    (d) equality of opportunity for all men and women.

2. The congress system
    (a) succeeded in repressing liberalism in continental Europe.
    *(b) sought to stifle liberalism through alliances of conservative regimes pledged to retain the status quo.
    (c) sought to establish stable, limited monarchies in Europe.
    (d) was Tsar Alexander's effort to create a Christian empire.

3. The Revolution of 1830 in France
    (a) resulted from Louis XVIII's refusal to deny his theoretical absolute power.
    *(b) benefited the upper middle class.
    (c) established Louis Napoleon as the new emperor of France.
    (d) put the working class in a position of political supremacy.

4. Many Tories opposed parliamentary reform on the grounds that
    (a) large landowners could not be trusted to legislate in the interests of middle-class businessmen.
    (b) dissenting Protestants must not be allowed to participate in the political life of the nation.
    (c) policies must be determined on the basis of the greatest good for the greatest number.
    *(d) despite a very limited franchise, the unreformed Parliament looked after the interests of the nation.

5. The Reform Bill of 1832
   (a) enfranchised the responsible working class.
   *(b) succeeded in averting a revolution by heading off a working-class–middle-class alliance.
   (c) abolished the Corn Laws and so reduced both the price of bread and the risk of revolution.
   (d) denied the concept of representation by interest.

6. Which of the following was NOT true of the reign of Tsar Nicholas?
   (a) Russia remained an autocratic state.
   (b) The bureaucracy grew more centralized and efficient.
   (c) A political police force was established to quell domestic disorder.
   *(d) Western innovations like railways were forbidden.

7. During the 1830s, middle-class revolutions or reform movements triumphed in all the following countries EXCEPT
   *(a) Poland.
   (b) Spain.
   (c) Belgium.
   (d) France.

8. The pace of liberal reform was slower in France than in Britain in the 1830s because of all the following reasons EXCEPT which one?
   (a) France had industrialized more slowly.
   (b) Free trade was less appealing in a country that did not enjoy Britain's domination of the world's markets.
   (c) The powerful members of the French upper-middle class tended to be bankers and merchants rather than industrialists.
   *(d) Louis Philippe was such a popular monarch that public discontent remained at low levels during his lifetime.

9. The new poor law in Britain
   (a) established a system of doles for the support of the unemployed.
   (b) established the government's responsibility to regulate prices and wages for the good of society.
   *(c) expressed the liberal belief that poverty was an individual rather than an institutional problem.
   (d) declared that the poor were the Church's responsibility.

10. Significant social reforms in Britain, such as the abolition of the slave trade and the restriction of child labor, resulted from
   *(a) religious conviction.
   (b) the recognition that classical liberalism had failed.
   (c) competition between Tories and Whigs in appealing to the newly enfranchised working class.
   (d) upper-class fear of revolution.

11. The Chartists
   (a) succeeded in bringing Britain to revolution.
   *(b) met defeat because of both the well-organized resistance of the government, and defections from their own ranks brought on by increasing prosperity.
   (c) agreed that only violent means could achieve the end of full and equal political participation.
   (d) attacked factories and smashed machines that they believed led to unemployment.

12. All of the following contributed to the outbreak of revolution in France in 1848 EXCEPT
   (a) radical disillusionment with middle-class liberalism.
   (b) Louis Philippe's repressive measures against radicals.
   *(c) the increasing unpopularity of Louis Philippe's military campaigns.
   (d) the government's refusal to extend the franchise to middle-class moderates.

13. The provisional government established after Louis Philippe's abdication failed because of
   *(a) increasing tensions between middle-class liberals and radical socialists.
   (b) the aristocracy's refusal to abolish the Corn Laws.
   (c) the widespread dislike of the New Poor Law.
   (d) the government's refusal to hold elections.

14. The election of Louis Napoleon as president was part of the imposition of order following the
   (a) Luddite riots.
   (b) February revolution of 1848.
   *(c) June Days.
   (d) Decembrist rebellion.

15. Which of the following does NOT help to explain Louis Napoleon's success?
    (a) He had corresponded with radicals and seemed to have a revolutionary new scheme for eliminating poverty.
    *(b) He established the long-desired democratic government in France.
    (c) He was the nephew of Napoleon and symbolized France's greatness.
    (d) He gained the Church's support by allowing Catholics to regain their control of the educational system.

16. The Revolution of 1848 in France revealed that
    *(a) the success of middle-class liberalism depended in part on its ability to accommodate working-class demands.
    (b) liberalism had little chance of succeeding anywhere but Britain.
    (c) the key actors in political revolution were the peasants.
    (d) the working class would support only democratic governments.

17. Under Napoleon III
    (a) the middle class achieved its political goals.
    (b) the working class found that, once again, it had been deprived of any benefits resulting from revolution.
    *(c) France appeared to have reemerged as a world power.
    (d) France embarked on a period of peace and prosperity.

18. What is the definition of the British labor "aristocracy"?
    (a) a group of landed gentlemen who advocated enfranchising the working class
    (b) members of the working class who rose to the very top of the social and political hierarchy by their own skill and hard work
    (c) leaders of the Whig party
    *(d) skilled workers who earned relatively high wages

19. Passage of the Reform Bill of 1867 in Britain was engineered by
    (a) William Gladstone.
    *(b) Benjamin Disraeli.
    (c) William Pitt.
    (d) Robert Peel.

20. With the passage of the Reform Bill of 1867
    (a) Britain attained universal male suffrage.
    (b) democratic government became a principle of the British political system.
    *(c) Britain entered the period of liberalism's triumph.
    (d) the Liberals upstaged the Conservatives and won the loyalty of new voters.

IDENTIFICATIONS

Concert of Europe	William Wilberforce
Quintuple Alliance	dissenter
Troppau	François Guizot
Monroe Doctrine	Luddites
"Peterloo"	Friendly Societies
George Canning	People's Charter
rotten boroughs	Auguste Blanqui
Charles X	Louis Blanc
Carlist Wars	June Days
Anti-Corn Law League	labor aristocracy

TRUE OR FALSE

F 1. In Naples and Spain, the congress system succeeded in suppressing liberal revolts.

F 2. The Whigs defended the rights of the working class and called for political democracy in Britain.

F 3. The major beneficiaries of the French Revolution of 1830 were the skilled workers.

F 4. The Decembrists succeeded in establishing a liberal, constitutional monarchy in Russia.

F 5. Both France and Britain established a national system of primary education as a result of liberal reforms in the 1830s.

T 6. In the 1830s, the British Government succeeded in defeating the Grand National Consolidated Trades Union and the threat of a general strike.

T 7. In 1848 the French assembly ended the workshop system for political as well as economic reasons.

T 8. By 1853 Louis Napoleon had obtained nearly absolute political power in France.

T 9. To demonstrate the grandeur and might of his regime, Napoleon III pursued an aggressive foreign policy.

T 10. Unlike in France in 1848, the British governing classes in both 1832 and 1867 proved successful in accommodating the forces of change and so avoiding a revolution.

DISCUSSION AND/OR ESSAY QUESTIONS

1. "Though the [Reform Act of 1832] was the product of change and itself brought change in its wake, it was understood as a conservative measure" (p. 792). Could the same be said of the French Revolution of 1830? Why or why not?
2. "The laws of classical economics clashed with other prejudices and beliefs, pulling men and women in various directions at once. Their uncertainty mirrored the extent to which no one could discern a right course in this world of new difficulties and fresh options" (p. 797). Discuss in reference to the British middle class from 1815 to 1870.
3. How do you explain Napoleon III's rise to power?
4. Agree or disagree: "In France in the nineteenth century, pursuit of the ideal of economic liberty led to the abandonment of the ideal of political liberty."
5. Defend or refute this statement: "The labor aristocrats in Britain achieved victory in 1867 by selling out their fellow workers and by denying the ideals of Chartism."

SUGGESTED FEATURE FILMS

Les Enfants du Paradis (Children of Paradise). 195 min. B/W. 1945. Pathe. Depiction of the dark side of Paris in the 1840s.

Juarez. 132 min. B/W. 1939. Warner. With Claude Rains as Napoleon III, Brian Aherne as Emperor Maximilian von Habsburg, and Paul Muni as Juarez. Study guide available through the AHA.

Princess Caraboo. 97 min. Color. 1994. Columbia/Tri-Star. Set in 1817, this true story looks at the impact of a royal imposter on English high society.

Sense and Sensibility. Approx. 2 hrs. Color. 1995. Columbia. Emma Thompson wrote and starred in this stunning adaptation of Austen's novel.

SUGGESTED CLASSROOM FILMS

Daumier's France. 60 min. Color. 1985. Films for the Humanities. Portrait of Daumier, and of France during the July Monarchy and the Second Empire.

The Industrial Revolution and the Industrial World: Part Two. 30 min. Color. 1989. Insight Media. Focuses on the political and cultural changes that accompanied industrialization.

London: The Making of a City. Part V: Early Victorian London 1837–1870. 20 min. Color. 1990. Films for the Humanities. A look at economic and social changes in what had become the largest city in the world.

Queen Victoria: A Profile in Power. 30 min. Color. 1976. Learning Corporation of America. An imaginary interview with the queen.

Seven Ages of Fashion: The Victorians. 1837–1901. 26 min. Color. 1992. Films for the Humanities. Uses changes in clothing styles to illuminate social and cultural shifts.

CHAPTER 23. NATIONALISM AND NATION-BUILDING (1815–1870)

Outline

I. Nationalism as an artificial construct
  A. Nationalism and linguistic identity
  B. Nationalism and liberalism
  C. Nationalism and nation-building
II. Romanticism and nationalism
  A. Romanticism defined
    1. Reaction against the Enlightenment
    2. Exaltation of the individual
  B. Romantic nationalism
    1. Herder and the *Volksgeist*
    2. Hegel and the organic evolution of society
    3. Fichte and the example of the French Revolution
    4. The cultural products of Romantic nationalism
III. Nationalism and nation-building: 1880–1848
  A. Nationalism and reform in Prussia
    1. Military reforms
    2. Domestic reforms: Stein
  B. Economic nationalism
  C. Failure of liberalism in Germany
  D. Nationalism in the Austrian Empire
  E. Nationalism in Italy and Ireland
IV. Nationalism, liberalism, and revolution, 1848
  A. Failure of revolution in Austria
    1. The March Days
    2. Counternationalism
    3. Imperial nation-building
  B. Failure of revolution in Prussia
  C. The Frankfurt Assembly
    1. Great Germans versus Little Germans
    2. Liberalism versus nationalism
V. Nation-building, 1850–1870
  A. Bismarck and the building of Germany
    1. Defeat of the liberals
    2. The Crimean War
    3. The Seven Weeks' War
    4. Universal suffrage
    5. The Franco-Prussian War

   B. Italian unification
       1. Cavour and the use of war
       2. Garibaldi and the conquest of the Kingdom of the Two Sicilies
       3. The occupation of Rome
   C. Nation-building in Russia
   D. Nation-building in the United States
       1. The growth of democracy
       2. Immigration
       3. Slavery and the South
       4. The Civil War

MULTIPLE CHOICE
Choose the best response.

1. Which of the following statements is INACCURATE?
    (a) Nationalism depended for its existence on an increasingly literate
         population.
    *(b) European liberals recognized the inherent conservatism of nationalism
         and fought to reduce its appeal.
    (c) Nationalism is a sentiment created by a political elite to serve its own
         purposes.
    (d) In central and eastern Europe, nation-building was the political
         expression of nationalism.

2. Unlike Enlightenment thinkers, romantics stressed the importance of
    _____ in obtaining knowledge.
    *(a) the soul
    (b) the mind
    (c) the senses
    (d) experiment

3. According to the theory of the organic evolution of society and state,
    (a) each ethnic group should possess its own state.
    (b) each state needed a strong ruler to defend its best interests.
    *(c) institutions are the products of historical growth, not simply abstract ideas.
    (d) since each state evolved according to its own nature, past experience
         was of no use to determine present action.

4. The concept of the dialectic pattern of change is associated with the
    writings of
    (a) Bismarck.
    (b) Beethoven.
    *(c) Hegel.
    (d) Goethe.

5. French successes in the revolutionary and Napoleonic wars taught that
 *(a) soldiers who believe that they have a personal stake in the war's outcome make much more effective fighters.
 (b) weapons rather than numbers would win wars in the industrial age.
 (c) careful discipline and precise training would enable a small army to defeat a much larger foe.
 (d) victory depended on a solid industrial base.

6. Stein's reforms of Prussia
 (a) were motivated by the desire to establish liberal democracy in Germany.
 *(b) sought to foster in Germans a sense of national loyalty.
 (c) failed because of Bismarck's opposition.
 (d) sought to increase working-class participation in the state.

7. Friedrich List argued that
 (a) the state must reward its citizens if they were to develop a sense of national loyalty.
 (b) the German middle classes have to be given more opportunities for financial success.
 (c) Prussia had to adopt British free-trade policies if it expected to compete with Britain in world markets.
 *(d) Prussia must adopt protectionist policies in order to build a prosperous economy.

8. Frederick William IV
 *(a) combined romantic nationalism with authoritarian rule.
 (b) crushed the revolt of the *carbonari*.
 (c) consolidated British rule in Ireland.
 (d) granted the Prussian people limited national autonomy.

9. In the Austrian Empire
 (a) nationalism served as the one bond that could tie together the diverse groups.
 *(b) nationalism threatened to dissolve the empire into rival ethnic nation-states.
 (c) Pan-Slavism served to unite the people out of fear of Russian takeover.
 (d) the establishment of a constitutional monarchy stabilized the state.

10. The cultural nationalist movement that stressed the unity of many eastern European peoples was called
 (a) the Liberation.
 (b) Chartism.
 (c) *carbonari*.
 *(d) Pan-Slavism.

11. Which of the following nationalist movements derived its strength from peasant support?
     (a) the Italian
     *(b) the Irish
     (c) the English
     (d) the German

12. The imperial government was able to reassert control after the revolution of 1848 in the Austrian empire because
     (a) Metternich refused to give in to the revolutionaries.
     (b) the Frankfurt Assembly could not agree on a constitution.
     (c) of the lack of a liberal reform movement in the empire.
     *(d) of the divisive impact of nationalism.

13. The Frankfurt Assembly failed because
     (a) it endeavored to establish a radical rather than a liberal state.
     *(b) it did not resolve the contradictions between liberalism and nationalism in the building of a German state.
     (c) the Prussian army quickly blocked its revolutionary efforts.
     (d) its refusal to support Hungarian nationalism turned the army against the Assembly.

14. Great Germans and Little Germans disagreed over
     (a) the need for Germany to possess an empire to prove its world-power status.
     *(b) the position of Austria in a unified Germany.
     (c) tariff policies governing both trade within the German states and with other countries.
     (d) the role of the army in the new state.

15. As a result of the 1848 revolution,
     (a) a unified German nation-state was created.
     (b) Austria became the leader of the German nationalist movement.
     *(c) German liberalism gave way to German nationalism.
     (d) Germany became part of the Habsburg empire.

16. In order to unify Germany, Bismarck
     (a) provoked Austria into beginning the Crimean War.
     (b) cultivated the favor of the liberal Prussian parliament.
     *(c) used a diplomatic crisis to provoke war with France.
     (d) formed an alliance with Britain against Russia.

17. Bismarck believed that
    (a) the destiny of the German people was a German Empire.
    *(b) German unification under Austria threatened Prussian interests.
    (c) only a unified Germany could provide the stable basis for a liberal democracy in Germany.
    (d) only a unified Germany could withstand the threat of socialism.

18. Consolidation of Italian unification required all of the following EXCEPT
    (a) the expulsion of the Austrians from Italy.
    (b) the conquest of the Kingdom of the Two Sicilies.
    (c) compromise between republicans, Catholics, and moderates.
    *(d) papal approval.

19. The question of how Russia could fulfill her nationalist destiny divided mid-nineteenth-century intellectuals into two camps:
    *(a) the slavophiles versus the westernizers.
    (b) the *carbonari* versus the Pan-Slavists.
    (c) the Liberationists versus the Pan-Slavists.
    (d) the slavophiles versus the Catholics.

20. The Jeffersonians believed that the United States should be a
    *(a) republic led by an aristocracy of virtue and talent.
    (b) limited monarchy.
    (c) democracy in which all adults had the right to vote.
    (d) multicultural society which treated all ethnic groups equally.

IDENTIFICATIONS

Johann von Herder	Guiseppe Mazzini
Volksgeist	Daniel O'Connell
William Wordsworth	March Days
Georg Wilhelm Hegel	*Realpolitik*
J. G. Fichte	*risorgimento*
Johann Wolfgang von Goethe	Camillo di Cavour
Zollverein	Guiseppe Garibaldi
German Confederation	

TRUE OR FALSE

T   1.   Johann von Herder argued that each people has its own unique historical character, or *Volksgeist*.

T   2.   Beethoven's music illustrates the romantic commitment to the power and freedom of the individual will.

T   3.   During the first half of the nineteenth century, Prussia sought to rebuild its economic and military strength.

F   4.   Because of the Habsburgs' policies of repression, neither nationalism nor liberalism attracted adherents in the Austrian Empire before 1850.

F   5.   Like the nationalist movement in northern Italy, Irish nationalism took the form of middle-class protest against a foreign occupying power.

T   6.   The French Revolution of 1848 inspired similar events within the Austrian Empire, Germany, and Italy.

F   7.   The Frankfurt Assembly failed because it attempted to ally with working-class radicals and so alienated its moderate, middle-class support.

T   8.   The Crimean War weakened both the defeated Russia and the victorious Austria.

T   9.   The Seven Weeks' War left Austria severely weakened and so aided both the unification of Germany under Prussia and the unification of Italy.

T   10.   The majority of the founders of the United States were anti-democratic.

DISCUSSION AND/OR ESSAY QUESTIONS

1.   Some historians have argued that because no clear and precise definition of "romanticism" has been accepted, the terms should be discarded. Examine the ideas of Goethe, von Herder, Hegel, and Fichte. Should these men all be labeled "romantic"?

2.   Write an essay entitled "Romanticism, Nationalism, and Liberalism: Connections and Contradictions."

3.   Bismarck declared, "The great questions of the day will not be decided by speeches or by majority decisions . . . but by blood and by iron." Was he right? Did blood and iron decide the course of German history in the nineteenth century?

4.   Many of the delegates of the Frankfurt Assembly went home "convinced that their dual goal of liberalism and nationalism was an impossible one" (p. 830). Were these men correct? Examine this question with regard to the nineteenth-century political history of two of the following: Germany, Italy, Austria, the United States.

5.   Defend or refute this statement: "The beneficiary of nineteenth-century nation-building was neither liberalism nor romanticism but capitalism."

SUGGESTED FEATURE FILMS

The Charge of the Light Brigade. 141 min. Color. 1968. United Artists. Tony Richardson directed this film version of the tragedy and glory of the Crimean War. Based in part on Cecil Woodham Smith's *The Reason Why.*

Immortal Beloved. 121 min. Color. 1994. Columbia/Tri-Star. Unforgettable although sometimes inaccurate account of Beethoven's life; includes a poignant dramatization of the first performance of the Ninth Symphony.

The Leopard. 125 min. Color. 1963. Twentieth-Century Fox. Based on the Guiseppe de Lampedusa novel about a nineteenth-century Sicilian noble family.

SUGGESTED CLASSROOM FILMS

Beethoven: Ordeal and Triumph. 53 min. Color. 1967. McGraw-Hill. Features Eric Leinsdorf and the Boston Symphony Orchestra.

Bismarck: Germany from Blood and Iron. 30 min. Color. 1976. Learning Corporation of America. Uses Bismarck's words to describe the process of German unification.

Blake. 53 min. Color. 1974. BBC/Time-Life Films. Malcolm Muggeridge narrates this account of Blake's life and work.

Civilisation: A Personal View by Kenneth Clark. No. 11—The Worship of Nature. 52 min. Color. 1970. BBC/Time-Life Films. A look at eighteenth-century romanticism. *No. 12—The Fallacies of Hope.* Byron, Beethoven, Napoleon, Delacroix, and Rodin are used to illustrate the theme of eighteenth-century hopes betrayed by nineteenth-century realities.

Karl Marx: The Massive Dissent. 57 min. Color. 1977. Films, Inc. A look at Marx and other socialist thinkers.

The Making of the German Nation: Part One—The Struggle for Unity. 20 min. Color. 1983. Insight Media. Covers the Congress of Vienna, Bismarck, and the Franco-Prussian War.

Revolution and the Romantics. 2 parts. 30 min. each. Color. 1989. Insight Media. Explores the links between romanticism and the revolutionary spirit.

The Spirit of Romanticism. 27 min. Color. 1978. Encyclopaedia Britannica Educational Corporation. Dramatizations based on letters and documents.

The Unification of Germany. 33 min. Color. 1986. Insight Media. Covers the period from 1815 through 1871.

The Unification of Italy. 30 min. Color. 1989. Insight Media. A look at both process and players.

PART SIX.   THE WEST AT THE WORLD'S CENTER

CHAPTER 24.   INTERNATIONAL INDUSTRIALIZATION AND
              IMPERIALISM (1870–1914)

Outline

 I. New technologies
     A. Mass production of steel
     B. Widespread availability of electricity
     C. Technical advances in the chemical industry
 II. Changes in scope and scale
     A. Population increases
     B. Higher living standards and the rise of the consumer society
     C. Changes in industry
         1. Expansion and consolidation
         2. Effects of increases in scale on workers
III. The new capitalism
     A. The emergence of finance capitalism
     B. The spread of industrial unification
     C. The intertwining of business and government
 IV. International competition: imperialism
     A. The rise of the global economy and dependency on "invisible" exports
     B. Disruption of less developed societies
     C. The role of technology
     D. Causes of the new imperialism
         1. The economic argument: Hobson and Lenin
         2. Political considerations and the balance of power
     E. The idea of imperialism: the missionary spirit and patriotic propaganda
     F. The colonization of Africa
     G. British India
     H. Russian and American imperial patterns

MULTIPLE CHOICE
Choose the best response.

1. Important technological developments that undergirded the second phase of
    industrialization included all of the following EXCEPT
    (a) the mass production of steel.
    (b) availability of electric power.
    (c) improved design and expanded capacity of steam engines.
    *(d) the mass production of cotton.

2. Steel came to be produced cheaply and in great quantities as a result of
   - (a) the recognition that steel was harder, more malleable, and stronger than iron.
   - *(b) the Bessemer, Siemens-Martin, and Gilchrest processes.
   - (c) the puddling process.
   - (d) German government-sponsored research designed to overtake Britain as industrial leader.

3. The increased availability of electric power caused all of the following results EXCEPT which one?
   - (a) Individual homes as well as industrial work places were electrified.
   - (b) Transportation within and between cities became easier with the electrification of subways, tramways, and eventually long-distance railways.
   - (c) Factory organization became more flexible.
   - *(d) Small workshops were replaced by large industrial concerns.

4. By the turn of the century, the leaders in the chemical industry were the
   - (a) British.
   - (b) French.
   - *(c) Germans.
   - (d) Dutch.

5. Population growth between 1870 and 1914 resulted from
   - (a) middle-class prosperity and the resulting desire to have large families.
   - (b) the need of the working class to have many children to ensure themselves of security in their old age.
   - *(c) a sharp decline in infant mortality.
   - (d) a rising birth rate in western Europe.

6. In the period between 1870 and 1914
   - (a) the European death rate began to move steadily upward.
   - (b) poverty was largely eliminated from urban areas in western Europe.
   - (c) cholera outbreaks reached epidemic proportions.
   - *(d) more people enjoyed a higher standard of living than ever before.

7. The consumer boom
   - (a) was an entirely middle-class phenomenon as workers continued to struggle for subsistence.
   - (b) was confined to the new urban areas.
   - (c) occurred only in Britain and Germany.
   - *(d) resulted in a great increase in the production of manufactured goods.

8. Changes in the scale and organization of industry meant that
    * (a) both management and production techniques had to adapt to meet the
        new demand for efficiency.
    (b) workers found themselves with increased bargaining power and
        therefore higher wages and a higher standard of living.
    (c) small workshops were eliminated from industrial production in the
        clothing trade.
    (d) the prices of consumer goods increased as production processes
        became more and more expensive.

9. For workers, the consequences of the increased scale of manufacturing
    included all of the following EXCEPT
    (a) a tendency to lose pay and/or prestige as a result of adapting older
        skills to new machines.
    * (b) growing pride in their ability to run the new and complex machinery.
    (c) acceptance of a wage scale based on piece rates.
    (d) loss of the right to "a fair day's wage for a fair day's work."

10. The increased scope of production and the need for efficiency produced the
    following changes in the institution of capitalism EXCEPT
    (a) the growth of incorporation.
    (b) vertical integration.
    (c) the formation of cartels.
    * (d) the victory of laissez-faire ideology.

11. The emergence of finance capital
    (a) occurred only in those nations that abandoned free trade.
    (b) signaled an increase in intra-industrial competition.
    (c) meant a decline in rates of production and a shift from industrial to
        service-oriented economies.
    * (d) depended on the emergence of a stockholding class and legislation
        favorable to incorporation.

12. Which nation clung to free trade until well into the twentieth century?
    (a) Germany
    (b) The United States
    * (c) Britain
    (d) France

13. Although most European countries imported more goods than they exported,
    they avoided huge deficits by relying on
    (a) the gold standard.
    (b) vertical integration.
    (c) scientific management.
    * (d) "invisible" exports.

14. Lenin argued that imperialism resulted from
    *(a) the internal contradictions of capitalism.
    (b) a series of pragmatic responses to particular situations.
    (c) the economic interests of a small group of influential financiers.
    (d) governments' desire to divert their populace's attention from domestic hardships.

15. According to your textbook, late-nineteenth-century imperialism resulted from a combination of economic factors and
    *(a) concerns over national security and the balance of power.
    (b) the threat of an expanding communist Russia.
    (c) the desire to prevent American control of Africa.
    (d) the militarist culture of the middle class.

16. The imperialist idea encompassed all of the following EXCEPT the
    (a) belief that Europeans had a duty to "civilize" Asia and Africa.
    *(b) hope that contact with other societies would create a multi-racial culture in Europe.
    (c) moral appeal of combatting the slave trade.
    (d) link between national greatness and imperial possessions.

17. After 1875, European imperial competition centered in
    (a) Japan.
    *(b) Africa.
    (c) China.
    (d) India.

18. The Boer War resulted in
    (a) the shift from informal to formal British rule in India.
    (b) a continuing British presence in Egypt.
    *(c) a British victory in South Africa and a loss of international prestige.
    (d) Britain's loss of control over the Congo to the Germans.

19. Russian rulers
    (a) refused to participate in imperial expansion.
    (b) concentrated on expanding Russian colonies in southern Africa.
    (c) used their vast military might to establish economic hegemony over Japan.
    *(d) pursued colonization policies that threatened British interests in both the Middle East and India.

20. The United States
    (a) joined in the scramble for Africa.
  *(b) concentrated on South America, the Pacific, and the Caribbean as its arena for empire.
    (c) opted out of the imperial game and acted instead as a protector of underdeveloped nations in the Western Hemisphere.
    (d) possessed an internal market of such great potential that it did not need or want an empire.

IDENTIFICATIONS

Henry Bessemer	the cartel
Alessandro Volta	invisible exports
Isaac Singer	J. A. Hobson
limited liability	Leopold II
finance capitalism	Cecil Rhodes
vertical organization	the "Indian Mutiny"

TRUE OR FALSE

T   1. Germany seized the lead in the development and utilization of new techniques in the chemical industry.

F   2. Between 1900 and 1914, the automobile and airplane transformed the economic and industrial structure of the Western world.

F   3. The years after 1870 saw the elimination of the periods of unemployment that had made a worker's life so uncertain.

T   4. The new consumer boom demonstrated the increasing role of women in determining consumption patterns.

F   5. After 1870, European and American businesses embarked on a period of consolidation, reduction, and retraction.

T   6. Vertical organization ensured that a company would possess both a ready stock of raw materials and a guaranteed market for its products.

T   7. J. A. Hobson argued that the scramble for Africa was a result of the economic interests of a small group of European financiers.

T   8. European governments found the idea of imperialism useful in diverting the public's attention from domestic troubles.

F   9. In the 1870s, a private trading company headed by Bismarck opened up the Congo region for colonial exploitation.

F   10. The Boer War provides one of the examples of successful black African resistance against white European expansion.

DISCUSSION AND/OR ESSAY QUESTIONS

1. Defend or refute this statement: "The economic and social changes after 1870 are so striking and so qualitatively different from the developments of the first Industrial Revolution that they deserve to be labeled 'The Second Industrial Revolution.' "
2. Compare and contrast the life of a worker in 1830 and in 1890. How had his or her working and living conditions changed? Did the worker's lot improve in these sixty years?
3. Describe the emergence of finance capitalism. In what ways did its structures differ from those of early-nineteenth-century capitalism?
4. How did economic developments and political concerns combine to produce the imperialism of the late nineteenth century?
5. Describe the course of British expansion into Africa during the nineteenth century. What motivated this expansion?

SUGGESTED FEATURE FILMS

Burn. 112 min. Color. 1970. United Artists. A look at economic imperialism on a fictive nineteenth-century Caribbean island. With Marlon Brando.

Khartoum. 134 min. Color. 1966. United Artists. Charlton Heston and Lawrence Olivier starred in this account of General Gordon's unsuccessful Sudanese campaign in the 1880s.

The River. 99 min. B/W. 1950. Jean Renoir. A look at British colonialism in India.

Zulu. 135 min. Color. 1964. Paramount. This depiction of the Zulu Wars and the clash of primitive peoples and European technology features Michael Caine.

SUGGESTED CLASSROOM FILMS

Civilisation: A Personal View by Kenneth Clark. No. 13—Heroic Materialism. 52 min. Color. 1970. BBC/Time-Life. Examines the industrial revolution and the triumph of the scientific worldview.

The Colonial Idea. 56 min. Color. 1977. BBC/Films Inc. A study of imperialism from the Crusades through the twentieth century

Europe, the Mighty Continent: Day of Empire Has Arrived. 52 min. Color. 1976. Time-Life Films. Colonial and artistic unrest at the turn of the century.

Europe, the Mighty Continent: Hey-Day Fever. 52 min. Color. 1976. Time-Life Films. The glory of Europe in 1900.

Maharajas: Imperialism by Conspiracy. 25 min. Color. 1974. Centron Educational Films. History of the interrelationship between the Indian princes and the British Raj.

The Scramble for Africa. 37 min. Color. 1986. Insight Media. Examines the link between European nationalism and the colonization of Africa.

The Triumph of the West. 13 parts. 50 min. each. Color. 1987. Insight Media. BBC series featuring British historian John Roberts in a discussion of the interactions between Western and non-Western cultures.

The West and the Wider World. 26 min. Color. 1985. Insight Media. A broad survey, extending from Magellan to the scramble for Africa.

CHAPTER 25.   THE MIDDLE CLASS CHALLENGED

Outline

I. The challenge of socialism
   A. The ideas and influence of Marx: *The Communist Manifesto*, *Capital*, and communism
   B. The First International
      1. Obstacles to formation
      2. Marx versus Lassalle and Bakunin
      3. The demise of the International
   C. The Paris Commune
   D. The spread of socialism and its internal disunity
      1. The uniqueness of Russian socialism
      2. Revisionists versus purists
      2. Anarchism and syndicalism
II. The challenge of science and philosophy
   A. The disruption: evolutionary theory
      1. Lamarck and acquired characteristics
      2. Darwin and natural selection
      3. Refinements of the Darwinian hypothesis
   B. Philosophical and psychological challenges
      1. Huxley and agnosticism
      2. Spencer and Social Darwinism
      3. Pavlov and behaviorism
      4. Freud and psychoanalytic theory
      5. Nietzsche's philosophy
   C. The response of the Church
      1. Differing Protestant responses
      2. Roman Catholicism: Pius IX and Leo XIII
   D. The impact of scientific and philosophical challenges
III. The challenge of literature and the arts
   A. Increased literacy and a new reading public
   B. The gap between artists and the public
   C. Realism and the critique of middle-class society
      1. In France: Balzac and Zola
      2. In Britain: Dickens and Hardy
      3. In Germany and Scandinavia: Hauptmann and Ibsen
      4. In Russia: Turgenev, Dostoevsky, Tolstoy
   D. Art: the turn away from the public
      1. Impressionism: Monet and Renoir
      2. Expressionism: Cézanne
      3. Post-Impressionism: Gauguin and van Gogh
      4. Picasso

182

E. New directions in literature, music, and drama
1. Symbolist poetry
2. Strauss and Debussy
3. Avant-garde theater

MULTIPLE CHOICE
Choose the best response.

1. Marx's theory of history was influenced by the philosophy of
  *(a) Hegel.
   (b) Nietzsche.
   (c) Zola.
   (d) Lyell.

2. Marx taught that
   (a) peasant nations could bypass capitalism and move directly to socialism.
   (b) the proletarian revolution would succeed only if it adopted non-violent means of change.
   (c) socialists should work with middle-class political parties to win improved working conditions.
  *(d) under communism both private property and the class system would be eliminated.

3. Revisionist socialism did NOT
   (a) originate in Bernstein's *Evolutionary Socialism*.
   (b) view social reform and participation in parliamentary politics as the means of achieving socialism.
  *(c) serve as the basic rallying point for the Second International.
   (d) have a far greater number of followers than did purist socialism in France, Britain, and Germany.

4. The anarchists
  *(a) worked for the immediate abolition of state bureaucracy.
   (b) denied that the long-term goal of socialism would be postponed by working with middle-class politicians for short-term reforms.
   (c) viewed the general strike as the main tool for building socialism.
   (d) won control of the Labour party in Britain and the German Social Democratic party.

5. Syndicalism's most effective spokesman was
   (a) Ivan Turgenev.
   (b) Herbert Spencer.
   (c) Ernest Renan.
   *(d) Georges Sorel.

6. In the years before the First World War, socialism did NOT
   (a) battle the more radical proposals of the anarchists and syndicalists.
   (b) suffer from internal divisions between the revisionists and the purists.
   (c) gain ground in the industrially developed areas of Europe such as Britain, France, and Germany.
   *(d) cease to be seen as a threat by the European middle class.

7. Darwin contended that
   (a) evolution results from radical mutations favorable to survival in a given environment.
   *(b) variation and natural selection serve as the primary factors in the origins of new species.
   (c) the universe is composed of matter alone; even memory, imagination, and thought are functions of matter.
   (d) like nature, societies compete for survival, with the fittest always the victor.

8. Darwinism *most seriously* threatened the Christian worldview because it
   (a) denied the doctrine of papal infallibility.
   (b) declared that science had proven that God did not exist.
   (c) contradicted a literal reading of the account of God's creation of the world given in the first chapters of Genesis.
   *(d) depicted the natural world as a ceaseless and directionless struggle in which the ability to survive, not moral truth, defined good and bad.

9. The Social Darwinists
   (a) argued that competition for survival would eventually produce a race of supermen.
   (b) argued that because Darwin had undermined Christianity, men and women should focus their efforts on social reform here and now.
   *(c) believed that Western civilization had proved itself the fittest society to rule the world.
   (d) developed the concept of cultural relativism.

10. The work of Pavlov inaugurated the school of psychology called
    * (a) behaviorism.
    (b) psychoanalysis.
    (c) empiricism.
    (d) modernism.

11. Freud regarded human beings as
    * (a) egoistic creatures motivated by urges of power, self-preservation, and sex.
    (b) purely physiological organisms.
    (c) a collection of moral weaklings dominated by the few supermen.
    (d) the special creation of a loving God.

12. Nietzsche argued all of the following EXCEPT that
    (a) natural selection should operate unhindered among human beings.
    (b) Christianity and Judaism exalt vices as virtues.
    (c) elimination of the unfit would result in a race of supermen.
    * (d) the future of the human race is biologically determined.

13. The Vatican Council of 1869 declared the dogma of
    * (a) papal infallibility.
    (b) the immaculate conception of Mary.
    (c) Biblical inerrancy.
    (d) the Social Gospel.

14. The realists
    (a) believed that art should depict life as it is, without regard for morality or social reform.
    (b) depicted a reality of the inner soul that ordinary people could not understand.
    * (c) criticized industrial society by depicting the injustices inflicted on humanity.
    (d) argued that art should outline the program of change needed to create a new and more just reality.

15. Zola and Dickens did NOT
    (a) criticize crucial assumptions of the middle-class worldview.
    (b) write in a language accessible to middle-class readers.
    (c) demonstrate deep sympathy for the oppressed.
    * (d) abandon hope for the improvement of humanity.

16. A lecture on realist literature would NOT include
    * (a) Paul Valéry.
    (b) Thomas Hardy.
    (c) Gerhard Hauptmann.
    (d) Ivan Turgenev.

17. The impressionists
    (a) taught that making a good impression was more important than acting according to a moral code.
    (b) endeavored to impress the public with the need for social reform.
  *(c) regarded light as the key factor in determining the appearance of an object.
    (d) argued that most people acted on the basis of faulty impressions and so should be denied the vote.

18. The artist who laid the foundations of expressionism was
    (a) Arthur Schopenhauer.
    (b) Auguste Rodin.
    (c) Hugo DeVries.
  *(d) Paul Cézanne.

19. Each of the following statements is true of Picasso's cubism EXCEPT which one?
    (a) It was frequently incomprehensible to the ordinary middle-class viewer.
  *(b) Its subject matter, the South Sea islands, revealed the artist's rejection of modern Western society for more primitive culture.
    (c) It symbolized the chaos of modern life.
    (d) It repudiated traditional notions of form and the traditional view of art as a pretty picture of the world.

20. By the turn of the century, artists and writers tended to believe that art should be created
    (a) as a political tool.
    (b) to inspire the newly educated masses.
  *(c) for art's sake.
    (d) to unite society with its forgotten past.

IDENTIFICATIONS

Capital	Friedrich Nietzsche
dictatorship of the proletariat	Ivan Pavlov
the Paris Commune	Sigmund Freud
Rosa Luxemburg	social gospel
Georges Sorel	*Syllabus of Errors*
Jean Lamarck	Leo Tolstoy
Origin of Species	Claude Monet
Hugo DeVries	Paul Cézanne
T. H. Huxley	the symbolists
Herbert Spencer	Claude Debussy

TRUE OR FALSE

F   1.   The largely lower-middle-class Paris Communards advocated the abolition of private property.

F   2.   The revisionists advocated the destruction of the state through terrorism.

T   3.   Like socialism, syndicalism demands that workers share in the ownership of the means of production.

T   4.   Charles Darwin's theory of organic evolution was influenced by developments in the field of geology.

T   5.   Thomas Huxley argued that the existence and nature of God is unknowable.

T   6.   Behaviorism reduces all human behavior to a series of physical responses.

F   7.   The institution of state-financed education and the resulting mass literacy meant that late-nineteenth-century authors now could trust that their works would be read by and influence almost all of society.

T   8.   An important characteristic of the art world in the years before World War I was a withdrawal from the conventions and concerns of the world at large.

F   9.   The expressionists argued that art existed to express a moral message.

T   10.   At the end of the nineteenth century and beginning of the twentieth, composers moved away from formal structure toward personal expression.

DISCUSSION AND/OR ESSAY QUESTIONS

1. Compare and contrast the basis tenets of Marxist socialism, revisionism, syndicalism, and anarchism. Which seemed the most appealing and likely to succeed in late-nineteenth-century Britain? France? Russia?

2. Discuss this statement: "Developments in the biological and psychological sciences challenged the middle-class faith in progress by depicting the human being as an animal with little control over a hostile and arbitrary world."

3. Describe the basic tenets of Social Darwinists. Who would be most likely to embrace this ideology and why?

4. "In European literature of the late nineteenth and early twentieth centuries, we see a world at war with itself." Do you agree? Why or why not?

5. Imagine you have been asked to give a lecture entitled "The Fragmentation of Western Culture in the Years before World War I," with the paintings on pages 898–907 as your illustrations. What will be the main points of your lecture?

SUGGESTED FEATURE FILMS

Angels and Insects. Approx. 2 hrs. Color. 1996. Samuel Goldwyn Home Entertainment. A perceptive and often hilarious look at the impact of evolutionary ideas on British culture.

A Doll's House. 109 min. Color. 1974. Learning Corporation of America. Jane Fonda stars in David Mercer's screenplay, which was filmed in Norway.

Far from the Madding Crowd. 175 min. Color. 1967. EMI. Film version of Hardy's novel.

Freud. 120 min. B/W. 1962. Universal. The John Huston film of Freud's life.

Lust for Life. 122 min. Color. 1956. MGM. Directed by Vincente Minnelli and starring Kirk Douglas. Looks at both Van Gogh's work and the changing art world in which he lived.

Madame Curie. 124 min. B/W. 1943. MGM. Based on the book by Eve Curie.

Modern Times. 87 min. B/W. 1936. United Artists. Chaplin's classic film about industrialization.

Tess. 172 min. Color. 1979. Columbia. Roman Polanski's version of Hardy's *Tess of the D'Urbervilles.*

SUGGESTED CLASSROOM FILMS

The Christians: The Roots of Disbelief (1848–1962). 42 min. Color. 1978. McGraw-Hill. The effect of nationalism, Victorianism, and Darwinism on Christianity.

Charles Darwin. 23 min. Color. 1973. Extension Media Center. Uses excerpts from *The Journal of the Voyage of the Beagle* to describe Darwin's achievement.

Darwin's Revolution. 52 min. Color. 1986. Insight Media. James Burke hosts this examination of Darwin's ideas and the social ideologies built upon them.

Karl Marx and Marxism. 52 min. Color. 1983. Films for the Humanities. Covers the biography of Marx, the development of his ideas, and the efforts to embody his ideas in the political world.

Paris, 1900. 72 min. B/W. 1950. Macmillan Films. Documentary uses newsreels and silent films.

The Paris Commune. 30 min. Color. 1990. Films for the Humanities. Looks at both the context and consequences of the Commune.

A Third Testament: Tolstoy. 53 min. Color. 1974. BBC/Time-Life Films. Malcolm Muggeridge on location in Russia.

CHAPTER 26. A DELICATE EQUILIBRIUM (1870–1914)

Outline

I. Germany: the search for imperial unity
  A. The imperial structure
    1. The states
    2. The parliament
  B. The *Kulturkampf*
  C. Attacks against the socialists
    1. Dissolution of the Social Democratic party
    2. Social welfare legislation
  D. Bismarck's loss of power and William II's politics
  E. Socialist gains and political stalemate
II. France: the embattled Third Republic
  A. The formation of the Third Republic
  B. Reactionary radicals and the republic's response
    1. The Dreyfus affair
    2. Anticlericalism and the curbing of the Church
  C. Threats from the Left and the republic's response
III. Great Britain: from moderation to militance
  A. Political stability
    1. Gladstone and Disraeli
    2. Ministerial responsibility and a moderate ruling class
  B. Challenges to stability
    1. Labor unrest and Liberal reforms
    2. Lloyd George's budget and the House of Lords
    3. Militant revolts: the trade unions, Ireland, the suffragettes
IV. Russia: the road to revolution
  A. Reform and reaction in nineteenth-century Russia
    1. Liberation of the serfs
    2. The structure of local government
    3. Repression and reaction
  B. Alexander III: Russification and autocracy
  C. Westernization and a working class
    1. Industrialization and working-class consciousness
    2. Emergence of new political parties: Lenin and the Bolsheviks
  D. The Revolution of 1905
    1. The Russo-Japanese War
    2. Bloody Sunday and urban strikes
    3. Success and setback
    4. Gains from the revolutionary movement

V. The search for equilibrium elsewhere in the West
   A. Italy
      1. The gap between north and south
      2. Giolitti's *trasformismo*
      3. Socialist split
   B. Austria-Hungary: the Dual Monarchy and nationalist divisions
   C. The Ottoman Empire
      1. Nationalism and disintegration
      2. The Congress of Berlin
      3. The Young Turk revolution
   D. The United States: economic crisis and progressivism
VI. International rivalries: the road to the First World War
   A. The century of peace
   B. Steps to World War I
      1. The balance of power: Bismarck and the isolation of France
      2. The diplomatic revolution: the Triple Alliance versus the Triple Entente
   C. Other causes of World War I
      1. The question of German war guilt
      2. The impact of nationalism
      3. Militarism and domestic unrest
   D. Crises between 1905 and 1913: Morocco, Serbia, the Balkan Wars

MULTIPLE CHOICE
Choose the best response.

1. A lower house elected by universal male suffrage with no power to initiate legislation was characteristic of which parliamentary system?
   (a) the British
   (b) the French
   *(c) the German
   (d) the Italian

2. Prussia dominated the German Empire for all the following reasons EXCEPT that
   (a) the emperor was also the king of Prussia.
   (b) Prussia possessed a strong military tradition.
   (c) Prussia retained economic dominance.
   *(d) Prussians staffed the emperor's cabinet.

3. What was the *Kulturkampf*?
   (a) Bismarck's effort to repress the German socialists
   (b) William II's dismissal of Bismarck
   (c) the creation of the German elementary education system
   *(d) Bismarck's campaign against the Catholic Church

4. The European nation that led the way in establishing social welfare legislation was
   (a) Britain.
   (b) France.
   *(c) Germany.
   (d) the United States.

5. A premier or prime minister answerable to, and with no authority to dissolve, the legislature characterized the political system of
   (a) Britain.
   *(b) France.
   (c) Germany.
   (d) Italy.

6. In the years after 1875, the Third Republic faced its most dangerous threat in the form of
   (a) a revolutionary form of agrarian socialism.
   *(b) monarchists, authoritarian Roman Catholics, and other reactionaries.
   (c) militant suffragettes.
   (d) colonial independence movements.

7. The Dreyfus affair
   (a) signaled the start of anti-Semitic persecutions in Europe.
   (b) demonstrated the stability of the British parliamentary system and the moderation of its two ruling parties.
   (c) sparked the Revolution of 1905.
   *(d) was symptomatic of the divisions that threatened the survival of the Third Republic.

8. Which of the following statements is INCORRECT concerning France in the years between 1870 and 1914?
   *(a) Socialism was effectively crushed by a series of anti-socialist laws.
   (b) The revisionist versus purist debate divided and weakened French socialists.
   (c) The Catholic hierarchy aided the monarchists in their struggle against the Third Republic.
   (d) Anti-Semitism became an issue in the battle between republicans and monarchists.

9. British stability after 1875 rested on
   * (a) the moderation and social homogeneity of the leadership of the opposing political parties.
   (b) an authoritarian but efficient political system.
   (c) national unity based on a common religious and ethnic identity.
   (d) universal manhood suffrage and representative democracy.

10. Much of the social reform legislation passed in Britain was the work of
    * (a) David Lloyd George.
    (b) Alfred Dreyfus.
    (c) Eugene Debs.
    (d) Robert Peel.

11. In the years before 1914, political and social instability grew in England as a result of all of the following EXCEPT
    (a) increasing trade-union militancy.
    * (b) the 1912 election in which socialists won the largest bloc of votes in the House of Commons.
    (c) the constitutional crisis arising from the controversy over the 1909 budget.
    (d) the spread of militant female suffragism.

12. The Russian radicals who viewed the village commune as the model for a future socialist society were called
    (a) Futurists.
    (b) Social Democrats.
    (c) Communards.
    * (d) Populists.

13. Tsar Alexander III believed that
    (a) parliamentary democracy must be implemented gradually in Russia to avoid revolution.
    * (b) the Russian people would be lost without despotic rule.
    (c) only a policy of rapid industrialization and Westernization would guarantee Russia's security.
    (d) the Catholic Church constituted the chief threat to Russian stability.

14. Lenin argued that
    (a) socialists should participate in nonsocialist governments.
    (b) Marxism required that Russia pass through a capitalist stage before achieving socialism.
    * (c) immediate revolution must be achieved by a highly disciplined party.
    (d) Russian socialism depended on transforming the situation of the peasants.

15. The reasons for the Russian revolutionaries' setback after 1905 do NOT include
    (a) the loyalty of the army to the tsar.
    (b) the split between members of the middle class.
    (c) disaffection among the workers.
    *(d) the opposition of western European governments.

16. As a result of Giolitti's policies
    (a) socialism disappeared as a viable force in Italian politics.
    (b) the advance of industrialization in Italy was halted.
    *(c) the division between northern and southern Italy widened.
    (d) Catholicism was outlawed in Italy.

17. The history of the Ottoman Empire after 1875 demonstrated each of the following EXCEPT that
    (a) nationalism was a force for division as well as for unity.
    (b) instability in eastern Europe threatened the stability of Europe as a whole.
    (c) universal male suffrage did not guarantee the establishment of liberal democracy.
    *(d) unionization of unskilled workers threatened the power of the ruling class.

18. Bismarck aimed his diplomatic maneuvering at
    (a) isolating Russia in order to defeat Pan-Slavism.
    *(b) isolating France to prevent it from initiating a war of revenge against Germany.
    (c) weakening Britain to enable Germany to seize the political and economic leadership of Europe.
    (d) forming an alliance of conservative regimes to ensure the defeat of socialism.

19. The Triple Alliance did NOT include
    (a) Germany.
    (b) Italy.
    (c) Austria-Hungary.
    *(d) France.

20. Explanations of why world war broke out in 1914 would NOT include
    (a) the breakdown of Bismarck's diplomatic system.
    (b) arms buildup and the formation of opposing alliance systems.
    *(c) Bismarck's willingness to risk war for the sake of Prussian gain.
    (d) the internal instability of Europe's nations.

193

IDENTIFICATIONS

Kulturkampf
William II
Georges Boulanger
William Gladstone
Herbert Asquith
Emmeline Pankhurst
Populist Party
Nicholas II

Sergei Witte
Duma
Bolsheviks
Bloody Sunday
trasformismo
Congress of Berlin
Young Turks
Triple Alliance

TRUE OR FALSE

T 1. One factor in Bismarck's decision to attack the socialists was his need to retain the favor of German industrialists.

F 2. The slow pace of social reform in France led French socialists to conclude that they had to participate in the parliamentary system in order to make progress.

F 3. The militancy and radicalism of the British suffragette movement so threatened authorities that they granted the franchise to women in 1914.

T 4. The liberation of the serfs did not effect drastic changes in the pattern of rural life in Russia.

T 5. The tsar succeeded in negating most of the gains of the Revolution of 1905 because he retained the loyalty of the army.

T 6. A growing number of opponents to the tsarist regime embraced violent revolution and terrorism as the method of achieving change.

F 7. The establishment of the Dual Monarchy relieved nationalist tensions in Austria-Hungary.

F 8. The Progressive movement argued that a restricted money supply and the lack of an income tax had led the United States to economic crisis.

T 9. The shift in the balance of power between 1890 and 1907 convinced the Germans that they were surrounded by hostile powers and that they therefore had to maintain their alliance with Austria-Hungary.

T 10. Fritz Fischer argued that the chief cause of World War I was Germany's aggressive policies of expansion.

DISCUSSION AND/OR ESSAY QUESTIONS

1. Describe Bismarck's goals and the path he followed to reach them. Did he succeed?

2. The Holocaust, the attempted extermination of European Jews during World War II, forms one of the darkest stains on the record of human history. It can be argued that Hitler's anti-Jewish policies were rooted in the events and attitudes of late-nineteenth- and early-twentieth-century Europe. Examine the interaction between nationalism and anti-Semitism in Europe between 1875 and 1914.

3. Consider the political and social history of Germany, France, and Great Britain between 1870 and 1914.What were the factors that made these nations receptive to war in 1914?

4. Why did Russia fail to develop into a stable parliamentary democracy? Why did more and more opponents of the tsarist regime view violent revolution rather than gradual reform as an effective means of change?

5. Imagine that you have been asked to deliver a lecture on "The Road to World War I." Outline your talk.

SUGGESTED FEATURE FILMS

Battleship Potemkin. 75 min. (Sound version: 60 min.) B/W. 1925. Goskino. Eisenstein's study of the 1903 Odessa Mutiny. Judged the best film ever made in 1948 and in 1958.

The Childhood of Maxim Gorky. 101 min. B/W. 1938. Soyuz det film. *Out in the World.* 98 min. 1939. *My Universities.* 104 min. 1940. Film biography of the Russian writer.

SUGGESTED CLASSROOM FILMS

Battleship Potemkin: Odessa Steps Sequence. 10 min. Color. Fleetwood Films. The most famous sequence of this famous film.

Churchill and British History, 1874–1918. 29 min. B/W. 1974. Centron Educational Films. Still and newsreel film are used to outline the world that shaped Churchill.

The Decline of Czarism. 30 min. Color. 1986. Insight Media. Covers the decline of the Romanov dynasty.

The Dreyfus Affair. 15 min. B/W. 1970. Texture. Uses contemporary graphics to tell the story.

Europe, the Mighty Continent: The Drums Begin to Roll. 52 min. Color. 1976. Time-Life Films. Examines the preparations for war between 1904 and 1914.

Europe, the Mighty Continent: A World to Win. 52 min. Color. 1976. Time-Life Films. Intellectual, political, and social ferment in prewar Europe.

The Life of Emile Zola. 32 min. B/W. 1937. Warner. Excerpts from the feature film.

Nicholas and Alexandra: Prelude to Revolution, 1904–1905. 30 min. Color. 1971. Learning Corporation of America. Excerpts from the feature film *Nicholas and Alexandra.*

The Social Classes—1900: A World to Win. 52 min. Color. 1990. Insight Media. Examines the intellectual and political turmoil that marked Europe at the turn of the century.

Stalin and Russian History, 1879–1927. 29 min. B/W. 1974. Centron Films. Biography of Stalin from his seminary days through Lenin's death. Includes actual films of the industrialization of Russia.

CHAPTER 27.   THE FIRST WORLD WAR

Outline

I. Prelude to war
   A. Serbia versus Austria
      1. The assassination of Francis Ferdinand
      2. The Austrian ultimatum
      3. The attitudes of Russia, France, and Germany
   B. Mobilization and war
   C. The entry of Britain
   D. The question of guilt
II. The ordeal of battle
   A. The patriotic war: propaganda efforts
   B. War of attrition
      1. Life and death in the trenches
      2. The high costs
      3. Total victory
   C. Expansion of the conflict: the entry of the United States
III. Revolution in the midst of war
   A. Limits of leadership in Russia
   B. The March 1917 Revolution
      1. The overthrow of the tsar
      2. The Kerensky government
   C. The Bolshevik Revolution: peace, bread, land
   D. The Easter Rebellion in Ireland
IV. Armistice and peace
   A. The Fourteen Points
   B. Domestic conflict in Germany
   C. The collapse of the Central Powers
      1. The disintegration of the Habsburg Empire
      2. Revolution in Germany
      3. The signing of the armistice
   D. A harsh peace
      1. The Paris Conference
      2. The Big Three
      3. The Treaty of Versailles
   E. Treaties with Germany's allies: the problem of national self-determination
   F. Results of the war
      1. The League of Nations
      2. A war of waste: the armed camp remains
      3. Other changes

MULTIPLE CHOICE
Choose the best response.

1. The conflict between Serbia and Austria-Hungary erupted into a Europe-wide war for all the following reasons EXCEPT which one?
   (a) The time needed to gear up Russia's military machine required that Russia mobilize against Germany as well as Austria.
   (b) France was committed to its alliance with Russia.
   (c) The quickest route for the German army to France lay through neutral Belgium.
   *(d) Britain had publicly committed itself to support France.

2. The historian seeking to explain Britain's entry into the war would include all of the following EXCEPT
   *(a) the unanimous approval of the three political parties for a policy of war.
   (b) the British military's commitment to send an expeditionary force to support France in case of war.
   (c) conversations and informal diplomatic agreements between Britain and France, and Britain and Russia.
   (d) Britain's commitment to guarantee Belgium's neutrality.

3. Which of the following is in correct chronological order?
   *(a) Austrian declaration of war on Serbia; Russian mobilization; German declaration of war on France
   (b) German declaration of war on France; Russian mobilization; British declaration of war on Germany
   (c) Austrian declaration of war on Russia; British declaration of war on Germany; German declaration of war on France
   (d) Russian mobilization; Austrian declaration of war on Belgium; French declaration of war on Austria

4. The historiographical controversy over the origins of the First World War sparked by Fritz Fischer centers on the question of
   (a) the necessity of Russia's declaration of full-scale mobilization.
   *(b) Germany's eagerness to go to war against Russia and France before they became sufficiently powerful to resist a German onslaught.
   (c) Serbia's refusal to comply with Austria's ultimatum in its entirety.
   (d) Britain's insistence on defending Belgium's neutrality.

5. Governments felt compelled to depict the war as a conflict between good and evil rather than a battle among national powers because
   (a) the Church played a leading role in most European states.
   (b) public allegiance to the war effort was so low that governments needed to arouse support.
   *(c) the war required the engagement of the civilian as well as the military populations.
   (d) they realized the war would last a long time and would exact a high price from their peoples.

6. The Schlieffen Plan
   (a) utilized Austria's ultimatum to Serbia as a pretext for war.
   (b) allowed Lenin to return to Russia to seize control of the revolution.
   *(c) required that Austria hold off Russia while Germany quickly defeated France.
   (d) called for drawing France into the war to undermine her industrial and imperial supremacy.

7. On the Western Front
   (a) generals quickly realized the value of the tank in breaking through trench defenses.
   *(b) the war settled into a stalemate.
   (c) the Allies quickly and decisively defeated the Austrians.
   (d) trench warfare meant monotony but very little actual danger for the ordinary soldier.

8. By 1916, the human cost of the war was so high that
   (a) governments called for a negotiated peace.
   (b) mutiny of the French troops spread throughout the Allied armies and forced negotiations for a truce.
   (c) voters in Britain, France, and Germany demanded and received more moderate leadership.
   *(d) new leaders came to power and called for total victory.

9. The United States entered the war because
   (a) the American public demanded a war against communism.
   *(b) the government feared that a German victory would upset the balance of power in Europe.
   (c) of treaty obligations to protect neutral Belgium.
   (d) Germany had declared war on the United States.

10. Factors in the outbreak of the Russian Revolution in 1917 do NOT include
    (a) the weak and irrational leadership provided by the tsar.
    (b) a series of military defeats.
    (c) inflation and shortages of food and fuel.
    *(d) widespread public support for the Bolsheviks.

11. The March 1917 Revolution
    (a) overthrew the tsar and placed power in the hands of the Bolsheviks.
    *(b) gave power to middle-class liberals who aimed to establish a limited monarchy.
    (c) followed a bloody civil war between middle-class moderates and working-class revolutionaries.
    (d) gave to the peasants "Peace, Bread, and Land."

12. After the March Revolution, the increasingly powerful soviets demanded
    (a) a redoubled war effort.
    (b) the institution of a communist dictatorship.
    (c) the establishment of a consitutional monarchy and capitalist economic policies.
    *(d) the redistribution of land and an end to the war.

13. The Bolsheviks overturned the provisional government led by
    (a) Clemenceau.
    (b) Lenin.
    *(c) Kerensky.
    (d) Rasputin.

14. Upon seizing power, Lenin did NOT
    (a) order the distribution of land to the peasants.
    (b) nationalize the banks and confiscate private accounts.
    (c) surrender Poland, Finland, and the Ukraine to Germany.
    *(d) end the civil war with his policies of "Peace, Bread, and Land."

15. Wilson's plan for peace was called the
    (a) League of Nations.
    *(b) Fourteen Points.
    (c) Allied Pact.
    (d) Democratic Promise.

16. The Big Three consisted of
   (a) Francis Ferdinand, William II, and Nicholas II.
   (b) Lenin, Trotsky, and Stalin.
   (c) Grey, Poincaré, and Wilson.
   *(d) Lloyd George, Clemenceau, and Wilson.

17. As a result of the Treaty of Versailles,
   (a) Serbia was held responsible for starting the war.
   *(b) Germany was required to pay reparations to the Allies.
   (c) Austria was united with Germany.
   (d) Russia was allowed to dictate what form of government would be established in the new nations of eastern Europe.

18. The peace treaties provided for all the following EXCEPT the
   (a) loss of three-quarters of Austria's area and three-quarters of its population.
   (b) independence of Hungary, Czechoslovakia, Yugoslavia, and Poland.
   *(c) division of eastern Europe in accordance with the principle of self-determination of peoples.
   (d) establishment of the League of Nations.

19. The League of Nations
   (a) included all Western nations.
   (b) reduced armaments to the lowest level possible consistent with domestic safety.
   *(c) helped in the settlement of racial and political refugees.
   (d) backed the claims of small nations against the Great Powers throughout the 1920s and 1930s.

20. The First World War did NOT
   (a) highlight the efficacy of central planning.
   (b) make Europe a debtor to the United States.
   (c) produce worldwide inflation.
   *(d) redraw the map of Europe along clear-cut ethnic lines.

201

IDENTIFICATIONS

Francis Ferdinand	Gregory Rasputin
trialism	Alexander Kerensky
Bethmann-Hollweg	Leon Trotsky
Sergei Sazonov	Lavr Kornilov
Fritz Fischer	Easter Rebellion
Western Front	Caporetto
Gallipoli	Paris Conference
the Somme	the Big Three
Georges Clemenceau	Treaty of St. Germain
Paul von Hindenburg	Kemal Atatürk

TRUE OR FALSE

F   1.   The Serbian government's refusal to comply with any of the demands of the Austro-Hungarian ultimatum led to mobilization for war.

F   2.   Germany recognized that Britain's treaties with Russia and France made inevitable her entry into the war on the side of the Entente.

F   3.   Italy fought on the side of the Triple Alliance.

T   4.   According to Entente propaganda, the war was a crusade to cleanse humanity of the stain of militarism.

T   5.   Woodrow Wilson perceived the war as a struggle to make the world safe for democracy.

F   6.   Military commanders recognized the important strategic potential of such industrial contributions to the war as the airplane and the tank.

T   7.   Shortages of food, clothing, and weapons, as well as transport breakdowns, explain much of Russia's military failure.

T   8.   The provisional government established after the March 1917 Revolution refused to abandon Russia's commitment to the war.

T   9.   Conflict within Germany over war aims brought the nation to the brink of civil war in the fall of 1918.

F   10.   The Treaty of Versailles ceded all Slavic territories to the new Soviet Union.

DISCUSSION AND/OR ESSAY QUESTIONS

1. What sequence of events led from an assassination in Bosnia to the British declaration of war on Germany?
2. "When the dust had settled and the carnage had been cleared away, all of Europe stood as the losers of the First World War. Only the United States emerged victorious." Do you agree? Why or why not?
3. Describe the course of the Russian Revolution. At what point, if any, could the Bolsheviks have been defeated?
4. "The war that took place between 1914 and 1918 . . . sowed the seeds of new and even more deadly conflicts in the future" (p. 947). Compare and contrast the map of Europe before and after World War I. Where do you perceive the seedbeds of future conflict?
5. Discuss this statement: "The First World War disillusioned the European middle classes and exposed the nineteenth-century faith in progress as a groundless illusion and a peril to peace."

SUGGESTED FEATURE FILMS

All Quiet on the Western Front. 130 min. B/W. 1930. Universal. Effective film version of Erich Maria Remarque's antiwar novel.

Arsenal. 99 min. B/W. 1929. VUFKU. A look at the workers of the Ukraine during the Great War. Silent.

Dr. Zhivago. 192 min. Color. 1965. MGM. Omar Sharif stars in this colorful version of Boris Pasternak's look at the Russian Revolution.

The End of St. Petersburg. 120 min. B/W. 1927. Mezhrabpom-Russ. Chronicles the years from 1905 to 1918 through the eyes of a peasant.

Gallipoli. 110 min. Color. 1980. Paramount. Peter Weir's film about the Australian experience very effectively demonstrates the failure of traditional notions of heroism and courage to comprehend the reality of the Great War. Starring Mel Gibson.

La Grande Illusion. 117 min. B/W. 1937. Cinedis-RAC. A 1917 POW camp provides the setting for Jean Renoir's examination of the decay of the aristocracy.

The Informer. 91 min. B/W. 1935. RKO. Liam O'Flaherty's story of Dublin during the Time of Troubles.

King and Country. 86 min. B/W. 1964. British Home Entertainments. A disturbing portrait of trench warfare, which focuses on the court-martial and execution of a private.

Lenin in October. 111 min. B/W. 1937. Mosfilm. Soviet version of Lenin's activities during the war.

Nicholas and Alexandra. 189 min. Color. 1971. Columbia. Covers the life and death of the tsar and his family.

October. 105 min. B/W. 1928. Sovkino. Based on John Reed's *Ten Days That Shook the World.* Eisenstein's account of the Bolshevik seizure of power.

Oh! What a Lovely War. 144 min. Color. 1969. Paramount. A bitter British examination of the First World War. Film version of Joan Littlewood's stage show.

The Tin Drum. 142 min. Color. Film Polski. Based on Günter Grass's best-seller about a boy who plays his drum to the beat of Germany's tragic history in the twentieth century.

SUGGESTED CLASSROOM FILMS

Bolshevik Victory. 20 min. B/W. 1969. Films, Inc. Granada Television documentary on the October Revolution.

Causes and Immediate Effects of the First World War. 22 min. B/W. 1940. International Geographic Pictures. Newsreels and maps are used in this older interpretation of the war.

The Decline of Czarism. 30 min. Color. 1986. Insight Media. Covers the decline of the Romanov dynasty.

Europe, the Mighty Continent: Are We Making a Good Peace? 52 min. Color. 1976. Time-Life Films. Examines the Treaty of Versailles and its results.

Europe, the Mighty Continent: This Generation Has No Future. 52 min. Color. 1976. Time-Life Films. Looks at the unimagined horrors of trench warfare.

The First Casualty. 55 min. Color. 1974. Heritage Visual Sales. John Terraine narrates the story of British use of propaganda during the First World War.

The Great War. 52 min. B/W. 1965. McGraw-Hill. Shows actual battle scenes.

The Great War—Fifty Years After. 25 min. Color. 1968. NBC. Includes film clips from the war.

Nightmare in Red. 55 min. B/W. nd. Contemporary Films. Shows actual scenes from the Bolshevik Revolution.

The Russian Revolution. 36 min. Color and B/W. 1989. Insight Media. Excerpts from Eisenstein films and documentaries are used to set the revolution within the context of Russian history.

Versailles—the Lost Peace. 26 min. Color. 1978. Films, Inc. The frustration of Wilson's idealistic hopes for postwar Europe.

Wilfred Owen: The Pity of War. 58 min. Color. 1987. Films for the Humanities. Uses Owen's poems, diaries, and letters.

CHAPTER 28. TURMOIL BETWEEN THE WARS

Outline

I. The Soviet experience and the rise of Stalin
  A. Lenin and Trotsky
  B. The civil war and economic crisis
  C. Lenin's communism versus Marxism
  D. Trotsky versus Stalin
    1. Stalin and the party
    2. The issue of world revolution
  E. The party, the state, and foreign policy under Stalin
    1. The Five-Year Plan
    2. Collectivization
    3. The Third International
    4. The 1936 Constitution
    5. The purge trials
  F. Costs and consequences of the Soviet revolution
II. The emergence of fascism in Italy
  A. Italy's long-term problems
  B. The effects of World War I
  C. The evolution of fascism
    1. Mussolini's career
    2. The *Fasci*
    3. The doctrines of Fascism
    4. Mussolini's fascist state
    5. Corporatism
III. The rise of Nazi Germany
  A. The Spartacist rebellion
  B. The Weimar Republic
  C. Causes of the collapse of German democracy
    1. Defeat in World War I
    2. Economics
  D. Weimar's later years and political polarization
  E. Hitler's rise to power
  F. The Nazi revolution
  G. Nazi rule
    1. Economic policies
    2. Social structures
    3. Anti-Semitism
  H. The significance of German Nazism and Italian Fascism

IV. The democracies between the wars
   A. Class conflict in France
   B. Economic difficulties in Britain
   C. Conservatism in the United States
   D. The Great Depression and its results
     1. Economic nationalism
     2. The Popular Front
     3. The New Deal
V. Intellectual and cultural trends in the interwar years
   A. "Antimetaphysics": Logical Positivism and the sociology of religion
   B. Antidemocratic philosophies: Pareto and Spengler
   C. Einstein and the revolution in physics
   D. Literature: from isolation to engagement
   E. Saving capitalism: Keynesian economics
   F. Art, music, architecture: the discovery of new forms
   G. Propaganda and the media

MULTIPLE CHOICE
Choose the best response.

1. Lenin
  (a) quarreled with Stalin over the issue of world revolution.
  (b) repudiated the use of violence as a means of establishing a socialist state.
 *(c) sought neither material gain nor personal glory.
  (d) adopted a policy of cooperation with the Western powers.

2. Bolshevism or communism differed from Marxism because it
 *(a) subscribed to the necessity of the dictatorship of an elite.
  (b) saw the middle class as an ally rather than an enemy of the proletariat.
  (c) argued that revolutionary socialism would follow capitalism.
  (d) sought a worker-controlled state as well as economy.

3. Stalin differed from Trotsky in his insistence on
  (a) the necessity of worldwide communist revolution.
 *(b) placing Soviet interests ahead of those of international communism.
  (c) encouraging the spread of small, privately owned businesses in order to improve Soviet economic life.
  (d) making no alliances with non-communist nations.

4. Collectivization involved all of the followng EXCEPT the
    *(a) spread of small, peasant-owned farms.
    (b) liquidation of the kulak class.
    (c) mechanization of agricultural production.
    (d) extension of centralized control over Soviet agriculture.

5. As a result of World War I, Italy did NOT
    (a) gain territory from Austria.
    (b) make a financial sacrifice it could ill afford.
    (c) suffer from high inflation rates and a labor glut.
    *(d) witness the rejection of socialism by the working class.

6. The principle doctrines of Italian fascism included the
    (a) belief in a dictatorship of the elite.
    (b) belief that the Jews caused Italy's failures.
    *(c) belief that military conflict strengthened both individuals and nations.
    (d) rescue of capitalism through state-directed economic planning.

7. Under Mussolini
    *(a) public works programs, building projects, and state-sponsored social
        security made life easier for the working class.
    (b) the gap between the north and south of Italy finally closed.
    (c) workers were placed in control of industry.
    (d) Roman Catholics faced systematic persecution.

8. The Weimar Republic rested on a fragile foundation because
    (a) the economic and social gap between north and south threatened the
        nation's stability.
    (b) civil war sapped the nation of manpower and economic resources.
    *(c) the German people had had little experience with democratic
        government.
    (d) nationalist sentiment raised discontent among ethnic minorities.

9. Nazism triumphed in Germany for all of the following reasons EXCEPT
    which one?
    *(a) The Entente countries refused to renegotiate reparations payments.
    (b) German cultural, political, and economic prestige before 1914 made its
        defeat seem incomprehensible.
    (c) The demilitarization of Germany angered the politically powerful army
        officer corps.
    (d) Inflation destroyed not only savings but also faith in government.

10. Hitler came to power in Germany
    (a) by marching on Berlin and seizing control in a bloodless revolution.
    *(b) because a group of industrialists, landowners, and bankers backed him for chancellor.
    (c) by manipulating the growing state bureaucracy to increase his own power and influence.
    (d) because his brownshirt "putsch" destroyed the parliamentary government.

11. Nazi Germany was NOT characterized by
    (a) a one-party state.
    (b) use of paramilitary troops to maintain order and discipline.
    (c) generous treatment of the peasant class.
    *(d) high unemployment rates.

12. The historian seeking to explain the Nazi persecution of the Jews would include all of the following EXCEPT
    (a) Hitler's own anti-Semitism.
    *(b) the anti-war activities of Jews during the First World War.
    (c) popular perception of a link between Jewishness and Marxism.
    (d) fear of urbanization and reform.

13. In both Britain and France between the wars
    *(a) class conflict grew more severe.
    (b) authoritarian regimes replaced democratic governments.
    (c) economic resentments resulted in the spread of anti-Semitism and the forced emigration of Jewish citizens.
    (d) the Great Depression had little impact.

14. All of the following contributed to the Great Depression of 1929 EXCEPT
    (a) a worldwide fall in agricultural prices.
    (b) increasing competition from non-European economies.
    (c) the collapse of prices on the New York Stock Exchange.
    *(d) the abandonment of protective tariffs.

15. The New Deal
    (a) was a less drastic change in policy than occurred in Europe.
    *(b) involved programs of currency management and social security.
    (c) aimed to introduce socialism gradually to the United States.
    (d) solved the problem of unemployment.

16. The Logical Positivists
    (a) argued that religion assisted directly in the spread of capitalism.
    (b) proclaimed the existence of the collective unconscious.
    *(c) rejected values or ideals that did not correspond with something in the physical universe.
    (d) viewed philosophy as a means of answering questions about the nature of ultimate reality.

17. Who argued that Protestantism led directly to the spread of capitalism?
    (a) Adolf Hitler
    (b) Walter Gropius
    *(c) Max Weber
    (d) Benito Mussolini

18. Who adopted an antidemocratic stance and maintained that human beings are merely "beasts of prey"?
    (a) George Orwell
    (b) John Steinbeck
    *(c) Oswald Spengler
    (d) John Maynard Keynes

19. As a result of the depression
    (a) artists and writers withdrew to a position of self-imposed isolation, and wrote and painted for an elite group.
    *(b) art and literature were to a degree politicized as artists and writers reached out to a mass audience.
    (c) pessimism, particularly about any sort of involvement in human affairs, dominated Western art and literature.
    (d) writers linked the crisis of capitalism to the decline in religious belief.

20. Hitler
    (a) encouraged artists to experiment with bizarre new art forms.
    (b) patronized the Bauhaus school of architecture to increase German cultural prestige.
    (c) ignored cultural matters as unimportant.
    *(d) used art as part of his larger propaganda campaign.

IDENTIFICATIONS

Leon Trotsky
Five-Year Plan
kulaks
corporatism
Spartacists
Karl Liebknecht
Dawes Plan
Mein Kampf
Third Reich
Blut und Boden

Edouard Herriot
Logical Positivism
Max Weber
existentialism
John Maynard Keynes
expressionism
dada-ists
atonality
Bauhaus
Triumph of the Will

TRUE OR FALSE

F   1. With the New Economic Policy, Lenin established a five-year schedule for the industrialization of the Russian economy.

T   2. Stalin was able to seize control of the Soviet Union because he had filled the government with party members loyal to him.

F   3. The consistency of Mussolini's ideas and actions is revealed by the history of fascism in Italy in the 1920s and 1930s.

T   4. The Weimar Republic faced opposition from industrialists, landowners, and army and civil service officials.

F   5. Although Hitler used anti-Semitic slogans to win followers, he was not himself an anti-Semite.

F   6. The Great Depression began with the collapse of prices on the New York Stock Exchange but hit Europe much harder than the United States.

T   7. The formation of the Popular Front government was a reaction to both the Great Depression and the efforts of ultraconservatives to overthrow the French Republic.

F   8. The New Deal, through management of the economy and programs of relief and public works, solved the problem of unemployment in the United States.

T   9. Functionalists argued that a building should declare its actual use and purpose as well as reflect the age of science and technology in its ornamentation.

T 10. The rise of the mass media gave totalitarian regimes an important tool in their efforts to indoctrinate their populations.

DISCUSSION AND/OR ESSAY QUESTIONS

1. Discuss this statement: "Instead of making the world 'safe for democracy,' World War I seriously threatened the continued survival of democratic government in Europe."
2. In what ways did the Soviet Union in 1939 differ from Russia in 1918? How do you explain the changes? How do you account for what *did not* change?
3. Compare and contrast Italian fascism and German Nazism. How do you account for the similarities? The differences?
4. Examine Wassily Kandinsky's *Panel (3)* and José Clemente Orozco's *Barricade* (pp. 1010–1011). How would you use these works to illustrate a lecture on the topic "Cultural Crisis between the Wars"?
5. Explain the ideas and significance of Max Weber, Oswald Spengler, Jean-Paul Sartre, and John Maynard Keynes. Would you agree that without understanding the devastating impact of the First World War, you cannot fully comprehend the works of these thinkers? Why or why not?

SUGGESTED FEATURE FILMS

Animal Farm. 75 min. Color. 1955. Louis de Rochemont. Animated version of Orwell's story.

Burnt by the Sun. 152 min. Color. 1994. Sony Pictures Classics. Written, produced, and directed by Nikita Mikhalkov, this film won the 1995 Oscar for Best Foreign Film. A portrait of the intelligentsia in 1930s Soviet Union.

Cabaret. 123 min. Color. 1972. ABC Pictures. A memorable picture of Berlin in the 1930s.

Earth. 63 min. B/W. 1930. VUFKU. Silent film depicts the clash between the kulaks and the collective farmers.

The Great Dictator. 129 min. B/W. 1940. United Artists. Chaplin's indictment of fascism.

The Joyless Street (Die Freudlose Gasse or Street of Sorrow). 139 min. B/W. 1925. Hirschel Sofar. Silent movie with Greta Garbo in Vienna in the 1920s.

1900. 320 min. Color. 1976. Twentieth-Century Fox. Unforgettable interpretation of the rise of fascism in Italy between 1900 and 1945. With Donald Sutherland.

The Triumph of the Will. 120 min. B/W. 1934. Leni Riefenstahl. Riefenstahl's documentary of the 1934 Nuremberg Rallies.

SUGGESTED CLASSROOM FILMS

Adolf Hitler, Part I: The Rise to Power. 27 min. B/W. 1963. Contemporary Films. Newsreel footage tells the story of Hitler's rise.

Benito Mussolini. 26 min. B/W. 1978. Contemporary Films. A biographical account.

The End of the Old Order 1900–1929. 26 min. Color. 1985. Insight Media. A survey of political and social changes in both Europe and America.

Europe, the Mighty Continent: Form, Riflemen, Form! 52 min. Color. 1976. Time-Life Films. Growing desperation and militarism in Europe in the 1930s.

Expressionism. 26 min. Color. 1971. International Film Bureau. Explores German expressionism from its Dresden beginnings to the "Blue Rider" group in Munich.

Franklin D. Roosevelt: The New Deal. 26 min. B/W. 1973. McGraw-Hill. Uses documentary footage to relate the life of Roosevelt through his third term.

Germany—Dada. 55 min. Color. 1968. University Educational and Visual Arts. Filmed with the aid of Dada-ists Hans Richter and Richard Huelsenbeck.

The Great Depression: A Human Diary. 53 min. B/W. 1970. Mass Media Ministries. Uses photographs to demonstrate the extent of the suffering in the United States.

Hitler and Mussolini, 1937. 18 min. B/W. 1937. Obern. Nazi propaganda footage; no English subtitles.

Igor Stravinski. 42 min. B/W. 1966. Carousel. Narrated by Charles Kuralt; includes interviews and scenes from ballet and concert performances.

The Life and Times of Bertrand Russell, Parts I and II. 50 min. B/W. 1967. BBC/Time-Life Films. Includes interviews with Russell as well as his contemporaries.

The Making of the German Nation. Part III: The Weimar Republic. 20 min. Color. 1983. Insight Media. From the Versailles Treaty through Hitler's rise to power.

Marcel Proust: From a Masterpiece to a Master's Work. 21 min. Color. 1961. Contemporary Films. Award-winning film uses not only Proust's writings but also the art and music of which he wrote to describe his life and society.

Memories of Berlin: Twilight of Weimar Culture. 72 min. Color. 1977. Insight Media. A look at the intellectual and cultural ferment of interwar Berlin.

Minister of Hate: Goebbels. 25 min. B/W. 1959. McGraw-Hill. Interviews with historian H. R. Trevor-Roper and producer Fritz Lang on the Nazis' mastery of propaganda.

Mussolini and Italian Fascism. 32 min. Color. 1992. Insight Media. Exploration of the contradictions of Mussolini's ideas and career.

The Rise of Adolf Hitler. 28 min. B/W. 1972. Films, Inc. Looks at Germany in the 1920s as well as at Hitler's career.

Stalin and Russian History, 1928–1953. 31 min. B/W. 1974. Centron Films. Includes the major events and policies of Stalin's era.

Surrealism. 24 min. Color. 1972. International Film Bureau. Account of the surrealist movement, with descriptions of both techniques and aesthetics.

The World of the '30s. 30 min. each. Color. 1989. Films for the Humanities.
  I. America in the '30s: Depression and Optimism.
  II. Losing the Peace. Focuses on the problems with implementing the Versailles Treaty, the failure of the Popular Front, and the Blum government.
  III. The End of a Revolution. Examines the Soviet experience.
  IV. Years of Gloom and Hope. Focuses on Britain, Belgium, and Holland.
  V. The Fuhrer's Germany.
  VI. Disaster in a Pleasant Climate: Trouble in Italy and Spain.
  XI. The Dawn of Tomorrow. Looks at technological and social change.
  XII. The End of the World. The coming of World War II.

World War I and the Rise of Fascism. 2 parts. 30 min. Color. 1989. Insight Media. Examines the First World War and its consequences for Europe in the 1920s and 1930s.

CHAPTER 29.   THE SECOND WORLD WAR

Outline

Introduction: comparison of the two world wars
  I. The causes of the war
      A. Defects of the peace treaties
      B. Power politics
      C. Economic conditions
      D. Nationalism
      E. Appeasement policies
          1. Hitler's expansionism
          2. The Spanish Civil War
          3. Munich and after
          4. Nazi-Soviet pact
 II. The outbreak of hostilities
      A. European war
          1. Attack on Poland
          2. The phony war and blitzkrieg
          3. The Battle of Britain
          4. Germany's invasion of Russia
      B. Global war
          1. Pearl Harbor
          2. Allied offensives
          3. The Holocaust
          4. Stalingrad
          5. The D-Day invasion
      C. The end of the war
          1. In Europe
          2. The atomic bomb
III. The peace settlement
      A. Postwar plans and Allied conflicts
          1. The Atlantic Charter
          2. The Teheran conference
          3. The Yalta conference
          4. The Potsdam conference
      B. The treaty with Japan
      C. Establishment of the U.N.
          1. Structure
          2. Achievements and failures

MULTIPLE CHOICE
Choose the best response.

1. In BOTH the First and Second World Wars,
    * (a) threats to the balance of power precipitated the conflict.
    (b) trench warfare characterized the conflict.
    (c) the European peoples cheered the outbreak of hostilities.
    (d) European Jews were rounded up and sent to death camps.

2. The causes of World War II do NOT include
    (a) the failure of the peace treaties after World War I.
    (b) a precarious balance of power on the European continent.
    * (c) the Allied nations' refusal to accede to German demands.
    (d) nationalist discontent.

3. Nearly all the nations of the world signed _____, renouncing war
    as an instrument of national policy.
    (a) the Yalta Agreement
    (b) the Potsdam Treaty
    * (c) the Kellogg-Briand Pact
    (d) the Versailles Treaty

4. The depression of the 1930s contributed to the outbreak of the Second World
    War by playing a role in each of the following EXCEPT
    (a) national construction of high tariff walls.
    (b) significant increases in arms production.
    (c) the appeal of Nazism to Germans.
    * (d) the appeal of pacifism in France and Britain.

5. The policy of appeasement was based on
    (a) the pessimistic conviction that Germany would inevitably triumph.
    * (b) the belief that Germany had legitimate grievances that needed to be
        addressed.
    (c) faith in the League of Nations as an instrument of world peace.
    (d) the desire to aid the Soviet Union in spreading socialism.

6. The Spanish Civil War did NOT
    (a) reveal Hitler's and Mussolini's willingness to ignore the terms of
        international agreements.
    (b) highlight the indecision and inaction of both France and Britain.
    * (c) reveal Stalin's refusal to lend Soviet aid to Western communist
        movements.
    (d) show the horrible effects of the use of aerial bombing on civilian centers.

7. "Peace in our time" was declared in 1938 by
   (a) Adolf Hitler.
   *(b) Neville Chamberlain.
   (c) Franklin Roosevelt.
   (d) Henri-Philippe Pétain.

8. Place the following in correct chronological order.
   (a) bombing of Hiroshima; German invasion of Poland; Spanish Civil War
   (b) U.S. entry into the war; German invasion of Poland; Spanish Civil War
   *(c) Spanish Civil War; German invasion of Poland; U.S. entry into the war
   (d) German invasion of Poland; U.S. entry into the war; the Spanish Civil War

9. Place the following in correct chronological order.
   *(a) German invasion of Poland; Battle of Britain; German invasion of the Soviet Union
   (b) German invasion of Poland; German annexation of Austria; German invasion of the Soviet Union
   (c) German invasion of the Soviet Union; German invasion of Poland; German annexation of Austria
   (d) Battle of Britain; German annexation of Austria; German invasion of the Soviet Union

10. Which of the following caused the Allies to declare war against Germany?
   (a) Hitler's annexation of Austria
   *(b) Hitler's invasion of Poland
   (c) Hitler's invasion of Czechoslovakia
   (d) Hitler's invasion of the Rhineland

11. Which of the following is INCORRECT?
   (a) Beginning in the spring of 1940, the Germans conquered Norway, Denmark, Belgium, the Netherlands, and France.
   (b) *Blitzkrieg* means lightning war.
   *(c) At Dunkirk, the Germans sustained their first serious defeat.
   (d) During the Battle of Britain, Germany bombed whole sections of British cities and killed tens of thousands of civilians.

12. What event brought the United States into World War II?
   (a) the sinking of the *Lusitania*
   (b) the German aerial campaigns against British cities
   *(c) Japan's bombing of Pearl Harbor
   (d) the Japanese invasion of Manchuria

13. Hitler decided to invade the Soviet Union after
    (a) the Soviet Union allied with Britain and the United States.
    (b) his defeat of France and Britain left him free to turn eastward.
    (c) the U.S. entry into the war made a quick victory essential.
    *(d) British resistance frustrated his attempts to bomb the island into submission.

14. The American decision to use the atomic bomb was based on the
    *(a) desire to end the war with Japan quickly.
    (b) desire to end the war with Germany quickly.
    (c) need to remove Japan from the conflict so that the Allies could concentrate their forces against Germany.
    (d) wish for vengeance because of the brutal Axis fire-bombings of civilian centers.

15. The Allied leaders disagreed about
    (a) whether or not to invade Britain.
    (b) the war aim of unconditional surrender.
    *(c) the future national boundaries and political complexion of Poland.
    (d) the necessity of fire-bombing civilian centers.

16. The postwar planning conferences of the Allied leaders were characterized by all of the following EXCEPT
    (a) conflict over control of the political outlines of postwar Eastern Europe.
    *(b) commitment to realize the goals of the Atlantic Charter.
    (c) conflict over the democratic nature of future Eastern European governments.
    (d) refusal to address fundamental disagreements.

17. At _____, Allied leaders outlined plans for Russian expansion into Poland and the establishment of the United Nations.
    (a) Locarno
    (b) Versailles
    *(c) Yalta
    (d) Berlin

18. Which was NOT a result of the postwar peace settlement?
    (a) Soviet-backed Communist governments in Eastern Europe
    *(b) Allied acceptance of a Soviet-dominated Germany
    (c) the "war crimes" trials of Nazi leaders
    (d) the establishment of the United Nations

19. The most important functions of the United Nations were assigned to the
    (a) General Assembly.
    *(b) Security Council.
    (c) League of Nations.
    (d) International Court of Justice.

20. The United Nations
    (a) abandoned the League of Nations' idealistic belief in the equality of all peaceful nations.
    (b) refused to allow the Soviet Union membership after its plans to dominate Poland were revealed.
    (c) was assigned the job of keeping peace in the world but given no armed force to do so.
    *(d) proved powerless in blocking determined action by major powers.

IDENTIFICATIONS

Locarno Agreements	D-Day
Neville Chamberlain	Nagasaki
phony war	the Holocaust
blitzkrieg	Dresden
Vichy	Teheran conference
Battle of Britain	Potsdam conference
Lend-Lease Act	Clement Attlee
Battle of Stalingrad	Nuremberg trials

TRUE OR FALSE

T   1. Armaments expansion proved to be an effective means of reducing unemployment and revitalizing national economies.

F   2. The instability of ethnically diverse Czechoslovakia stemmed from the refusal of the dominant Slovaks to accede political rights to the ethnic minorities.

T   3. Both the annexation of Austria and of the Sudetenland could be justified on the grounds of national self-determination.

T   4. Stalin feared that the Western nations would bargain with Germany and so directed Hitler's aggression eastward.

F   5. Despite the failure of his appeasement policies, Neville Chamberlain led the British to eventual victory against Germany.

F   6.   The United States entered World War II out of fear that Germany
           would succeed in conquering Britain and thus would control all of
           Europe.
T   7.   From 1943 on, the war began to turn in the Allies' favor.
T   8.   Nearly six million Jews died during World War II as a result of
           Hitler's plan to eliminate the Jews from Europe.
T   9.   The focus of disagreement among the Allied leaders centered on the
           future of central Europe.
T   10.   Action by the Security Council required the unanimous consent of
           Britain, France, the United States, China, the Soviet Union, and two
           other member nations.

DISCUSSION AND/OR ESSAY QUESTIONS

1. Discuss this statement: "The Second World War was actually Phase Two of
   the First World War."
2. Examine the economic and political factors behind the outbreak of the
   Second World War. Would you agree that the Great Depression played a
   greater role than any political element?
3. Defend or refute this statement: "Appeasement has been given a bad name because of the outcome of events in the 1930s and 1940s. However, appeasement
   was a moral and rational approach to remedying the weaknesses of the World
   War I peace settlement. It failed only because Hitler was neither moral nor
   rational."
4. In total war, there are no noncombatants. Examine the role of the civilian
   populations in the course and impact of the Second World War.
5. What are the major features of the peace settlement after World War II? How
   do you explain the division of Europe into two hostile blocs, one led by the
   United States, the other led by the Soviet Union?

SUGGESTED FEATURE FILMS

Europa, Europa. 115 min. Color. 1991. Festival. The unbelievable but true story of
   Solomon Perel, a young German Jewish boy who fled to Poland in 1938, lived
   in a Soviet youth camp, was captured by the Germans, adopted by an SS
   Commander, and survived the war.

A Generation; Kanal; Ashes and Diamonds. 909 min. B/W. 1954; 1957; 1958.
   Film Polski. Andrzej Wajda's trilogy about Poland during World War II.

Hope and Glory. Color. 1987. Columbia/Tri-Star. Director and writer John Boorman's autobiographical account of his childhood in London during the Blitz. Nominated for five Academy Awards, including Best Picture, Best Director, and Best Original Screenplay.

Schindler's List. 197 min. Color. 1994. MCA Universal Home Video. Steven Spielberg's masterful telling of the story of Oskar Schindler, the Nazi party member and war profiteer who saved the lives of 1,100 Jews.

Shoah. 9 hours, 30 min. Color. 1985. Filmed on location in 14 countries, this epic documentary brings together the testimony of victims, perpetrators, and bystanders.

SUGGESTED CLASSROOM FILMS

The A-Bomb Dropped on Japan. 4 min. B/W. 1962. Fleetwood. Contemporary newsreel excerpts.

And the World Listened: Winston Churchill. 28 min. B/W. 1955. University of Wisconsin. Political Science Professor Leon B. Epstein comments.

Battle of Britain. 50 min. B/W. 1943. National Audio-Visual Center. From the *Why We Fight* series.

Chamberlain versus Hitler. 25 min. B/W. 1964. Films, Inc. The drafting of the Munich agreement.

D-Day. 50 min. B/W. 1962. Films, Inc. Uses actual German and Allied footage.

The Decision to Drop the Bomb. 32 min. B/W. 1966. Films, Inc. Explores the decision-making process that led to use of the atomic bomb.

Elie Wiesel: Witness to the Holocaust. 21 min. Color. 1990. Filmic Archives. Comes with 32-page student guide and 20-page teacher resource book.

Europe, the Mighty Continent: With Hardship in Their Garment. 52 min. Color. 1976. Time-Life Films. The horrors of total war.

Facing Hate. 60 min. Color. 1997. Films for the Humanities. Bill Moyers interviews Auschwitz survivor and Nobel Laureate Elie Wiesel.

Genocide. 52 min. Color. 1973. D. L. Taffner. Thames Television program on Hitler's Final Solution.

The Hero City—Leningrad, Parts I and II. 23 min. 30 min. B/W. 1968. Films, Inc. Covers the 900-day siege.

Holocaust: Liberation of Auschwitz. 18 min. Color and B/W. 1985. Filmic Archives. A Soviet cameraman photographed the liberation of Auschwitz on Jan. 27, 1945; this is the film footage.

Josef Goebbels. 23 min. B/W. 1965. Sterled. Goebbels's life and use of propaganda.

Memory of the Camps. 58 min. B/W. 1985. Filmic Archives. Film shot by British and American soldiers in 1945.

The Music of Auschwitz. 16 min. Color. 1978. Carousel. *60 Minutes* interview with musician and Auschwitz survivor Fania Fenelon.

Nazi Concentration Camps. 59 min. B/W. 1945. National Audio-Visual Center. The official film record made by the Allied forces as they advanced into Germany.

Night and Fog. 55 min. B/W. 1955. Alan Resnais's disturbing documentary of German concentration camps.

The Spanish Civil War. Part I: The War on Spain. 35 min.; *Part II: The War Beyond Spain.* 26 min. B/W. 1972. Kraus Thomson Organization. Uses newsreel footage, interviews with historians and survivors, and even cartoons.

The Spanish Turmoil. 64 min. B/W. 1967. Time-Life Films. Includes actual footage of the war.

Tale of Two Cities: Hiroshima and Nagasaki. 12 min. B/W. 1949. National Audio-Visual Center. Documentary of the effects of the atomic bombings.

Ten Seconds That Shook the World, Parts I and II. 25 min. each. B/W. 1963. Films, Inc. Chronological account of the atom bomb's development and the decision to use it.

Total War. 26 min. B/W. 1969. Learning Corporation of America. World War II as experienced by civilians.

Trial at Nuremberg. 55 min. B/W. 1964. Films, Inc. Archive film of the war crimes trial.

Verdict for Tomorrow. 28 min. B/W. 1962. Anti-Defamation League of B'nai B'rith. Examines the Eichmann trial and its significance.

The Warsaw Ghetto Uprising: Diary of the Last Heroes. 52 min. Color. 1997. Films for the Humanities. Archival footage and the reminiscences of five surviving fighters retell the story of the uprising.

The World at War Series. 26 parts. 51 min. each. Color. 1974. Heritage Visual Sales Ltd. Thames Television series beginning with Germany in 1933 and ending with a reunion of World War II veterans.

PART SEVEN.   THE EMERGENCE OF WORLD CIVILIZATION
CHAPTER 30.   THE POSTWAR YEARS: RIVALRY AND RECOVERY

Outline

Introduction: the costs of the war
  I. A divided continent
      A. The United States and the U.S.S.R. after the war
          1. The Soviet Union in Eastern Europe
          2. The Marshall Plan, NATO, and the Russian response
          3. A divided Germany
      B. The Cold War
          1. U.S. attitudes
          2. Soviet attitudes
          3. Stalinism
      C. After Stalin
          1. The Soviet Union under Khrushchev
          2. Challenges in Eastern Europe
          3. The Berlin Wall
          4. Revolt in Czechoslovakia
      D. Efforts to bridge the gap between East and West
 II. Economic renaissance
      A. Causes of postwar economic growth
      B. Mixed economies .
      C. Economic recovery and growth
          1. Economic revival in West Germany
          2. National planning in France
          3. Italy's industrial miracle
          4. Shared continental prosperity
          5. The British exception
      D. Steps toward European economic integration
      E. Economic development in Eastern Europe
      F. Expansion of social services in the West
III. The politics of European recovery
      A. New and moderate leadership
      B. French political fragmentation, de Gaulle, and the Fifth Republic
 IV. Intellectual and cultural patterns
      A. Isolation of the avant-garde
      B. Postwar literature and film: engagement, alienation, absurdity, and escape
      C. The visual arts

222

MULTIPLE CHOICE
Choose the best response.

1. Stalin's anti-Western policy did NOT stem from
    (a) personal paranoia.
    (b) the threat of American-inspired military and economic encirclement.
    (c) traditional Russian fears of Europe.
    *(d) the Allies' refusal at Teheran and Yalta to grant the Soviet claim to
         Eastern European hegemony.

2. In which country was a communist but non-Soviet-controlled regime
    established in 1948?
    (a) Poland
    (b) Greece
    (c) Czechoslovakia
    *(d) Yugoslavia

3. Which of the following would NOT belong in a lecture entitled "The
    Beginning of the Cold War: Soviet-American Relations 1946–1950"?
    (a) The formation of the Warsaw Pact
    (b) The Marshall Plan
    *(c) The construction of the Berlin Wall
    (d) The Berlin Airlift

4. The _____ provided American funds for the reconstruction of Western
    European economies after World War II.
    (a) Truman Doctrine
    (b) New Deal
    (c) Council for Mutual Economic Assistance
    *(d) Marshall Plan

5. In the late 1940s and early 1950s, U.S. leaders believed that
    (a) the Soviet system was essentially democratic.
    *(b) the Soviets were planning to establish communist dictatorships across
         Western Europe.
    (c) the Japanese-Soviet alliance threatened Western prosperity.
    (d) Stalin's paranoia about American economic imperialism was justified.

6. In the decade after Stalin's death
    (a) Soviet leaders rejected Stalin's authoritarian system of government.
    (b) the United States abandoned its policy of Soviet "containment."
    *(c) Soviet leaders eased some of the economic restrictions on client states.
    (d) the new Soviet leaders sought to escalate confrontations with the
        United States.

7. Nikita Khrushchev did NOT
    *(a) allow Hungary to leave the Soviet bloc.
    (b) institute a "thaw" in Soviet intellectual and cultural affairs.
    (c) abandon Stalin's policy of personal seclusion.
    (d) seek a policy of "peaceful coexistence" with the United States.

8. After Khrushchev's fall, the reins of Soviet power passed to
    (a) Alexander Dubcek.
    *(b) Leonid Brezhnev.
    (c) Lavrenty Beria.
    (d) Leon Trotsky.

9. According to your textbook author, which Western European politician was
   most effective at bridging the gap between East and West?
    (a) Leonid Brezhnev
    *(b) Willy Brandt
    (c) Charles de Gaulle
    (d) Margaret Thatcher

10. Factors in Western Europe's postwar economic renaissance did NOT include
    (a) wartime technological innovations with peacetime applications.
    (b) removal of obstacles to international trade and payments.
    *(c) adherence to the principles of the free-market economy.
    (d) consumer demand and the resulting capital investment.

11. Explanations of West Germany's economic revival include all of the
    following EXCEPT the
    (a) loss of East Germany and therefore the elimination of the economically
        conservative Junkers.
    *(b) adoption of the most socialized economy in Western Europe.
    (c) occupying powers' initial insistence that Germany spend no money on
        defense.
    (d) opportunity to rebuild factories with up-to-date equipment and
        techniques.

12. Britain's economy
    (a) led Europe in increase in growth rates after the war.
    (b) differed from other European nations in the postwar period in its
        failure to grow.
    (c) grew as a result of the rise of nationalist sentiment after the war and the
        resulting tendency to invest at home.
    *(d) remained sluggish in part because of the hostilities between labor and
        management.

13. The EEC was
   *(a) a Western European economic alliance aimed at the abolition of trade barriers among its members.
   (b) a military alliance of Western European countries alarmed at the thought of Soviet invasion.
   (c) an economic alliance between Britain and her European neighbors.
   (d) an American-dominated industrial organization aimed at reviving manufacturing in the poorer regions of Spain and Italy.

14. Which of the following is INCORRECT concerning the economies of Eastern Europe in the post–World War II years?
   (a) National incomes rose and output increased.
   (b) The Soviet Union's satellite states were compelled to trade with the Soviet Union to their disadvantage.
   (c) Early policies emphasized heavy industry and collectivized agriculture.
   *(d) Levels of unemployment soared and social services were almost nonexistent.

15. In Germany, France, and Italy during the 1950s and 1960s
   *(a) centrist parties affiliated with the Roman Catholic Church held power.
   (b) strongly doctrinaire socialist governments instituted radical reforms that alienated the middle classes.
   (c) feminism altered the political balance of power as women began to vote as a bloc.
   (d) the strength of the communist parties led to close affiliation with the Soviet Union.

16. De Gaulle's rise to power in France can be explained by all of the following EXCEPT
   *(a) France's failure to share in the postwar economic renaissance.
   (b) the crisis in Algeria.
   (c) the erosion of the political center in France.
   (d) the weakness of the French executive branch and the resulting tendency toward parliamentary deadlock.

17. The postwar governments of most of Western Europe can best be labeled as
   (a) communist.
   (b) laissez-faire.
   *(c) centrist.
   (d) reactionary.

18. Which of the following is associated with structuralism?
   *(a) Claude Levi-Strauss
    (b) Albert Camus
    (c) Günter Grass
    (d) Boris Pasternak

19. Which of the following statements concerning post–World War II culture is INCORRECT?
   *(a) Filmmakers were blocked by censorship from making anything but mindless entertainment.
    (b) A number of authors used the absurd to express their despair about the condition of humanity.
    (c) The gap between the avant-garde and the generally educated public remained wide.
    (d) Writers frequently addressed the problem of alienation in their work.

20. Protest against increasing state power and the resulting alienation of the individual can be found in the works of all of the following EXCEPT
    (a) Boris Pasternak.
    (b) Aleksandr Solzhenitsyn.
   *(c) Mark Rothko.
    (d) Herbert Marcuse.

IDENTIFICATIONS

NATO	Willy Brandt
Warsaw Pact	European Economic Community
Marshal Tito	Konrad Adenauer
Cominform	Charles de Gaulle
Nikita Khrushchev	Albert Camus
Brezhnev Doctrine	abstract expressionism

TRUE OR FALSE

T   1. By 1948, Soviet-dominated governments had been installed in Poland, Hungary, Rumania, Bulgaria, and Czechoslovakia.

T   2. The Truman Doctrine provided assistance programs to prevent communist infiltration in Greece and Turkey.

F   3.   The West responded to the creation of the Warsaw Pact with the establishment of NATO.

T   4.   Germany was the focal point of U.S.-Soviet tensions during the late 1940s.

T   5.   The Soviets viewed the Truman and Marshall programs as forms of neoimperialism.

T   6.   The Soviet invasion of Hungary in 1956 made it clear that Soviet leaders would not allow Eastern European nations to leave the Warsaw Pact.

F   7.   During the 1950s, Western Europe experienced an unprecedented combination of high inflation and high rates of unemployment.

T   8.   The creation of the Common Market contributed to the Continental prosperity of the 1960s.

F   9.   Both Britain and Spain failed to share in Western Europe's postwar prosperity.

F   10.   The postwar years saw the creation of state welfare systems only in those areas dominated by the Soviet Union.

F   11.   De Gaulle worked to strengthen France's ties with the United States and to increase American involvement in European affairs.

T   12.   Adenauer, de Gasperi, and de Gaulle all shared a certain apprehensiveness about parliamentary democracy.

F   13.   De Gaulle built an independent nuclear strike force because of his belief that the territorial ambitions of the Soviet Union posed a constant threat to Western Europe.

F   14.   Because of the expansion of higher education, the gulf between the avant-garde art world and the general public narrowed in the postwar years.

F   15.   Because of the cold war, Marxism appealed to few intellectuals in Western Europe.

DISCUSSION AND/OR ESSAY QUESTIONS

1.   Was the cold war an inevitable result of World War II, or could it have been avoided?

2.   Consider this statement: "The dominant theme in postwar European history is growing uniformity. In terms of political structures, economic life, and social divisions, the nations of Europe grew increasingly alike after 1945." Do you agree? If so, are there any exceptions?

3.   What factors explain the economic renaissance of Europe after World War II?

4.   Describe the extent, and assess the impact, of U.S. involvement in European affairs between 1945 and 1970.

5.   In the period between 1950 and 1970, Europeans experienced unprecedented economic prosperity; yet in those same decades, European writers and artists often produced works centering on themes of despair and alienation. Why?

SUGGESTED FEATURE FILMS

Akenfield. 98 min. Color. 1974. Angle Films. Film version of Ronald Blythe's vivid portrayal of postwar rural Britain.

JFK. 189 min. Color. 1991. Warner Home Video. This Oliver Stone film is sure to arouse debate about the difference between historical interpretation and fiction.

Plenty. 124 min. Color. 1985. Twentieth Century Fox. Meryl Streep stars in this film version of David Hare's play about postwar Britain's loss of power and purpose.

Thérèse Desqueyroux. 109 min. B/W. 1962. Filmel. Mauriac's novel about bourgeois boredom is here set in the 1960s.

Weekend. 105 min. Color. 1968. Lira Films. Godard's violent attack on modern capitalist society.

Z. 125 min. Color. 1969. Reggane. Suspense drama of assassination and governmental corruption.

The "Angry Young Men" movement in literature, "kitchen-sink" drama, and the renaissance in British film in the 1950s and 1960s coalesced in a host of films, including:

The Angry Silence. 94 min. B/W. 1960. British Lion. A look at class conflict in Britain through the story of a worker who refuses to join a strike.

The Entertainer, 96 min. B/W. 1960. British Lion. Lawrence Olivier stars in this version of John Osborne's play about the decline of Britain.

A Kind of Loving. 112 min. B/W. 1962. Anglo-Amalgamated. Working-class life, love, and marriage.

The Loneliness of the Long Distance Runner. 104 min. B/W. 1962. British Lion. This film expands Alan Sillitoe's short story about a boy at reform school.

Look Back in Anger. 99 min. B/W. 1959. Associated British Pictures Corporation. Richard Burton stars in this version of John Osborne's play about the quintessential "Angry Young Man."

Room at the Top. 117 min. B/W. 1959. Remus. John Braine's very funny novel on screen.

Saturday Night and Sunday Morning. 89 min. B/W. 1960. Bryanston. Alan Sillitoe wrote the screenplay for this version of his novel.

SUGGESTED CLASSROOM FILMS

Berlin: A Study in Two Worlds. 43 min. Color. nd. Gertrude Purple Gorham Agency. Comparison of East and West Berlin both before and after the building of the Berlin Wall.

Britain: A Changing Culture. 25 min. Color. nd. McGraw-Hill. Examination of the problem of British adaptation to the postwar world.

Europe, the Mighty Continent: A European Idea. 52 min. Color. 1976. Time-Life Films. Europe in the 1960s and 1970s.

Europe, the Mighty Continent: How Are the Mighty Fallen. 52 min. Color. 1976. Time-Life Films. Europe overshadowed by the superpowers.

Europe, the Mighty Continent: Human Rights, Fundamental Freedom. 52 min. Color. 1976. Time-Life Films. The crumbling of empires and the occupation of Eastern Europe.

History 1917–1967. Unit II. No. 7—Khrushchev and the Thaw. 21 min. B/W. 1970. Time-Life Films. Examination of de-Stalinization.

History 1917–1967. Unit III. No. 9—The Cold War. 23 min. B/W. 1970. Time-Life Films. From the Berlin airlift to the Cuban Missile Crisis.

Khrushchev: The Bear's Embrace. 24 min. Color. 1980. Learning Corporation of America. Part of the *Leaders of the 20th Century* series.

The Ordeal of Anatoly Kuznetsov. 52 min. B/W. 1969. CBS. Interview with the novelist one month after his defection from the Soviet Union.

The Second Battle of Britain. 47 min. Color. 1975. Coronet. Morly Safer looks at the problem of British decline. Includes interviews with Winston Churchill, Jr., Claud Cockburn, Malcolm Muggeridge, and unionist Jimmy Reid.

Triumph of the West. No. 13—Capitulations. 50 min. Color. 1985. BBC/Films Inc. British historian John Roberts looks at the second half of the twentieth century.

CHAPTER 31. FRAGMENTATION AND CHANGE: THE END OF POSTWAR CERTAINTIES

Outline

I. Patterns of social change and social protest
   A. Social change
      1. Population growth
      2. Altered class relations
      3. Educational reforms and the communications revolution
   B. Social protest
      1. Student revolts
      2. The women's movement
      3. The civil rights movement
II. Economic stagnation: the price of success
   A. The oil embargo and its aftermath
   B. The debt crisis
   C. Political responses
      1. Changes in governments and policies
      2. Constitutional crises
III. Europe recast: The collapse of communism and the end of the Soviet Union
   A. Gorbachev, *perestroika*, and *glasnost*
   B. The collapse of communism in Eastern Europe
   C. The fall of the Soviet Union
      1. The rise of Boris Yeltsin
      2. The aborted hardliner coup
      3. The secession of the republics
   D. The new eastern Europe
      1. Economic and political disarray
      2. Ethnic and religious conflict
   E. Civil war in the former Yugoslavia

MULTIPLE CHOICE
Choose the best response.

1. Changes in the nature of the middle class included
   (a) decreasing numbers due to widespread movement into the upper class.
   (b) increasing hostility toward the working class.
   (c) increasing intra-class hostilities between those with university educations and those without.
   *(d) increasing numbers of technocrats and managers.

229

2. Which of the following is NOT true of the working class in postwar Europe?
   (a) Its skills became more specialized and technologically oriented.
   (b) The number of manual laborers increased at a slower rate than that of salaried employees.
   *(c) It lost its political voice with the decline of trade unions.
   (d) It adapted to the more complex machinery of modern factories.

3. The student revolt in Paris in 1968
   (a) failed because of the hostilities between workers and students.
   (b) succeeded because it remained focused on the single issue of university modernization.
   *(c) was the most serious of a number of student revolts in Europe and the United States.
   (d) strengthened de Gaulle's position as president.

4. The women's movement of the late 1960s and 1970s
   (a) first arose within the ranks of the working class.
   (b) focused on obtaining the vote.
   *(c) called attention to discrimination in the workplace.
   (d) was confined only to the United States, France, and Great Britain.

5. Which American black leader did NOT espouse the ideal of a fully integrated nation?
   (a) Martin Luther King, Jr.
   *(b) Malcolm X
   (c) Julius Nyerere
   (d) Nelson Mandela

6. Which of the following was NOT an organization fighting for the advancement of American blacks in the decades after World War II?
   (a) CORE
   (b) the National Urban League
   (c) the NAACP
   *(d) the New Deal

7. In the 1970s the Western European economy
   (a) declined in a relentless deflationary spiral.
   (b) failed to respond to American competition.
   (c) continued on its postwar path of ever-rising growth rates.
   *(d) weakened under the pressures of inflation and high unemployment rates.

8. The oil embargo instituted by OPEC in 1973
   * (a) helped fuel the inflationary spiral
   (b) shook the United States but had little impact on Western Europe because of its supplies of North Sea oil.
   (c) introduced inflation to Western European economies.
   (d) spurred Eastern Europe on its drive toward self-sufficiency.

9. In the second half of the 1970s, the Eastern European economies were marked by
   (a) high unemployment rates.
   * (b) indebtedness to Western creditors.
   (c) a shift toward consumer goods production.
   (d) increasing ability to compete with the West.

10. In the early 1980s, the governments of all of the following countries moved Left EXCEPT in
   (a) France.
   * (b) Britain.
   (c) Italy.
   (d) Spain.

11. As a result of Mitterrand's economic reform policies,
   (a) France recovered quickly from its economic malaise.
   (b) France experienced a period of unprecedented full employment.
   * (c) a drain on government resources led to devaluation of the franc.
   (d) French unions and the French Communist Party led a widespread citizen's revolt.

12. Which is NOT true of the 1970s and 1980s?
   (a) A number of politicians and thinkers challenged the idea of the centralized welfare state.
   * (b) Both Spain and Italy repudiated the policy of nationalizing industries.
   (c) A number of U.S. governments acted with little regard for constitutional legalities.
   (d) Governments of both Right and Left faltered as European economies declined.

13. Mikhail Gorbachev
   (a) wanted to destroy communism in the Soviet Union.
   (b) was overthrown after attempting to block the process of reform in Eastern Europe.
   * (c) sought to introduce the elements of a mixed economy to the Soviet Union.
   (d) believed that Russia should liberate itself from the rest of the Soviet Union.

14. *Glasnost* meant
    (a) that the Soviet Union abandoned communism for free-market capitalism.
    (b) the steady reduction of nuclear weapons from the Soviet arsenal.
    (c) any Soviet republic that wished to become independent from the Soviet Union was encouraged to do so.
    *(d) Soviet citizens were encouraged to discuss and debate openly.

15. The trade-union movement that succeeded in bringing democracy to Poland is called
    *(a) Solidarity.
    (b) Glasnost.
    (c) Perestroika.
    (d) Civic Forum.

16. In East Germany, mass emigration to the West and evidence of widespread political corruption forced the resignation of
    *(a) Erich Honecker.
    (b) Vaclav Havel.
    (c) Lech Walesa.
    (d) Boris Yeltsin.

17. Who played a crucial role in rallying the Soviet people to defeat the attempted communist coup in 1991?
    (a) Erich Honecker.
    (b) Vaclav Havel.
    (c) Lech Walesa.
    *(d) Boris Yeltsin.

18. In the 1990s, the former Soviet republics experienced all of the following EXCEPT
    (a) ethnic and religious conflict.
    (b) food shortages and inflation.
    *(c) an increase in average life expectancy.
    (d) a communist resurgence.

19. The warring factions in Bosnia included all of the following EXCEPT
    (a) Serbs.
    *(b) Chechens.
    (c) Muslims.
    (d) Croats.

20. In the Bosnian civil war
   (a) American military intervention ensured the defeat of the Serbs.
   (b) Russian troops experienced a series of humiliating military defeats.
   (c) the communist forces were wiped out.
   *(d) all sides engaged in "ethnic cleansing."

IDENTIFICATIONS

Common Market	OPEC
Simone de Beauvoir	*perestroika*
Martin Luther King, Jr.	Vaclav Havel
Margaret Thatcher	Boris Yeltsin
François Mitterrand	ethnic cleansing

TRUE OR FALSE

T   1. Both social welfare programs and improved health care resulted in an increase in the European birth rate after World War II.

F   2. Post–World War II prosperity fueled the movement of middle-class Europeans out of managerial positions and into the ownership of their own businesses.

T   3. In post–World War II Europe, more children went to school for longer periods of time.

T   4. Revolts against oppressive regimes, student unrest, and protests against the Vietnam War all played a role in the youth movement of the 1960s and early 1970s.

F   5. Many of the early activists in the women's movement had been part of the radical trade-union movement.

F   6. The civil rights legislation of the 1960s resulted in economic, although not political, equality for blacks in the United States.

T   7. During the 1960s, new industries in Europe prospered, but the basic or heavy industries such as coal and steel ran up deficits.

T   8. During the 1970s, labor relations in Europe worsened.

F   9. Eastern Europe erupted in revolt after Mikhail Gorbachev insisted that Soviet-style communism constituted the only acceptable form of government in the region.

F   10. Boris Yeltsin's commitment to the free enterprise economy resulted in full employment and economic growth in Russia.

DISCUSSION AND/OR ESSAY QUESTIONS

1. Why is this chapter entitled "Fragmentation and Change: The End of Postwar Certainties"? What fragmented? What certainties ended?
2. In what ways can the patterns of social change in postwar Europe be linked to the social protests that erupted in this period?
3. Describe the response of political leaders to the economic difficulties that troubled Europe in the 1970s and 1980s. Which responses proved the most effective and why?
4. Discuss the statement: "From 1945 to 1989, Soviet-style communism served as the lid on the pot of Eastern European ethnic and religious tensions. Once the lid was removed, the pot boiled over."
5. Mikail Gorbachev instituted the policies of *glasnost* and *perestroika* to save the Soviet Union. Instead, these policies accelerated the disintegration of the Soviet empire and the collapse of Soviet-style communism. How and why?

SUGGESTED FEATURE FILMS

At the River I Stand. 58 min. Color. 1993. California Newsreel. A portrait of the sanitation workers' strike that drew Martin Luther King, Jr., to Memphis, where he was assassinated.

Before the Rain. 114 min. Color. 1994. Gramercy Pictures. This look at post-Yugoslavia Macedonia was nominated for the 1995 Academy Award for Best Foreign Picture.

If. 111 min. Color. 1968. Paramount. Public-school rebellion in Britain in the 1960s.

Nixon. 192 min. Color. 1995. Buena Vista Home Video. Anthony Hopkins and Joan Allen star in this controversial Oliver Stone film about the controversial American president.

The Promise. 115 min. Color. 1995. NL Home Video. Separated by the Berlin Wall, a young couple experiences the two sides of German life from the early 1960s through 1989.

SUGGESTED CLASSROOM FILMS

The Battle of Chicago. 22 min. B/W. 1968. Footage from the Democratic National Convention in 1968.

Conversations with Gorbachev. 90 min. Color. 1994. Films for the Humanities. Historian Stephen Cohen interviewed Gorbachev after he fell from power.

The Germans: Portrait of a New Nation. 58 min. Color. 1995. Films for the Humanities. Includes profiles of families and individuals from both the former West and East Germanies.

Oh! Woodstock! 26 min. Color. 1969. Films, Inc. Two groups, young Woodstock participants and older professionals, comment on film clips from the Woodstock Rock Festival.

Soviets: The True Story of Perestroika. 5 parts. 53 min. each. Color. 1991. Films for the Humanities. Documentary series that focuses on the concerns, such as the degradation of the environment, that led to grassroots protests and political awakening.

A Woman's Place. 52 min. Color. 1973. Xerox Films. The changing roles of American women.

CHAPTER 32. PROBLEMS OF WORLD CIVILIZATION

Outline

I. Decolonization and the emergence of the developing world
   A. An independent developing world: Assets and liabilities
   B. The Chinese Revolution
   C. The end of colonial rule
      1. India
      2. Egypt and the Suez crisis
      3. Sub-Saharan Africa
      4. South Africa
      5. Algeria
   D. African economic decline
   E. The developing world and racial conflict
II. Warmaking and peacekeeping in the nuclear age
   A. The Korean War
   B. The Vietnam War
   C. The United States in Central America
   D. The U.S.S.R. in Afghanistan
   E. The Middle East
   F. Terrorism
   G. The threat of nuclear destruction
III. The problems of ecology and population
   A. Assaults upon nature
   B. The population explosion
      1. Link with ecology
      2. Causes and effects
IV. The achievements and limitations of science and technology
   A. Medicine and health
   B. Space exploration
   C. Nuclear science
   D. Electronics and the computer

MULTIPLE CHOICE
Choose the best response.

1. The developing world has become an important factor in the world power equation in part because of the
   *(a) wealth of these nations in terms of vital natural resources.
   (b) threat of these newly prosperous nations to dominate world commerce.
   (c) commitment of these nations to communist ideology.
   (d) uniting of these nations into an independent bloc.

2. The leader of the communists in the Chinese civil war was
* (a) Mao Zedong.
   (b) Ho Chi Minh.
   (c) Jawaharlal Nehru.
   (d) Deng Xiaoping.

3. In 1947
   (a) violence between blacks and whites led to a British takeover of Rhodesia.
   (b) the Ayatollah Khomeini seized control of Iran and embarked on a policy of thoroughgoing Westernization.
   (c) the French army, under de Gaulle's leadership, succeeded in destroying the Egyptian nationalist movement.
* (d) Britain granted autonomy to India and Pakistan.

4. Which of the following did NOT join in the invasion of the Suez Canal in 1956?
   (a) Britain
   (b) France
   (c) Israel
* (d) the United States

5. France's most painful and protracted withdrawal from a colonial possession occurred in
   (a) Tunisia.
   (b) Palestine.
* (c) Algeria.
   (d) Kenya.

6. "Apartheid" refers to the
   (a) Israeli policy of confining Palestinians to specific regions of Israel.
   (b) ethnic separatist movement that tore apart Nigeria.
   (c) division of the Indian subcontinent into the nation-states of India, Pakistan, and Bangladesh.
* (d) South African policy of segregating blacks and whites.

7. In the Korean War
* (a) stalemate followed the Chinese invasion to aid North Korea.
   (b) the United States and U.S.S.R. fought over domination of the Far East.
   (c) the United States and Japan continued their fight in another arena.
   (d) American possession of nuclear weapons proved the decisive factor in ending the conflict quickly.

8. Which of the following is NOT true concerning the Vietnam War?
   (a) Vietnamese nationalists had fought various foreign-backed and foreign troops since 1945.
   (b) Vietnamese nationalists drove out the French in 1954.
   *(c) The Viet Cong refused to allow the elections provided by the Geneva Agreement.
   (d) Under President Johnson, American involvement in Vietnam escalated steadily.

9. Tensions between Israel and the Arab nations remained high for all of the following reasons EXCEPT
   *(a) the refusal of any Arab leader to negotiate with the Israeli government.
   (b) Israel's inability to resolve the question of the rights of the Palestinian Arabs.
   (c) the Arabs' refusal to recognize Israel as a legitimate state.
   (d) the use of terrorism by the dispossessed Palestinians.

10. In the 1991 Gulf War, the United States led a coalition of twenty-nine other countries in war against
   (a) Kuwait.
   *(b) Iraq.
   (c) Israel.
   (d) Libya.

11. As a result of the SALT talks,
   (a) the breakup of the Soviet Union was assured.
   (b) the threat of detente was defeated.
   *(c) little in the way of concrete agreement was achieved.
   (d) the Soviet Union agreed to dismantle its nuclear arsenal.

12. The term "ecology" most accurately refers to
   (a) the interrelationships of human beings.
   (b) pollution problems.
   (c) the effect of the population explosion on the natural environment.
   *(d) the chain of life extending from microorganisms to human beings.

13. "Acid rain" is the term used for the
   (a) radioactive fallout from the Chernobyl disaster.
   (b) erosion of topsoil.
   *(c) effects of the sulfur dioxide discharged into the air by industrial and utilities plants.
   (d) massive aerial bombardment of Vietnam that was employed by U.S. troops.

14. The most serious nuclear accident to date occurred in 1986 at
    (a) Valdez, Alaska.
    (b) Times Beach, Missouri.
   *(c) Chernobyl, in the Soviet Union.
    (d) Bhopal, India.

15. The world's population explosion is best explained by
   *(a) a drop in the death rate combined with an uncurbed reproduction rate.
    (b) the growth in the wealth of the West and the subsequent rise in the birth rate of industrialized countries.
    (c) the longer average life span resulting from better medicine.
    (d) the failure of most Western nations to adopt population-control plans.

16. The discovery of DNA was significant because it enabled scientists to
   *(a) understand the causes of hereditary disease.
    (b) check the spread of diseases like scarlet fever.
    (c) develop the hydrogen bomb.
    (d) devise the American space program.

17. Space exploration was to a large degree motivated by
    (a) the desire to find solutions to the world's ecological problems.
   *(b) competition between the United States and the U.S.S.R.
    (c) pessimism about the earth's future.
    (d) recognition of the importance of electronics for the world economy.

18. The first hydrogen bomb was exploded in
    (a) 1945.
   *(b) 1952.
    (c) 1968.
    (d) 1980.

19. The field of electronics has played an important role in all of the following EXCEPT
    (a) the space industry.
    (b) automation.
    (c) the development of missile technology.
   *(d) the reduction of unemployment.

20. The personal computer has been linked to
   *(a) the privatization of life on a scale that may be dangerous.
    (b) the shift of manufacturing jobs to developing-world countries.
    (c) increasing gender inequalities in the workplace.
    (d) increasing corporate profits.

IDENTIFICATIONS

Mao Zedong	Persian Gulf War
Mohandas Gandhi	Chernobyl
apartheid	F. H. C. Crick and James D. Watson
Ho Chi Minh	*Sputnik*
PLO	Michel Foucault

TRUE OR FALSE

F   1.   In the 1960s and 1970s, most newly independent developing-world nations rejected the Western-oriented goals of industrialization and urbanization.

F   2.   Britain's gradual withdrawal from her colonial territories enabled these areas to avoid the ethnic and regional conflicts that tore apart the lands abandoned by the French.

T   3.   The combination of the worldwide escalation of petroleum prices, recurring droughts, and the failure of government-sponsored corporations resulted in the massive economic decline of Africa in the 1970s.

F   4.   Although the United States was supported by the majority of the Vietnamese, the greater military resources of the North Vietnamese rebels ensured communist victory in Vietnam.

T   5.   In Vietnam, El Salvador, and Nicaragua, the United States intervened, directly or indirectly, in civil-war situations.

F   6.   The breakup of the Soviet Union meant the end of the nuclear threat.

T   7.   By the 1970s, the United States, the Soviet Union, Britain, France, India, and Israel possessed either nuclear weapons or the technology necessary to create these weapons.

F   8.   The SALT treaties succeeded in eliminating major categories of weapons from the nuclear arsenals of both the United States and the Soviet Union.

T   9.   Environmental threats receiving attention in the 1990s included the destruction of the rain forests and global warming.

T   10.   The demographic revolution has been most conspicuous in Central and South America, Africa, and Asia.

DISCUSSION AND/OR ESSAY QUESTIONS

1.   Agree or disagree, in whole or in part: "Democracy is a luxury which the developing world cannot yet afford. History has shown that, in a country without a strong economy and a unified people, democratic political structures are bound to collapse. Democracy in the developing world must wait."

2. In what ways have economic developments determined political events in Asia, Africa, and South America since 1945?
3. Did the possession of nuclear weapons limit or strengthen the power of the United States and the Soviet Union to shape the world to suit their own ends? Discuss in reference to events in Korea, Cuba, Vietnam, and Afghanistan.
4. "Technology has enabled us to live longer while destroying the conditions needed to allow us to live *better*." Do you agree? Be sure to consider the demographic explosion, the ecological crisis, changes in medicine, and the advance of nuclear science in your argument.
5. Imagine you are the keynote speaker at a conference on "The Future of World Civilization." Your lecture is entitled "The Number One Problem." Outline your points.

SUGGESTED FEATURE FILMS

Atomic Cafe. 92 min. Color. 1982. Thorn EMI Video. Hilarious and highly disturbing look at the U.S. government's efforts to promote the atomic bomb in the early days of the atomic age.

The Battle of Algiers. 135 min. B/W. 1965. Casbah. Set in 1954, in the midst of the Algerian terrorist campaign against the French.

Dr. Strangelove, or, How I Learned to Stop Worrying and Love the Bomb. 93 min. Color. 1963. Columbia Pictures. Peter Sellers and George C. Scott star in this black comedy.

Fail Safe. 111 min. B/W. 1964. Sidney Lumet. A classic nuclear war film, with Henry Fonda as the American president.

On The Beach. 132 min. B/W. 1959. Universal. Film version of Neville Shute's novel about the final nuclear cataclysm.

Ramparts of Clay. Subtitled. 87 min. Color. 1970. J. I. Bertucelli. Set in southern Tunisia in the early 1960s, this is the story of a village woman who learns to read and finds herself out of place in both the traditional and the Western world.

Threads. 110 min. Color. 1985. BBC-TV. Explores the effects of a limited nuclear war on the town of Sheffield, England.

War Games. 110 min. Color. 1983. CBS/Fox. A young computer whiz unintentionally breaks into the U.S. missile defense system and brings the world to the brink of nuclear war.

The last several years have seen the making of a number of excellent films about the Vietnam War. All of the following are guaranteed to provoke intense discussion; most include very graphic and disturbing scenes.

Apocalypse Now. 150 min. Color. 1981. Paramount.
Casualties of War. 120 min. Color. 1989. Columbia.

The Deerhunter. 183 min. Color. 1978. MCA. Winner of five Academy
 Awards, including Best Picture.
Full Metal Jacket. 116 min. Color. 1987. Warner.
Platoon. 120 min. Color. 1986. Hemdale. Voted the Best Picture of 1986.

For an exploration of the Vietnam War as fought on the home front:

Born on the Fourth of July. 145 min. Color. 1990. Universal.
Coming Home. 127 min. Color. 1978. United Artists. One of the earliest and
 still one of the best of the Vietnam films.

SUGGESTED CLASSROOM FILMS

And Who Shall Feed the World? 47 min. Color. 1975. McGraw-Hill. Explores the
 political and economic issues involved in the questions of population growth
 and resource consumption by contrasting farm families in India and North
 America.

The Bomb. 30 min. B/W. 1966. Indiana University. Looks at the development of
 the nuclear bomb and its implications.

The H-Bomb Detonated. 4 min. Color. 1962. Fleetwood. Newsreel excerpts of the
 1952 Pacific test, the fallout from which contaminated a Japanese fishing crew.

History 1917–1967. 22 min. each. B/W. 1970. BBC/Time-Life Inc.
 Unit VI. No. 17—The Shrinking World. Looks at the the development and
  impact of modern communications.
 Unit VI. No 18—The Great Divide. Explores the problem of the gap between the
  developed nations and the developing world.

Indira Gandhi of India. 60 min. Color. 1973. Time-Life Films. An interview.

Mirror, Mirror: Northern Ireland. 58 min. Color. 1994. Films for the Humanities.
 Focuses not on the IRA but on the Protestant loyalists.

Miseries of War: Paintings by Felix Labisse. 10 min. Color. 1962. International
 Film Bureau. Labisse's paintings as a protest against the nuclear age.

Viet Nam. 8 min. B/W. Associated Press. A series of still photographs taken by AP
 photographers.

Vietnam: A Television History. 60 min. each. Color. 1983. Films, Inc. With
 correspondent Stanley Karnow.
 1. Roots of War.
 2. The First Vietnam War.
 3. America's Mandarin 1954–1963.
 4. LBJ Goes to War 1964–1965.
 5. America Takes Charge 1965–1967.
 6. America's Enemy 1954–1967.

  7. *Tet, 1968.*
  8. *Vietnamizing the War 1968–1973.*
  9. *No Neutral Ground: Cambodia and Laos.*
  10. *Peace Is at Hand 1968–1973.*
  11. *Homefront USA.*
  12. *End of the Tunnel 1973–1975.*
  13. *Legacies.*

Vietnam: Images of War. 26 min. Color. 1975. Journal Films. Contains graphic scenes.

The War Game. 49 min. B/W. 1966. Films, Inc. Dramatization of the effects of nuclear war on Britain.